Theodor Storm:
The Dano-German Poet and Writer

North American Studies
in 19th-Century German Literature

Jeffrey L. Sammons
General Editor

Vol. 33

PETER LANG
Oxford·Bern·Berlin·Bruxelles·Frankfurt am Main·New York·Wien

Clifford Albrecht Bernd

Theodor Storm

The Dano-German Poet and Writer

Er ist ein Meister, er bleibt.
(He is a master, he remains.)
— Thomas Mann on Theodor Storm

PETER LANG
Oxford·Bern·Berlin·Bruxelles·Frankfurt am Main·New York·Wien

Bibliographic information published by Die Deutsche Bibliothek
Die Deutsche Bibliothek lists this publication in the Deutsche National-
bibliografie; detailed bibliographic data is available on the Internet at
‹http://dnb.ddb.de›.

British Library and Library of Congress Cataloguing-in-Publication Data:
A catalogue record for this book is available from The British Library, Great
Britain, and from The Library of Congress, USA

ISSN 0891-4095
ISBN 3-03910-652-X
US-ISBN 0-8204-7170-4

Second printing 2005

© Peter Lang AG, European Academic Publishers, Bern 2003, 2005
Hochfeldstrasse 32, Postfach 746, CH-3000 Bern 9, Switzerland
info@peterlang.com, www.peterlang.com, www.peterlang.net

All rights reserved.
All parts of this publication are protected by copyright.
Any utilisation outside the strict limits of the copyright law, without
the permission of the publisher, is forbidden and liable to prosecution.
This applies in particular to reproductions, translations, microfilming,
and storage and processing in electronic retrieval systems.

Printed in Germany

TO
HEINKE AND KARL ERNST LAAGE

"Storm: ein vergeistigter Schifferkopf, etwas schräg gehalten, Wetterfältchen in den Winkeln der zugleich träumerischen und spähenden blauen Augen" (Storm's head is that of a sailor refined and spiritualized, held slightly to one side, with tiny wrinkles at the corners of the dreamy, peering blue eyes)
— Thomas Mann, Essay on Theodor Storm, 1930.

Contents

Acknowledgments	9
List of Illustrations	11
List of Abbreviations	13
Introduction	15
Storm's Exposure to Danish Culture in Early Life	27
1. The Danish orientation of the duchy of Schleswig	27
2. Husum's patriotic association with the Danish crown	35
3. The Copenhagen Style of architecture comes to Husum	42
4. Storm's schooling in Danish letters	47
5. The capstone: Storm's exposure to the Danish spirit at the University of Kiel	54
The Poems	75
1. Storm's calling to poetry	75
2. Storm's poetry in the judgment of Theodor Fontane and Thomas Mann	78
3. Danish verse melody as the source of Storm's poetry	81
4. Early verse: "Der Entfernten"	86
5. Reaping the benefit of a poetic apprenticeship: Liederbuch dreier Freunde	89
6. The breakthrough: "Nixen-Chor zur Begrüßung König Christians VIII. in Husum"	92
7. The immortal poem: "Oktoberlied"	99
8. Poetry and life: "Hyazinthen"	118
9. The chef d'oeuvre: "Meeresstrand"	134
10. From poetry to the novella	147

The Novellas	149
1. The Danish heritage	149
2. Early glory: Immensee	151
3. A Danish novella in German disguise: In St. Jürgen	160
4. Painting in oils: Aquis submersus	171
5. Final triumph: Der Schimmelreiter	193
The Last Months	215
Selected Bibliography	217
Index of Names	229

Acknowledgments

It is a pleasure to acknowledge my gratitude to others. My debt to those who have written on Storm before me is great, far greater than any set of footnotes or any bibliography, however extensive, could possibly indicate. If I were to single out a particular debt, it would be to Storm's Danish critics. They have opened my eyes to a radically new way to interpret the author's life and works.

I am grateful, too, to the staffs of the various archives and libraries I have visited in the course of writing this book, especially the Storm-Archiv in Husum, the Schleswig-Holsteinische Landesbibliothek in Kiel, and the Royal Library in Copenhagen, but a host of other institutions as well. I have tried to record my specific thanks in the footnotes.

I also want to thank my Danish friends Leif Ludwig Albertsen and Anna Simonsen for the encouragement they have given me over the years. My friend and former student Richard Hacken generously and intelligently supplied many of the translations for the volume. Marit MacArthur provided helpful editorial suggestions throughout and competently prepared my manuscript for submission to the publisher. Eline Bernd proved again to be a valuable editorial assistant.

My sincere thanks must go, furthermore, to Jeffrey L. Sammons, the General Editor of the *North American Studies in Nineteenth-Century German Literature*, for his careful scrutiny of the final manuscript; his shrewd observations and thoughtful advice, given in such a generous spirit, have much improved this book.

Last but not least, I should like to avail myself of this opportunity to thank the Executive Board of the Theodor-Storm-Gesellschaft for making me a Corresponding Member. I deeply appreciate that honor.

Clifford Albrecht Bernd
University of California, Davis   February 2003

List of Illustrations

Theodor Storm. Photograph by G. Constabel, July 7, 1886 (Courtesy of Theodor-Storm-Gesellschaft)	6
Gertrud Storm. Photograph (Courtesy of Theodor-Storm-Gesellschaft)	19
Ernst Matthias von Köller. Photograph (Courtesy of Professor Kai Detlev Sievers, Kiel)	20
Map showing the distribution of languages spoken in the Duchy of Schleswig in 1857 (Adapted from C. F. Allen, *Det danske Sprogs Historie i Hertugdømmet Slesvig eller Sønderjylland*. Vol. 2. Copenhagen: Reitzel, 1858)	29
Christian Paulsen's Danish gravestone in Flensburg (Courtesy of Dansk Centralbibliotek for Sydslesvig, Flensburg)	67
Nicolaus Falck. Portrait by Carl Rahl (Courtesy of Kunsthalle, Kiel)	71
Illustration for "Nixen-Chor zur Begrüßung König Christians VIII. in Husum." Lithograph by Sievert Steenbock (Courtesy of Dr. Carl Häberlin Friesenmuseum, Wyk auf Föhr)	97
Illustration for "Oktoberlied." Back cover of the first edition of Storm's *Gedichte*, Kiel 1852 (Courtesy of Theodor-Storm-Gesellschaft)	101
Illustration for "Meeresstrand" (Courtesy of Theodor-Storm-Gesellschaft)	143
Illustration for *Immensee*. By Ludwig Pietsch. 5th edition. Berlin 1857 (Courtesy of Theodor-Storm-Gesellschaft)	155
Illustration for *In St. Jürgen*. Front cover of the first edition. Schleswig 1868 (Courtesy of Theodor-Storm-Gesellschaft)	169
Illustration for *Aquis submersus* (Courtesy of Theodor-Storm-Gesellschaft)	185
Illustration for *Der Schimmelreiter* (Courtesy of Theodor-Storm-Gesellschaft)	207

List of Abbreviations

LL   Theodor Storm, *Sämtliche Werke*, eds. K. E. Laage & D. Lohmeier, Frankfurt am Main: Deutscher Klassiker Verlag, 1987–1988.

NFA   Theodor Fontane, *Sämtliche Werke*, eds. E. Gross et al., Munich: Nymphenburg, 1959–1975.

Mann *Essay*   Thomas Mann, *Theodor Storm, Essay*, ed. K. E. Laage, Heide: Boyens, 1996.

Mann *Essays*   Thomas Mann, *Essays of Three Decades*, translated by H. T. Lowe-Porter, New York: Knopf, 1947.

STSG   *Schriften der Theodor-Storm-Gesellschaft*

Storm's correspondences are usually referred to in the abbreviated form *Storm–Fontane, Storm–Heyse, Storm–Keller*, etc.

Introduction

In March 1971 the German critic Peter Goldammer could make the claim that Theodor Storm had become one of the most widely read German authors of the second half of the nineteenth century, and what is more, he said, the world-wide interest in Storm was steadily rising.[1]

The years since have shown that this claim was no exaggeration. Year after year, new editions of various works by Storm have come off the printing presses to sell quickly to the reading public. From Europe to the Western Hemisphere, and especially in the Far East, new translations of Storm's works have enlisted the enthusiasm of countless additional readers. Again and again Japanese scholars have reported that Storm is one of the most popular German writers in Japan.[2] By 1983 interest in Storm in that country had risen so high that the Japanese Storm Society was founded. In China, too, we hear, there has been a remarkable upsurge of interest in Storm.[3]

The great fascination that Storm's fiction now holds for readers far and wide has led to a concomitant rise in innovative scholarship on Storm — professional criticism's highest form of flattery. The annual issues of the *MLA International Bibliography of Books and Articles on the Modern Languages and Literatures* during the last decade (1990–1999) show that Storm has now come to march at the head

---

1 *Theodor Storm. Briefe*, ed. P. Goldammer, I (Berlin & Weimar: Aufbau, 1972), 11.
2 For the most recent report see: Hiroyuki Tanaka & Mari Tanaka, "Theodor Storm in Japan — beliebt und hochgeschätzt" in *Storm-Essays aus japanischer Perspektive. Jubiläumsband aus Anlaß des fünfzehnjährigen Bestehens der Theodor-Storm-Gesellschaft Japan*, eds. H. Tanaka, S. Fukami, M. Ishihama (Husum: Husum Druck- und Verlagsgesellschaft, 1999), 9–23.
3 Zhiyou Wang, "Theodor Storm in China" in *Theodor Storm und das 19. Jahrhundert. Vorträge und Berichte des Internationalen Storm-Symposions aus Anlaß des 100. Todestages Theodor Storms*, eds. B. Coghlan & K. E. Laage (Berlin: Erich Schmidt, 1989), 173.

of the procession of the German Poetic Realists. The number of critical publications concerned with Storm has surpassed those addressed to, for instance, Gottfried Keller and Conrad Ferdinand Meyer. Meyer's standing with the critics has most noticeably declined in comparison with that of Storm. When Heinrich Henel published a much acclaimed book on Meyer a half century ago,[4] no authority on German literature would have dreamed that such a critical shift in favor of Storm would one day occur.

This new prominence that Storm has acquired is perhaps most apparent in his inclusion in the list of canonical masters of nineteenth-century world literature compiled by Harold Bloom in 1994.[5] Storm appears now as one of only three commanding German lyricists of the nineteenth century (together with Heinrich Heine and Eduard Mörike). Neither the poetry of Keller, nor that of Meyer, nor even the moving ballads of Theodor Fontane enjoy, according to Bloom, the light of the canonical that currently shines on Storm.

As both the reading public and professional critics have chosen to give Storm such remarkable visibility in our time, then today there may exist a particular urgency to renew and quicken the attempts to understand this author and his most characteristic works. Interpretive accounts that try to bring a great literary figure like Storm to life in a contemporary context are, of course, always welcome, but they are especially desirable when such an artist is riding the crest of newfound popularity.

Of course, any new biographical study of Storm should naturally honor, preserve, and transmit the depository of knowledge about him, yet at the same time it should also produce new knowledge, which means questioning received ideas and revising traditional beliefs about him. This biographical account is revisionist in many instances, but above all because it takes seriously, for the first time in Storm criticism, the heritage of the Danish muse in his literary life and oeuvre. His Danish intellectual and cultural education, I shall argue,

---

[4] Heinrich Henel, *The Poetry of Conrad Ferdinand Meyer* (Madison, WI: University of Wisconsin Press, 1954).
[5] Harold Bloom, *The Western Canon* (New York: Harcourt Brace, 1994), 544.

opened the path for Storm to write his poems and novellas and distinctly shaped them.

Storm was born in the United Monarchy of Greater Denmark, the *Helstat*, as it is called in Danish, or the *Gesamtstaat*, as the Germans say. This was a vast monarchy that included Denmark, the duchies of Schleswig, Holstein, and Lauenburg, as well as Greenland, Iceland, the Faeroe Islands, and many other overseas possessions. Thus Storm had Danish citizenship at birth. From the very beginning he stood squarely inside the Danish, rather than the German, political and cultural orbit. The German states he referred to as *Ausland* (foreign territory). Others in Schleswig, that part of Greater Denmark in which he was reared, did the same, for Schleswig had chosen at the Congress of Vienna, just two years before Storm's birth, not to join the Confederation of German States, preferring instead to remain exclusively under the jurisdiction of the Danish monarch and Danish law.

It followed from these circumstances of birth that Storm's schooling, especially in literature, was oriented almost entirely toward the Danish cultural world. Indeed, Danish literature was the only modern literature in his school's curriculum. Later, when Storm took his degree in law at the University of Kiel, he demonstrated before a representative of the Danish crown that he had acquired a competence in Danish at a level that could only follow from a study of the great masters of Danish literature. At an early age, therefore, Storm had been schooled by the Danish muse, and he had learned to stand on the shoulders of Danish poets and writers.

The history of Storm criticism, however, makes it rather difficult to recognize that his creative experience was nourished by the literary culture prevailing in the Danish monarchy of his time. Scholarship on Storm, for more than one hundred years, has been largely blind to what should have been obvious about a poet born and raised in Greater Denmark, who lived under the rule of its monarch until his thirty-sixth year.

Why has mainstream Storm criticism, in particular the biographies, failed to acknowledge that his flights of the imagination could be linked to the Danish literature in which he was schooled? The answer can be found in the cornerstone of all biographical study on Storm: the two-volume biography written by his daughter Gertrud,[6] whose intimate knowledge of his life and works cannot be surpassed by any other biographer. This is the sole biography of Storm that can never be supplanted; it can only be supplemented and emended. As the American Germanist Elmer O. Wooley once said, "all scholarly studies on Storm have leaned heavily on her work.... As long as scholars take an interest in Storm, they will always have occasion to consult the writings of his loyal daughter."[7] Today, ninety years after the daughter's biography of the father was published, it has lost nothing of its original interest. In 1991 the need was felt to reprint it.[8]

Although Gertrud's biography has remained an indispensable handbook for Storm critics, we must now begin to notice that her thinking and attitudes were conditioned by a tidal wave of officially sanctioned anti-Danish patriotism that swept across Schleswig at the time she took up her pen to write her *magnum opus*.

It was in 1903, as she once told Elmer O. Wooley,[9] that she began her work on the biography. The date is significant, for that year marked the height of the infamous von Köller era, or *Köllertiden*, a term coined by Danish historiographers to decry this reactionary period at the turn of the century in Schleswig's history.[10] In 1897 Ernst Matthias von Köller, a Prussian despot who had served as the notoriously ruthless chief of police in Frankfurt after that city was absorbed into the Prussian State, became the Governor General of the Prussian province of Schleswig-Holstein. As the most pliant of

---

6   Gertrud Storm, *Theodor Storm. Ein Bild seines Lebens*. 2 vols. (Berlin: Curtius, 1912–1913).
7   E.O. Wooley, "Gertrud Storm," *Monatshefte für Deutschen Unterricht* (Wisconsin) 28 (1936): 247–249.
8   Reprint (Hildesheim: Olms, 1991).
9   Wooley, "Gertrud Storm," 248.
10 See the chapter *Köllertiden* in Hans Lund, Valdemar Ammundsen & Mads Iversen, *Sønderjyllands Historie*, V (Copenhagen: Reitzel, 1942), 208–222.

Photograph of Gertrud Storm, who regarded it as "the best picture I have ever had taken"
— E. O. Wooley, *Theodor Storm's World in Pictures*, Bloomington IN, 1954.

Ernst Matthias von Köller, the Prussian Junker and highly decorated official of Kaiser Wilhelm's Germany.

all ministers of Kaiser Wilhelm II[11] and the latter's consort Augusta Viktoria, von Köller was well aware that the empress possessed a burning hatred for everything Danish.[12] She was a daughter of the Royal House of Augustenborg (Augustenburg in German) and could not forget how her father, Friedrich, Duke of Augustenburg, had suffered when the Danish government forced him into exile and sequestered the family's many sumptuous estates in the duchy of Schleswig.

The new governor took up his appointment, therefore, with the single determination to win more favor with the imperial pair by stamping out all vestiges of Danish culture remaining in Schleswig after Prussia had annexed the territory in 1867. He stopped at nothing to achieve this end. His policy of forcibly germanizing "das maßlos freche Dänentum"[13] (the shamelessly insolent Danes) in Schleswig was carried out with a harshness and severity that knew few parallels in history.[14] The Danes who protested were pushed across the border into Denmark. Others fled to the United States and elsewhere.[15] Those who remained had to pretend they were loyal Germans.

Herr von Köller's frenzied attacks on all things Danish, which continued with unabating rigor under his successor, Baron Kurt von Wilmowski, would have made it singularly inopportune for Gertrud, at that time, to admit that her father had had, at any stage of his life, links to Danish culture. If her biography were to "sell" in the von Köller era, it had to be purged of anything suggesting Danish influence. Indeed, such a biography had to exemplify and reinforce the very German, anti-Danish portrait of her father that had already been

---

11 Lamar Cecil, *Wilhelm II. Prince and Emperor, 1859–1900* (Chapel Hill, NC: University of North Carolina Press, 1989), 230.
12 Kai Detlev Sievers, *Die Köllerpolitik und ihr Echo in der deutschen Presse 1897–1901* (Neumünster: Wachholtz, 1964), 66–68.
13 Ibid., 162.
14 Documentation on the brutal policies of von Köller can be found in the Acten des Königlichen Ober-Präsidiums der Provinz Schleswig-Holstein, Abtlg. 301, Nr. 4384, located today in the Landesarchiv in Schleswig. I am indebted to Bettina Reichert for making the file available to me.
15 See "Slesvig Forum" in *The American-Scandinavian Review* 7 (1919): 53.

put forth by von Köller and the empress's brother, Duke Ernst Günther, when they organized an auspicious Prussian patriotic ceremony for the unveiling of a monument to Storm at Husum on September 14, 1898.

Gertrud knew, hence, that she had to give the biography of her father an anti-Danish coloration. She did not shrink from deception and forgery to achieve her goal. The best example of this is her invention of the story that Storm had studied at the University of Kiel under a "Professor Deller," a teacher with a non-Danish sounding name.[16]

No "Professor Deller," however, had ever taught at the University of Kiel. Gertrud substituted this fictitious name for another faculty member with whom her father did have a close student-teacher relationship throughout his education at Kiel: Christian Paulsen (1798–1854). Gertrud had to replace Paulsen, for he was known to have been a most enthusiastic champion of Danish cultural values and conspicuously loyal to the Danish crown, and that would have made him a *persona non grata* or worse in the von Köller era.

I learned about Storm's association with Paulsen from the latter's diaries, which were published in Copenhagen in 1946 and which have remained unknown to Storm critics. In these diaries Paulsen states that Storm was one of his outstanding students.[17] Paulsen lectured in Kiel on "Danish law." Tellingly, it was in this subject that Storm had performed best in his examinations.[18]

How imprudent, even disgraceful, if Gertrud had revealed that her father had been a very good student of such a notorious Danophile! Hence, she invented the fictitious name of Deller, which, she must have felt, would keep Storm's admirers (including von Köller) off Paulsen's track. Nobody would be able to challenge the invention with any authority, since her father had designated her as the

---

16 Gertrud Storm, I, 131.
17 *Flensborgeren, Professor Christian Paulsens Dagbøger*, eds. K. Fabricius & J. Lomholt-Thomsen (Copenhagen: Gyldendal, 1946), 293.
18 Otto v. Fisenne, "Theodor Storm als Jurist," STSG 8 (1959): 12.

sole guardian of his published and unpublished literary legacy.[19] Successfully, she had blotted out Paulsen's name from Storm criticism, almost forever.

Not all of Gertrud's attempts to cover up the possibility of any Danish cultural influences on her father's life and work were as blatant as this one. More often she simply resorted to the art of omission in order to paint a more "German" portrait of her father. In her biography of Storm we learn, for instance, almost nothing about his extensive exposure to Danish letters during the nine years he attended school in Husum. The reader of her biography would never gather that his school had placed, as we shall find out, an extraordinary emphasis on educating its pupils in the Danish language and its literature. Instead, the anti-Danish image of her father that Gertrud (together with von Köller and Duke Ernst Günther) had created has become an unquestioned tenet of Storm criticism. In 1955 Franz Stuckert, a notable post-World War II biographer, could still say that we do not have the slightest shred of evidence that Storm had learned and understood Danish.[20] This biographer acquired his "knowledge," doubtless, from Gertrud's study. Without checking, Stuckert also repeated the daughter's false claim that Storm had studied with "Professor Deller."[21] Others have done the same.[22] Inherited assumptions die hard.

Now it is time to put aside the stubborn accretion of Gertrud's nationalistic portrait around the figure of Storm. With the advent of a more transnational outlook in our age, the lingering prejudices from the von Köller era should be stripped away, giving way to the emergence of a truer picture, a new bicultural Dano-German Storm.

This does not mean, of course, that criticism, from now on, should attempt to "tag" every single influence Storm assimilated as coming from the Danish muse. Did a Renaissance poet have to read

---

19   Wooley, "Gertrud Storm," 248.
20   Franz Stuckert, *Theodor Storm. Sein Leben und seine Welt* (Bremen: Schünemann, 1955), 24.
21   Ibid., 34.
22   See, for instance, v. Fisenne, 10.

Petrarch in order to compose a Petrarchan sonnet? Storm did not have to read any particular Danish poem or novella in order to compose a work in the manner of Danish practitioners. Because it permeated his formative education, he was an heir to the Danish literary tradition no less than, for instance, many poets all across Europe in the late nineteenth and early twentieth century were the heirs to French Symbolist poetry, even though they may not have read Mallarmé.

As an heir to this tradition, Storm added a new tone to the German lyric. Moreover, he refashioned the German novella. These achievements continue to assure him a place among the best European literature.

This study attempts to give approximately equal consideration to Storm's poems and novellas. That, too, runs counter to traditional Storm scholarship, which reflects the deeply rooted belief that he should be remembered primarily for his contributions to the genre of the novella. In general studies, Storm's poetry is invariably shortchanged to allot more space to the discussion of his (ostensibly more praiseworthy) prose fiction. I believe, however, that Storm deserves to be remembered no less for his achievements in the lyric. Indeed, if I were asked to state which accomplishment ranks higher, I would raise his poems above his novellas. Theodor Fontane, never known for poor aesthetic judgment, understood his contemporary better, I think, than the modern sages who, often enough, could find hardly more than grudging praise for Storm's poetry: "Denn seine höchste Vorzüglichkeit," Fontane said, "ruht nicht in seinen vergleichsweise viel gelesenen und bewunderten Novellen, sondern in seiner Lyrik" (his preeminence rests not in his much read and much admired novellas, but rather in his lyrics).[23]

Of course, the view that Storm's verse should no longer be disparaged in favor of his novellas gives added weight to the argument that Storm took his inspiration from the creative mood of the Danish muse. It was, after all, in that national literature that the genre of the

---

23   NFA, XV, 207.

lyric had towered over all forms of literary expression, including the highly innovative Danish novella. In German literature at the time, in contrast, it was drama that had reigned supreme. As late as 1859 German cities rivaled one another in erecting more and more impressive monuments to the dramatist Schiller.

Storm's Exposure to Danish Culture in Early Life

1. The Danish orientation of the duchy of Schleswig

Theodor Storm was born on September 14, 1817, in Husum, a town located just below the Dano-German language frontier that stretched across the former duchy of Schleswig, as the region is commonly known today by its German spelling. Although the English name *Sleswick* is no longer used, the Danes continue to say *Slesvig*, as they have done for centuries. The two different names that Germans and Danes have for this region, even today, indicate a long history of two distinct and overlapping cultures that would influence Storm.

Schleswig should not be confused with the contiguous duchy of Holstein (*Holsten* in Danish) with which it was joined in a loose *nexus socialis*, a social and economic association without political links, in Storm's early life. Politically and historically, the two duchies were independent and quite different from one another. For over a thousand years, until 1806, Holstein had been an integral part of the Holy Roman Empire of the German Nation. The territory of the duchy of Schleswig, on the other hand, always extended beyond the northern frontier of that empire: *Eidora Romani terminus imperii* (The Roman Empire ends at the Eider River), and it was the Eider River that constituted the border between Holstein and Schleswig.

Each duchy had gone its own way in the course of history and had developed its own autonomous identity. Holstein, within the empire, had acquired a German cultural orientation. Schleswig, beyond the reach of the German emperor in Vienna, was almost untouched by the culture of that empire. Hence, when the map of Europe was redrawn at the Congress of Vienna in 1815, it seemed natural that Holstein should join the newly formed Confederation of German States, and it seemed equally natural that Schleswig should not become a part of that union.

a. The Danish orientation of Schleswig's population

Another important characteristic of Storm's native duchy of Schleswig was that it had always been divided between a Danish-speaking region in the north and a German-speaking region in the south. The Danish area was by far the larger. According to population statistics published and distributed in 1831 by the University of Kiel, 150,000 inhabitants of the duchy were ethnically Danes, whereas only 80,000 could claim some sort of German ethnic identity.[24] Obviously, this gave Storm's native duchy, from a demographic standpoint, a strong Danish orientation.

b. Schleswig's political, legal, economic, and religious ties to Denmark

Adding further to the duchy's Danish orientation was the fact that the hereditary duke, an absolute ruler, had always been, or at least for as long as anyone could remember, the king of Denmark, who governed his duchy from the royal capital at Copenhagen. The loyalty which the duchy felt towards the crown, a British historian tells us, acted as a powerful cement in preserving the association of Schleswig with Denmark.[25]

Even with the duchy's minority German-speaking population, the sense of belonging to Greater Denmark, the *Helstat*, was traditionally strong, and was officially reinforced. Danish law, the *Lex Regia*, prevailed as the highest law of the land.[26] Since 1813, the notes of the Danish State Bank, the *Rigsbanktaler*, constituted the only legal tender recognized by the authorities; invoices in other

---

24 C. v. Wimpfen, *Ueber die staatsrechtlichen Verhältnisse der Herzogthümer Schleswig und Holstein* (Kiel: Universitäts-Buchhandlung, 1831), 36.
25 William Carr, *Schleswig-Holstein 1815–48. A Study in National Conflict* (Manchester: University Press, 1963), 27.
26 See the standard study on this subject by Nicolaus Falck, under whom Storm studied law: *Handbuch des Schleswig-Holsteinischen Privatrechts*, I (Altona: Hammerich, 1825), 9.

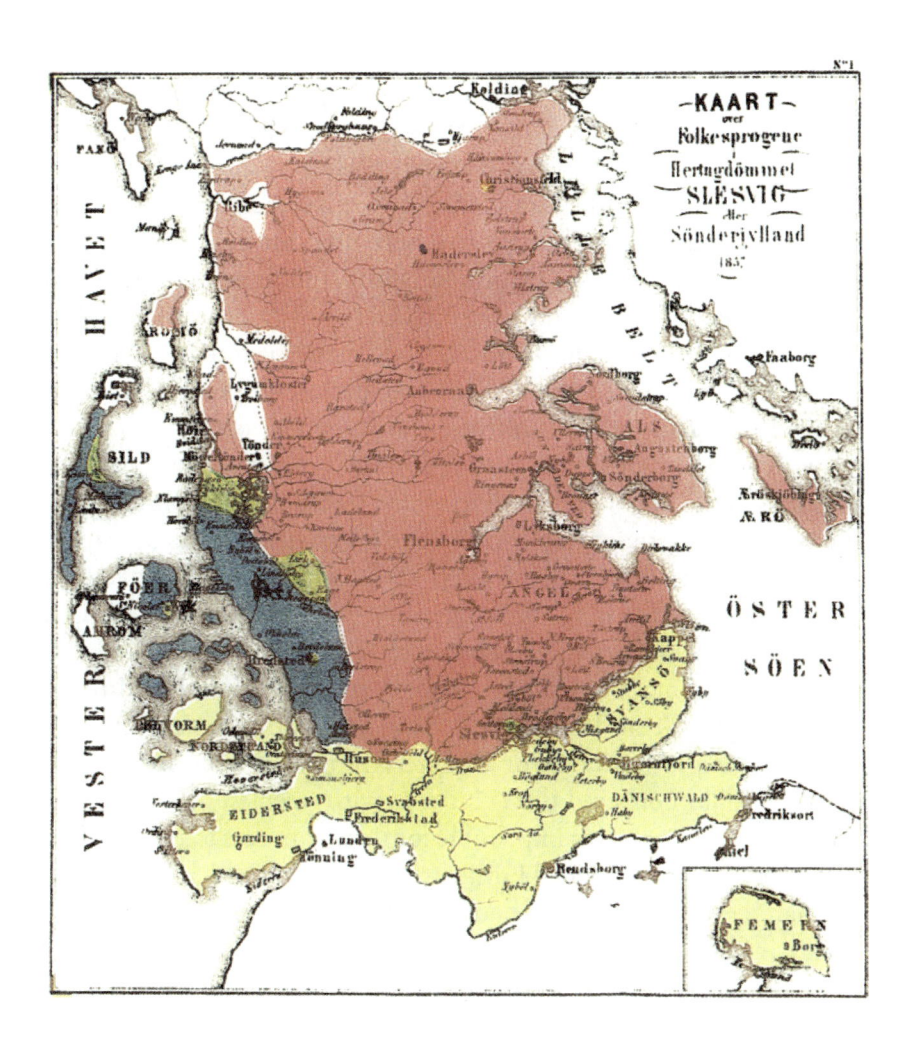

Storm's Exposure to Danish Culture in Early Life 29

Map showing the distribution of languages spoken in the Duchy of Schleswig in 1857. Red = Mostly Danish. Yellow = Mostly German. Green = Mixed Danish and Frisian. Blue = Mostly Frisian.

currencies had to be, for official purposes, recomputed according to the value of the Danish monetary unit.[27] Postal and stage coach services were provided by the Royal Danish Mail, with headquarters at the General Post Office in Copenhagen.[28] The uniforms of postal officials and mail coach drivers in Schleswig were identical to those of the entire Danish monarchy; the signs bearing the monogram of the reigning Danish monarch that were placed outside all post offices in the duchy were likewise identical to those seen everywhere in Denmark.[29] Domestic postal rates were used for mail between the duchy and all parts of the Danish kingdom, but higher international rates applied for letters and parcels to Germany.[30] Schleswig was, of course, also united with Denmark in the same customs' union, and this also strengthened the duchy's economic bond to Denmark at the expense of any close connection with the German states.

Religiously, Schleswig also followed Denmark. The Lutheran Church in the duchy, the faith to which virtually all inhabitants adhered, was the same as the Danish State Church. That was only to be expected, since the Lutheran king of Denmark was the sovereign head of the Church in all of the lands over which he ruled. The rigid form of Lutheranism in Schleswig and Denmark was unmarked by the tolerance practiced by German Protestants since the time of Frederick the Great. If there were a few non-Lutherans in Denmark and Schleswig — Catholics or dissenters from the Established Church — they could not build their churches with steeples, bell towers, or even bells.[31] Thus it was impossible for their churches to be mistaken for an edifice of the official Lutheran religion over which the Danish monarch presided. Such orthodoxy was unknown anywhere in Germany in the nineteenth century.

---

27 Otto Brandt, *Geschichte Schleswig-Holsteins*. (Kiel: Mühlau, [7]1976), 222.
28 Peter Jäger, *Postgeschichte Schleswig-Holsteins* (Kiel: Bezirksgruppe Kiel der Gesellschaft für deutsche Postgeschichte, 1970), 22.
29 A. Morell Nielsen, *The Danish Post and Telegraph Museum* (Copenhagen, 1987), 7, 16.
30 Jäger, 38.
31 Wilm Sanders, *St. Nikolaus Kiel* (Kiel: Schmidt & Klaunig, 1968), 7.

Many other practices also separated the Lutherans of Denmark and Schleswig from their brethren in Germany. Most conspicuously, perhaps, the difference could be noted in the vesture of the clergy. The Lutheran ministers in Schleswig wore the wide-collared *Præstekrave* identical to that of the Danish State Church, while the German Lutheran clerics wore the short, pointed *Beffchen*.

c. Schleswig's cultural ties to Denmark

With such strong demographic, political, economic, legal, and religious ties to Denmark, Schleswig had always been washed by the currents of culture that flowed from Copenhagen to the farthest corners of the dominions belonging to the Danish sovereign. And never in Denmark's long history did these currents spill over into Schleswig as much as they did during the years of Storm's early life. In these years, the arts in Denmark flowered more profusely than ever before; this era has come to be known as the *Guldalder* (Golden Age) of Danish art and culture.[32]

This was the age in which the heroic tragedies of Adam Oehlenschläger and the hilarious comedies of Johan Ludvig Heiberg gave the Royal Theater a new life, and the age in which the lilting poetry and ingenious fictional masterpieces of Hans Christian Andersen, the gripping novellas of Steen Steensen Blicher and Thomasine Gyllembourg, the cleverly contrived novels of Meïr Goldschmidt, and the inspirational lyrics of N.F.S. Grundtvig, all raised Danish literature to heights only reached by the very best of European wordsmiths. This was the age in which the bright colors of Christoffer Eckersberg and the grayer shades of Christen Købke suddenly gave Danish painting a European dimension. This was the age, moreover, in which the monumental art of Bertel Thorvaldsen had surpassed all other sculpture produced at the time. Above all, this was

---

32   The most informative books in English on the *Guldalder* are: *The Golden Age in Denmark* and *The Golden Age Revisited. Art and Culture in Denmark 1800–1850*, ed. B. Scavenius (Copenhagen: Gyldendal, 1994 & 1996). The volumes are also available in Danish and in German.

the age in which Christian Frederik Hansen's "Copenhagen Style" breathed extraordinary new life into Danish architecture, freeing it from the constraints of foreign domination to which that form of art had succumbed; for centuries previously, architects from all over Europe, never from Denmark, had received contracts to design the important buildings of the Danish nation.

The inhabitants of the duchy of Schleswig could not help but feel the impact of this Golden Age of Danish art, flowering so profusely immediately north of its borders. How could a Danish artistic current of such creative vigor and force have failed to spill over into the adjacent duchy governed from the same royal capital of Copenhagen? The populace of this Dano-German duchy must have been all the more impressed because this was the first time ever in Dano-German relations that Denmark, traditionally the recipient of German culture, had suddenly acquired the power to reverse that flow.

To comprehend the ramifications of this dramatic reversal, we must remember that ever since the time of Martin Luther, waves of German culture had regularly flooded the Danish cultural scene. Literary histories have long stressed Denmark's cultural debt to Germany, declaring that the form of the Danish Bible, and indeed the entire Danish literature it inspired, was unthinkable without the persuasive and pervasive influence of Luther's Protestant poetics. If we look especially at the flowering of the Lutheran religious lyrics in sixteenth- and seventeenth-century Denmark, we are tempted to declare such literary transference from Germany to Denmark as unparalleled in the annals of comparative literature.[33] Critics have long known, too, of the tremendous influence that Friedrich Gottlieb Klopstock, Johann Elias Schlegel, Schleswig's German writer Heinrich Wilhelm von Gerstenberg, and the members of the so-called

---

33 For a particularly convincing description of this instance of cultural borrowing see P. M. Mitchell, *A History of Danish Literature* (New York: Kraus-Thomson, ²1971), 51ff.

"German Circle" of Copenhagen had on the Danish muse of the eighteenth century.[34]

In short, the history of Danish and German literary influence prior to the time of Storm's youth offers incontestable evidence for the enormous debt that Danish literature of three centuries owed to German letters. Literary influence in the opposite direction, from Denmark to Germany, however, seldom occurred. It must have seemed all the more sensational, then, to people of literary taste in the bilingual duchy of Schleswig when the one-way current of literary influence was reversed. In the Golden Age, Danish literature had suddenly come into its own and had quickly found its way into the German-speaking world. Oehlenschläger, for example, soon became so famous in Germany that people considered him to be a German writer.[35] The German-reading public took so avidly to the translations of Denmark's new literature that by the 1830s audiences as far south in the German-speaking world as Vienna were discussing it.[36] Thomasine Gyllembourg, the famous female author of Denmark's Golden Age and the writer for whom Kierkegaard always reserved the highest praise in his discussions of Danish literature,[37] saw, for instance, two different multi-volume editions of her works translated into German between 1834 and 1836.[38]

---

34 John Wallace Eaton has presented us with such a powerful case for how much German literature had overwhelmed Denmark in the eighteenth century that few scholars, if indeed any at all, would try to refute him. See his *The German Influence in Danish Literature in the Eighteenth Century* (Cambridge, England: University Press, 1929).
35 Dieter Lohmeier, "Kopenhagen als kulturelles Zentrum der Goethezeit" in *Grenzgänge*, ed. H. Detering (Göttingen: Wallstein, 1996), 93.
36 Carl Bernhard, *Lebensbilder aus Dänemark in Novellen und Erzählungen*, I (Leipzig: Weber, 1840), xxvi.
37 Henning Fenger, *Kierkegaard, The Myths and their Origins*, Studies in the Kierkegaardian Papers and Letters, trans. G. C. Schoolfield (New Haven & London: Yale University Press, 1980), 3–4.
38 *Erzählungen aus der Copenhagener fliegenden Post*, trans. L. Kruse (Leipzig: Kollmann, 1834–1836); *Novellen vom Verfasser einer "Alltagsgeschichte,"* trans. W. C. Christiani (Leipzig: Kummer, 1835).

As one Danish writer of the *Guldalder* after another soon became known to readers far and wide in Germany, surely it was in the neighboring Danish duchy of Schleswig that they naturally made their greatest impact. Schleswig's linguistic and cultural orientation towards Denmark made this inevitable. In addition, the Danish artists of the Golden Age invariably made frequent visits to the duchy ruled by their sovereign and made their share of personal friends among Schleswig's populace. To read the diaries and letters of Hans Christian Andersen and Meïr Goldschmidt, for instance, is to discover how much these writers must have felt at home in the duchy of Schleswig.[39]

d. The weight of the stamp of Copenhagen in Schleswig

Hence, however we may care to define what was culturally "German" in the duchy of Schleswig at the time of Storm's early life, there was little, other than the language spoken in some southern districts, that did not in some way or other bear the stamp of Copenhagen.[40] Germany, without a national capital until late in the nineteenth century, had no similar seat of political, economic, religious, or cultural influence that could compete with the magnetic attraction of Denmark's fascinating "Paris of the North," at that time the hub of a

---

39   H. C. Andersens Dagbøger 1825–1875, eds. K. Olsen & H. Topsøe-Jensen (Copenhagen: Gad, 1971–1976); *Breve fra og til Meïr Goldschmidt*, ed. M. Borup (Copenhagen: Rosenkilde & Bagger, 1963).

40   The most comprehensive portrait of the duchy during this period of its history is in Danish: Knud Fabricius, *Sønderjyllands Historie*, IV (Copenhagen: Reitzel, 1936–1937). The most informative account in English is still, despite its Victorian limitations: Charles A. Gosch, *Denmark and Germany since 1815* (London: Murray, 1862). Several modern studies in English are also available, but often enough they reveal, as has been noted, an "ignorance of Danish historiography," which impairs their usefulness. See Holger Hjelholt, *British Mediation in the Danish-German Conflict 1848–1850*. Historisk-filosofiske Meddelelser udgivet af Det Kongelige Danske Videnskabernes Selskab 41:1. (Copenhagen: Munksgaard, 1965), 13. Of the many accounts in German, the most exciting (yet most controversial) one was written by Paul von Hedemann-Heespen, *Die Herzogtümer Schleswig-Holstein und die Neuzeit* (Kiel: Mühlau, 1926).

global monarchy. Denmark then had far-flung possessions on all of the populated continents of the world but Australia; its geographic reach extended from the coral strand of India in the east to as far west as the enchanted isles of the Caribbean, and from the sultry lowlands of African Guinea in the south to as far north as Greenland's icy mountains.[41]

Little wonder, then, that the principal highways in Schleswig at the time, the *chaussees*, ran east-west and not north-south. All important roads in the duchy led eastward, connecting with the ferries plying the Baltic to and from the royal capital. No such highways linked the duchy with the German states to the south. Germany was, after all, a "foreign" territory. Not surprisingly, the newspapers of the duchy always referred to events in the Danish-speaking world as *Nachrichten aus dem Vaterland* (news from the fatherland), whereas happenings occurring in Germany were reported, together with news from other parts of the world, under the heading *Nachrichten aus dem Ausland* (news from abroad).

2. Husum's patriotic association with the Danish crown

The currents that sprang up at the fountainhead of Danish political, economic, religious, and cultural life in Copenhagen, and which then trickled down into the Danish-orientated duchy of Schleswig, naturally also reached Husum, the duchy's fifth largest town.[42] As with the other principal towns of the duchy (Flensburg, Schleswig, Haderslev, Åbenrå), the Danish influence was taken for granted for centuries. And again, perhaps at no time in Husum's long history was this influence greater than during the years of Storm's early life.

---

41 For an unusually delightful picture of Denmark at the time, see the excellently written and handsomely illustrated volume by Leif Ludwig Albertsen, *On the Threshold of a Golden Age* (Copenhagen: The Royal Danish Ministry of Foreign Affairs, 1979).

42 Holger Hjelholt, *Sønderjylland under Treårskrigen*, I (Copenhagen: Gad, 1959), 10.

Emil Manicus, a former editor of Copenhagen's leading newspaper, the *Berlingske Tidende*, once reported that Husum at the time was basking in the sunshine of an unprecedented association with the Danish crown; the town was, from a Danish viewpoint, more loyal and patriotic than ever before.[43]

a. The Danish king regularly visits Husum

This loyalty and patriotism came about in large part because the king of Denmark, Frederik VI, who reigned from 1808 to 1839, regularly stopped over in Husum at least twice every summer, either on his way to and from his vacation spot on an island off the North Sea coast, or on his inspection trips to the dikes and polders built by royal concession along the coast and on the islands off the coast. Husum was the principal port of embarkation for the sea voyages from the mainland to the islands and for the trips along the coast. The sovereign's travel itinerary usually took him by boat from Copenhagen to the port of Flensburg on Schleswig's Baltic coast, and then from Flensburg overland to Husum, where he invariably spent a night or two at the town's castle before continuing his trip on another boat, sailing from Husum up and down the North Sea coast or to the islands off that coast. His return trip to Copenhagen later in the summer was via the same route.

The itinerary made it necessary for the monarch to visit the seaports of Flensburg and Husum more frequently than any other towns in the duchy, and of these two places Husum, with its beautiful castle and park, proved to be the king's favorite. In Flensburg the king had to stay at castles owned by the Royal House of Augustenborg (to which he was related), and he preferred not to do so because of dynastic disagreements. Hence, his unavoidable stops in Flensburg often entailed nothing more than a short parade down Flensburg's main thoroughfare and an obligatory luncheon with the town's magistrates, after which the monarch continued on his way. In

---

43 E. Manicus, "Efterretninger om Husum Latinskole i det 16., 17., og 18. Aarhundrede," *Slesvigske Provindsialefterretninger*, I (1860): 151.

Husum, however, he did not have to contend with the antagonism of his Augustenborgian relatives; he could live happily in a splendid castle of his own. As a result, Frederik VI came to love Husum.

b. Husum's affection for its Danish sovereign

Naturally the citizens of Husum, because of the favors the king bestowed upon them during the royal visits, also came to love their sovereign in turn. We have only to read the issues of Husum's weekly newspaper at the time, the *Königlich privilegirtes Wochenblatt*, to learn how the monarch's summer visits were occasions of great festivity for the town's populace. Again and again we read of the lavish welcomes for Frederik VI. A good example is the visit of June 29–30, 1825, when Storm, almost eight years old, was at a most impressionable age.

Three days prior to Frederik's arrival, on June 26, 1825, an honorific poem composed for the occasion was printed in the *Wochenblatt*. It received the maximum amount of publicity, covering the entire front page. We must assume that Husum's educated elite, the teachers at the local Latin School who gave Storm his thorough schooling in the craft of rhetoric, had been kept busy for some time preparing the eloquent verses. When the poem appeared in its final form, it had acquired a majestic tone appropriate to the majestic person to whom it was addressed. This was doubtless the intent of the rhetoricians who composed and approved the poem on behalf of the town's magistrates. The tone brings Husum and its Danish ruler together within a tight poetic form, which, for Storm and all of his fellow citizens young and old, both reflected and emphasized anew Husum's close patriotic association with the Danish crown.

Let us consider the verses and melody which heightened Husum's sense of blessed belonging to the Danish fatherland:

Königlich privilegirtes Wochenblatt
26. Juni 1825.

Ausdruck der Freude
über die abermalige Anwesenheit
unsers geliebten Landesvaters,
Sr. Majestät, Frederik VI.
in Husum.

Heil, Husum, Dir! Im Festgewande
Naht abermals *Dein König* Dir;
Ihn lieben All' im Vaterlande,
Nicht weniger auch wir.

Ihm, der mit hoher Vatergüte
Nach *Seines* Herzens eignem Drang,
Beschirmt des Landes Wohl und Blüte
Schon zwei Jahrzehend lang;

Ihm, *Fred'rik*, so gerecht und weise,
Ihm Husum's Freude, Lieb' und Dank,
Nach treuer Unterthanen Weise
Tönt froher Jubelsang.

Wir sehen freudevoll Dich wieder,
Wir sehen Dich von Angesicht.
Nimm an die dankerfüllten Lieder,
Nimm an den Kranz, den man Dir flicht!

Heil Dir, o *König!* ruhmbekränzet,
Stehst Du auf Deiner Väter Thron;
Und Recht und Liebe — unbegrenzet —
Ziert herrlich Deine Kron'.

Die Jugend nahet Dir mit Kränzen,
Das Herz von reiner Lieb' erfüllt,
Des treuen Volkes Augen glänzen,
Die Freudenthräne quillt.

Geleite Gott Dich! Deinen Spuren
Folgt heißer Dank und Liebe nach!
Dich grüßen jubelnd Stadt und Fluren
Mit jedem neuen Tag!

(Expression of Joy
at the Presence Once Again
in Husum
of Our Country's Beloved Father,
His Majesty, Frederik VI

Hail Husum! For your King is nearing
This town again in festive dress;
All Fatherland finds him endearing:
We also feel no less.

To him, whose heart to us connected
As noble father good and strong
His country's welfare has protected
For us two decades long;

To him, to Fred'rik wise and patient,
Husum's joy, our love and thanks,
In loyal songs of jubilation,
Rise happy from the ranks.

Again our view to you has opened;
Your face we see with joyful mood.
Accept this wreath: for you t'was woven.
Accept our songs of gratitude!

Hail King! To you with fame surrounded,
On patriarchal throne passed down;
And love and justice — full, unbounded —
Bedeck your splendid crown.

The young approach with wreaths o'erflowing;
Their hearts with purest love are blessed.
Your faithful subjects' eyes are glowing
With tears of joy expressed.

God guide you! We, beneath your shadows,
Send deepest thanks and love your way!
The jubilating town and meadows
Send greetings each new day!)

Translated by Richard D. Hacken

In the next issue of the *Wochenblatt*, on July 3, 1825, we read about the details of the monarch's visit. As the royal carriage approached the town, an honor guard of citizens rode out on horseback to greet and escort him and the accompanying members of his royal court to the entrance of Husum's castle. Trumpets filled the air with music upon his arrival. When the king stepped out of his carriage, the town's magistrates, clergy, and schoolmasters stood in line to welcome him with all the formalities befitting such a royal visit. A festive banquet in the castle followed. All night long, the town was lit up. According to the newspaper account, the citizens, as excited as they were over the king's stay in Husum, could hardly sleep that night and preferred to parade up and down the streets in festive rejoicing.

On the next morning the monarch paid an official visit to the school Storm attended. Then he toured Husum's harbor, where he was greeted by the thunder of cannon and the hurrahs of the crowds. Upon his return to the castle shortly before noon, a military band struck up a lively tune. After a festive luncheon with many invited guests, cannon fire again roared over the landscape and the monarch entered the royal carriage that took him to the ship awaiting him for the sea voyage to the isles off the coast. Such visits continued throughout Frederik VI's reign, until 1839, when Storm had reached the age of early manhood.

The royal summer visits, however, were not the only occasions of patriotic show in Husum. Numerous issues of Husum's *Wochenblatt* in Storm's boyhood and early manhood also tell about the festivities in Husum every year on the Danish king's birthday, January 28. Gaiety and merriment were always the order of the day. All over the town people attended gala birthday dinners and colorful balls.[44] Toasts to the beloved sovereign were everywhere to be heard.

---

44   See Friedrich Hoffmann, *Das alte Husum zur Zeit des jungen Storm* (Kiel: Institut für Weltwirtschaft, 1957), 13, 60. Hoffmann makes a special point of drawing attention to these dinners and balls.

Husum's happy sense of association with the Danish crown could also be felt on many other important occasions as well. Odes, sonnets, and other poetic expressions of honor and joy were composed and printed in the *Wochenblatt*, too, when the Queen Consort and the Royal Princess celebrated their birthdays on the same day every year, October 28: "Heil Dir und Deiner Caroline!" (Hail to Thee and Caroline!), we read, for example, in a poem on the front page of the *Wochenblatt* of October 29, 1826. The editorial staff of Husum's newspaper, it seems, took advantage of every royal birthday, baptism, confirmation, engagement, wedding, and all sorts of other anniversaries, to express the joy of the citizenry in belonging to the Danish monarchy.

Throughout Storm's early life, from his birth on September 14, 1817, to the death of Frederik VI on December 3, 1839, the *Wochenblatt* abounds with such statements as: "Und sie beten für Dich Alle zum Himmel auf, Gott erhalt' uns den Fürst, beten so Greis als Kind" (From the mouths of young and old the prayer ascends to heaven: God save our sovereign), September 28, 1817; "Hebet hoch jedes Glas . . . Gott segne Frederik!" (Let everyone raise the glass . . . God bless Frederik!), November 6, 1825; "Heil Dän'marks König und den Seinen" (Hail to Denmark's King and His Family), October 29, 1826; "Dem edlen Fürsten Heil und Segen! Ihn lieben wir, Und kommen dankend ihm entgegen" (Every blessing to our noble King! Him we love and to Him we give our thanks), October 28, 1827. Detlev Lorenz Lübker, one of Storm's teachers at the Latin School, even went so far as to use the millennium of the coming of Christianity to Denmark to remind the *Wochenblatt*'s readers that they were the "Bewohner dieses glücklichen Dänischen Staates" (inhabitants of this happy Danish state), on May 14, 1826.

Frederik VI's death gave the *Wochenblatt* another opportunity to reaffirm Husum's close association with the Danish crown. All the issues of the paper throughout the month of December 1839 were printed with a heavy black border so that the townspeople as well as the members of the Royal House in Copenhagen could see that Husum was united with the entire Danish nation in mourning the sovereign's passing.

3. The Copenhagen Style of architecture comes to Husum

If Husum's affection for Frederik VI had done much to strengthen the town's Danish orientation during Storm's early life, nothing gave that orientation greater visibility than Husum's new St. Mary's Church, which was erected at the center of the town in the years 1829–1833 and which, ever since its completion, has dominated Husum's skyline. Today the edifice is considered to be one of the most representative masterpieces of Denmark's chief architect of the Golden Age, Christian Frederik Hansen.[45]

Hansen had always worked hard for royal patronage and apparently had great success. After much of Copenhagen had been destroyed in the British bombardment of the city in 1807, Frederik VI entrusted Hansen with the demanding task of rebuilding many of the city's landmarks. Hansen devised a new style of architecture, known as the *Kjøbenhavnerstilen* (Copenhagen Style),[46] to give the city a unified appearance that would also provide the grandeur befitting a royal capital. Central to Hansen's architectural plan for a new Copenhagen was the king's palace, *Christiansborg Slot*, which had been damaged in the bombardment. It was now to be rebuilt in a grandiose classical style as the most impressive *monumentum Daniae* (monument of Denmark), to which the other important buildings in the city would relate in a subordinate fashion. The king would reign supreme and all the other new public buildings of the city would complement, in miniature, the dignity of his royal residence; the

---

[45] Hakon Lund & Anne Lise Thygesen, *C. F. Hansen*, II (Copenhagen: Arkitekten, 1995), 567–589. See, too, the commentary on Hansen by the leading German political figure of post-World War II Schleswig-Holstein, Gerhard Stoltenberg, in *Der Architekt C. F. Hansen*, ed. G. Wietak (Schleswig: Schleswig-Holsteinisches Landesmuseum, 1983), 13.

[46] On the widespread use of the term *Kjøbenhavnerstilen* (Copenhagen Style) to characterize Hansen's form of architecture see, above all, the monograph by C. M. Smidt, *Arkitekten C. F. Hansen og hans Bygninger* (Copenhagen: Gad, 1911), 32.

Copenhagen Style common to all of the new buildings would emphasize a sense of royal coordination with the palace.

The churches in Copenhagen which Hansen also had to rebuild were as much a part of his plan for a new, elegant royal city as any of the other public buildings. They, too, would have a majestic look, with stately Doric, Ionic, and Corinthian marble columns symbolizing the strength and rich diversity of one of the world's oldest kingdoms. They, too, would extend the classical grandeur of the royal palace to other parts of the capital city. They would, however, be smaller in scale and less imposing than the royal palace which, as the king's residence, had to enjoy a position of primacy in Copenhagen, according to Hansen's plan. High steeples, extensive naves, or overt ornamentation were not, therefore, a part of Hansen's overall design for the city. Nothing would tower over or deflect from the glory of the royal palace.

Frederik VI was naturally pleased with Hansen's patriotic values. When, in Husum, a new St. Mary's Church had to be erected (the former, ancient building had to be torn down because of irreparable structural defects), the king, as head of the State Church, quite predictably chose Hansen as architect for the task. The Copenhagen Style would then become visible in Husum, as in the royal capital and in other towns of the king's dominions, and through it the inhabitants would experience a feeling of close association with everything Copenhagen stood for. This feeling was intensified when the citizens of Husum were informed that Hansen would design their St. Mary's according to architectural plans he had used to rebuild the prominent St. Mary's Church in Copenhagen. It was assumed, therefore, that St. Mary's in Husum was intended to be a replica of St. Mary's in Copenhagen.[47] It would be hard to imagine a more telling association of Husum with Copenhagen. Nor could better proof be offered for the claim — made recently at an exhibition of

---

47   Stuckert, 15.

Hansen's art — that he symbolized the cultural and artistic bridge between the Danish capital and the duchy of Schleswig.[48]

Thus, the Copenhagen Style spread to Husum, with the church designed by the court-appointed Hansen and with the benefit of liberal funding from the royal coffers.[49] Of the building's specific Danish character there could be no doubt. Frederik VI had personally toured the building site on June 18, 1831 (according to a report in Husum's *Wochenblatt* of June 26, 1831) in order to formally approve the way Hansen's Copenhagen Style had been introduced to Husum's skyline. The architectural extension of Copenhagen's St. Mary's to the new St. Mary's in this far corner of Greater Denmark must have been a matter of considerable patriotic importance for Frederik. He had, we know, once taken a strong personal interest in the erection of that *monumentum Daniae* in the nation's capital.[50] The king must have been proud that the glory of Denmark's Golden Age architecture would now shine forth with new brilliance in another part of the monarchy over which he presided.

In Husum, so much importance was attached to this royal Danish approval of the church design that confusion arose as to whether the date of the king's visit or the subsequent date of the formal dedication ceremonies should be considered the actual date of the church's completion.[51] Without the sovereign's approval of the structure, certainly the court-appointed Hansen would never have marched at the head of the procession of dignitaries entering the church for its first official service.[52]

---

48 *C. F. Hansen in Hamburg, Altona und den Elbvororten*, ed. B. Hedinger (Munich & Berlin: Deutscher Kunstverlag, 2000), 7.
49 Documentation concerning the royal funding is in the Kreisarchiv Nordfriesland: Abt. D2, Nr. 126, folios 1 &2. I am indebted to Holger Borzikowsky, the archivist of Nordfriesland, for making this source material available to me.
50 Vilh. Lorenzen, *Vor Frue Kirke. Københavns Domkirke* (Copenhagen: Tryde, 1927), 126–128.
51 *Marienkirche Husum*, eds. U.v. Hielmcrone, P. Zubek, J. Henningsen (Husum: Schrift 7 des Kreisarchivs Nordfriesland, 1983), 24.
52 Documentation concerning the dedication ceremonies is in the Kreisarchiv Nordfriesland: Abt. D2, Nr. 126, folios 1 & 2.

Was this Frederik's or Hansen's church? Regardless of who may have been the guiding force behind the erection of Husum's St. Mary's, it turned out to be a highly conspicuous monument to Danish patriotic values. No one, perhaps, has seen this more clearly than the Prussian art historian Richard Haupt, who, in 1887, ruthlessly condemned the structure as a product of Danish minds which, he felt, should no longer have any place in the new Schleswig that Bismarck had wrested from Denmark and annexed to Prussia![53]

From the date the cornerstone of St. Mary's was laid on August 1, 1829, until the dedication on July 7, 1833, nothing, of course, was talked about more in Husum than this massive Danish importation. The townspeople quickly took sides over the erection of this, Husum's most impressive and important building. Much of the heated discussion, however, had little to do with the specifically Danish appearance Husum was acquiring. What bothered some patricians above all, including the Woldsens, Storm's maternal family, was the fact that 171 crypts below the floor of the former St. Mary's were ripped open and their contents scattered in order to make room for the foundation of the new church building.[54] Many of Husum's citizens were aghast at this violation of the bones of their ancestors. What they felt as an appalling lack of respect for the dead now became the subject of inflamed conversation all over the town and in Storm's own home as well. This, in turn, induced many, including Storm's mother and grandmother, to take a cynical attitude toward the structure that was destroying much that was considered sacred by Husum's venerable families.

More acute displeasure over the new St. Mary's also developed because Hansen stubbornly refused to allow memorials from the older church to be carried into his new building. He would not let his Copenhagen Style be compromised with artifacts that had their places

---

53   Richard Haupt, *Die Bau- und Kunstdenkmäler der Provinz Schleswig-Holstein*, I (Kiel: Homann, 1887), 457.
54   Ibid.

in earlier, less Danish periods of art history. He remained unmoved by the pleas of some of Husum's most established families, including the Woldsens, who had a sentimental attachment to these memorials and wanted them transferred to the new church.[55]

Storm, exposed almost daily to the sentiments of the older members of his family, became no less of a cynic than they and also expressed his reservations. He recorded these in his autobiographical sketch *Von heut' und ehedem* (About now and formerly). But there was little he or anyone else in Husum could do about the matter. Hansen enjoyed the strong support of both the sovereign and the town's magistrates who were, after all, only appointees of the crown and hardly in a position to veto what their king had approved. Thus, Hansen's uncompromised Copenhagen Style was imposed upon the townspeople from above, as we have been told, without regard to any reservations they expressed.[56] The new monument to Danish art became the imposing landmark of Husum. All that remained for those who objected was to talk more about this literal reproduction of a Copenhagen art form. Such discussion only served to heighten Storm's and other citizens' awareness of Husum's strengthened association with the Danish crown, which the new St. Mary's, in the Copenhagen Style, now so obviously proclaimed.

The discussion that had drawn everyone in Husum to focus more intensely on the king's new building was, of course, further fostered when the costs for erecting the structure had to be considered. Despite the generous funding from the crown, the citizens of Husum were also expected to carry their share of the expense for this architectural novelty in their midst. They did not, of course, at all relish this obligation, as Werner Jakstein has indicated.[57]

The practical implementation of the new Danish style of architecture also put demands on local contractors and artisans, which,

---

55   Documentation concerning the objections of Husum's patricians, including the Woldsens, is in the Kreisarchiv Nordfriesland: Abt. D2, Nr. 126, folios 1 & 2.
56   Haupt, 457.
57   Werner Jakstein, *Landesbaumeister Christian Friedrich Hansen. Der nordische Klassizist* (Neumünster: Wachholtz, 1937), 72.

because of their lack of experience and knowledge, they were unable to meet. Craftsmen were therefore imported from Copenhagen to work the masonry and to give expression to the melody of the Doric, Ionic, and Corinthian orders that was so central to Hansen's architectural scheme. It was judged that Husum's labor force also lacked the expertise necessary to handle the novelty of St. Mary's strange copper cupola; its construction, too, brought the importation of skilled laborers from Copenhagen, and this put more local men out of work. Of course, this painful loss of jobs and money gave the local population more reason to look with jaundiced eyes on the structure being erected in their midst. Thus every new building block that the imported artisans from Copenhagen put into place became the subject of renewed ill-humored comments, which in turn served as reminders that the town was fast becoming a part of the extended architectural horizon of Denmark's capital city.

4. Storm's schooling in Danish letters

If Danish culture continued to make its impact in the duchy of Schleswig and in the town of Husum, indeed all around Storm during the impressionable years of his boyhood and early manhood, nothing could have contributed more to providing him with a Danish cultural outlook in those years than the formal instruction in Danish he received at school in his native Husum. Instruction in Danish and particularly in Danish literature constituted an integral part of the curriculum at Husum's Latin School during Storm's time there. In fact, the teaching of Danish was taken so seriously that the principal himself, Peter Friedrichsen, took personal charge of it, as his Annual School Report for 1831 informs us (*Schulnachrichten. Bericht des Rektors*, 1831: 28).[58] In his earnest desire to give his pupils a thorough

---

58 The Annual Reports of the Latin School in Storm's time are preserved today in the archives of the Hermann Tast Gymnasium at Husum. I am indebted to Werner Stiebeling, the librarian at the school, for making these Reports and other documents available to me.

schooling in all aspects of Danish life and letters, the principal went to great lengths. In the same Report we find that, during vacation periods, he kept the school open and invited his pupils back to take part in the extracurricular dictation exercises (in Danish) he offered to broaden their knowledge of their Danish fatherland's history. The importance attached to Danish instruction at Friedrichsen's school becomes even more obvious when compared with such instruction at the time in the other Latin School in the southern part of the duchy: the *Domschule* in the town of Schleswig. There, we read, scheduled Danish classes were often canceled because of the lack of a teacher, and other subjects received a greater priority when teaching assignments were made.[59] Nothing of the sort occurred in Husum.

We should not be surprised at the principal's eagerness to strengthen Danish studies at his school. He had always headed the receiving line at the school's main entrance when the Danish monarch, Frederik VI, arrived for the periodic royal visits. As Husum's leading educator, moreover, Friedrichsen had always been an important person among the dignitaries who gathered in front of the town's castle to welcome the king, when the royal carriage rolled into the courtyard with all the fanfare befitting such a regal event. (One such visit by the monarch, as reported in Husum's weekly newspaper, is described above.) Frederik VI often visited his subjects in Husum, and the ceremonies that regularly took place on the welcoming carpets were, according to the various reports in Husum's *Wochenblatt*, always occasions of great festivity. Friedrichsen, of course, played his part in adding his share of patriotism, grace, dignity, and eloquence to these receptions.

Naturally, Frederik VI must have been pleased when he observed the extent to which this educator was beholden to him. It would have been difficult not to notice Friedrichsen's expressions of loyalty to the crown. It was all the more likely that the king would take note of this schoolmaster, since there were only four such prin-

---

59 According to the *Regulativ für die Königliche Domschule in Schleswig* (Schleswig: Königl. Taubstummen-Institut, 1826), 5.

cipals serving with royal approbation in the duchy at the time, at the Latin Schools in the towns of Husum, Haderslev, Flensburg, and Schleswig. By word and deed Frederik VI showed his appreciation to Friedrichsen: by word, doubtless, with oral expressions of gratitude, and by deed when he personally donated to the school's library gifts of books published in the nation's capital city.[60]

Of course, the monarch's patronage of Husum's Latin School and his repeated appreciative nods to its demonstratively patriotic principal would have served, in turn, to reaffirm the principal's efforts to give his pupils an excellent schooling in Denmark's language, literature, and culture. Friedrichsen apparently lost no time in implementing Frederik VI's royal directive of February 20, 1826, concerning the teaching of Danish in the duchy: seven hours per week were to be allocated henceforth to Danish instruction at higher institutions of learning.[61] That was a considerable amount of time to be spent on Danish in a school such as Husum's Latin School, which heavily emphasized Latin and Greek, but Friedrichsen promptly ensured that the study of the Ancients left sufficient time to accommodate His Majesty's request. At the end of Storm's first year at the school (1826–1827), Friedrichsen wrote in his Annual Report for 1827 (*Regulativ für die Gelehrtenschule der Stadt Husum*, 1827: 1–2) that seven hours of Danish instruction per week had been taught that year. The same degree of attention to the teaching of Danish persisted throughout the nine years (1826–1835) that Storm re-

---

60   The *Akzessionskatalog 1763–1834* of Husum's Latin School, now in the archives of Husum's Hermann Tast Gymnasium (T 145), duly records the titles of every book the king gave in each of the years the donations were made. The Christian Flor archive in the Royal Library at Copenhagen possesses five unpublished letters from Peter Friedrichsen to representatives of the Danish crown expressing appreciation for the gifts of Danish books to the school's library. Friedrichsen assures the crown that these gifts will quicken the growing interest in Danish literature amongst both the school's pupils and the town's citizenry. I am indebted to Palle Ringsted of the Royal Library for making these letters available to me.

61   E. Manicus, "Et Bidrag til den danske Nationalitets Historie i Slesvig," *Slesvigske Provindsialefterretninger*, I (1860): 198.

mained at the school, according to Friedrichsen's subsequent Annual Reports.

To fully appreciate the quality of Danish instruction Storm received, we need only compare it with the woefully deficient teaching of German at the school. According to Friedrichsen's Annual Reports for the period 1826–1835, instruction in German included only exercises in grammar and composition, which were surely dull and uninteresting for Storm's imaginative, poetic mind. The sole textbook for German instruction that Friedrichsen mentions is Johann Christian Heyse's *Theoretisch-praktische deutsche Grammatik* (Theoretical and Practical German Grammar).[62] Texts of German literature were evidently not considered important for pedagogical purposes.

Storm himself later reported on various occasions that he had learned little about modern German literature at school in Husum,[63] indeed little about anything from the whole of German literature.[64] In his final school year (1834–1835) he did not have the slightest idea that any noteworthy living German poets existed.[65] Today, to any student of German literature, Storm's statements seem incredible. Precisely at that time the *ars poetica* was flourishing profusely in Germany, with an amazing array of geniuses like Brentano, Tieck, Eichendorff, Heine, Mörike, and a host of other luminaries. Yet Storm, at school, had not heard of any of them! German instruction at a German-speaking school could hardly have been worse.

But if instruction in German rarely advanced beyond uninspiring grammar lessons at Storm's school, Danish studies, under Friedrichsen's patriotic tutelage, seem to have left nothing to be desired. Instruction included not only the essentials of vocabulary and grammar but also a thorough introduction to the best of Danish literature.

---

62 Johann Christian Heyse, *Theoretisch-praktische deutsche Grammatik* (Hannover: Hahn, 1814). Reprinted in numerous revised editions throughout the nineteenth century.
63 LL, IV, 442.
64 Ibid., 470.
65 Ibid., 488, 490.

The textbooks for Danish which Friedrichsen chose offer telling evidence of the difference between instruction in Danish and in German. These books from which Storm learned Danish were not merely "grammars" but rather "anthologies of literature," with additional grammatical and syntactical annotation. In Danish, the patriotic Friedrichsen wanted his pupils to acquire a superior level of knowledge, through study of the uses to which the language had been put by great masters of Danish literature.

Looking at Friedrichsen's Annual Reports for 1827–1835, we find that the most frequently mentioned textbook in Danish for the lower grades was the anthology compiled and edited by Ludolph Herrmann Tobiesen, an alumnus of the school.[66] For the upper grades, Friedrichsen used the more advanced anthology of Detlev Lorenz Lübker, a clergyman in Husum who wanted to make sure that candidates for ecclesiastical positions in the German-speaking districts of the duchy would also be able to preach effective sermons to their Danish-speaking flocks.[67]

These were the anthologies from which Storm prepared, week after week, his assignments, and these were the books that gave him his familiarity with contemporary literature, which he did not receive in German instruction at Friedrichsen's school. With these textbooks Storm was taught the patriotic value of studying Danish literature. He could read at the beginning of each anthology an extraordinarily reverent dedication to either King Frederik (Tobiesen) or the Queen Consort (Lübker). Storm could realize that the editors of both anthologies knew the policy of the royal Danish government well when they, like principal Friedrichsen, used their considerable pedagogical talents to encourage the educated youth in the duchy to become more Danish, in language as well as in spirit. "Ein Gott, ein König,

---

66 Ludolph Herrmann Tobiesen, *Neues dänisches Lesebuch zum Gebrauch in den gelehrten Schulen Schleswig-Holsteins und für alle, die die dänische Sprache erlernen wollen* (Altona: Hammerich, 1813).

67 Detlev Lorenz Lübker, *Neue dänische Blumenlese; oder Sammlung prosaisch-poetischer Stücke, zum Gebrauch für höhere Classen und für Freunde der dänischen Literatur* (Altona: Hammerich, 1826).

ein Gesetz, eine Sprache" (One Lord, one king, one law, one language) — this dictum of an earlier anthologist of Danish literature, Frederik Hoegh-Guldberg,[68] had become almost axiomatic for the teaching of Danish in the duchy; the Husum pedagogue Lübker specifically stated in his preface that with his new Danish anthology, he wished to continue the tradition that had been established by Hoegh-Guldberg.[69]

This meant, of course, not only deepening Danish patriotism with a sustained study of the Danish language, but also awakening an awareness that the most perfect command of the Danish language could only come through the study of the best of Denmark's wordsmiths. Judging by the selections from Danish literature included in their anthologies, Tobiesen and Lübker must have believed that poetry, above all, gave the student of Danish the sharpest insight into the possibilities of Danish literary expression and the ideal avenue of access to the Danish cultural scene. Shorter pieces of Danish prose in the form of novellas supplemented the pedagogical purpose of poetry in the two textbooks.

There can be no doubt about this: Storm received an enviable education in the Danish language, in Danish letters, and in Danish institutions. The claim of Franz Stuckert, the author of a long biography of the poet, that Storm in his school days had neither learned nor understood Danish,[70] is nonsense. That was an opinion Stuckert formed during World War II, when anti-Danish feeling ran high in Germany, and it was an opinion, furthermore, which presumably hardened in the early post-war period when Stuckert, while continuing to write Storm's biography, suffered unemployment and alienation in German society because of the particularly

---

68   F. Hoegh-Guldberg, *Dänisches Lesebuch für Schleswigholsteiner* (Kiel: Schulbuchdruckerey, 1809), viii.
69   Lübker, x.
70   Stuckert, 14.

overt patriotism he had displayed during the years of the Third Reich.[71]

The foundation in Danish which Storm acquired, up to the age of eighteen, was so strong that it could not have been dislodged when his father, in 1835, took him out of school at Husum and sent him to a finishing school in Lübeck, a city outside of the Danish political orbit. There the younger Storm was to receive a German education. Now he was introduced to outstanding works of German literature, such as Goethe's *Faust* and Heine's *Buch der Lieder*. A wholly new world of literary experience opened up for him and this, of course, broadened his education considerably.

Certainly this must have been the intent of Storm's father when he transferred his son to a school *im Ausland* (in a foreign territory), as his son referred to German-speaking territories not under the jurisdiction of the Danish monarch.[72] Storm's father himself had once studied at the University of Heidelberg, at precisely the time when German literary Romanticism was flowering there and contributing so much to the invigorating intellectual climate of that venerable seat of German learning. Storm's father had come to know, then, the valuable, broadening effect of complementing a Danish education with study in Germany.

Yet, as broadening and enriching as Storm's school days in the foreign world of Lübeck must have been (how could the reading and discussion of *Faust* be otherwise?), the stay abroad was not long enough to allow the influence of German literature to weaken the sure foundation in Danish letters which Storm had acquired in Husum. The experience of studying German literature and culture at Lübeck lasted only one and a half years, which was brief in comparison with the nine years of schooling in Danish culture in Husum.

71　*Bremische Biographie 1912–1962*, ed. W. Lührs (Bremen: Hauschild, 1969), 511; Helmut Peitsch, "Ein Storm aus Blut und Boden? Zur literarhistorischen Biographik aus der Zeit des Faschismus am Beispiel Franz Stuckerts" in *Theodor Storm – Narrative Strategies and Patriarchy*, eds. D. A. Jackson & M. G. Ward (Lewiston, NY: Mellen, 1999), 259–260.
72　*Storm–Ernst Esmarch*, 38, 151.

Whatever Storm may have learned in Germany, therefore, he remained essentially a product of his early Danish schooling and environment in Husum, a *Schuckelmeyer* (the disparaging name for a Dane), as his German schoolmates in Lübeck called him because of his curious foreign accent, manners, and ways of thinking.[73]

5. The capstone: Storm's exposure to the Danish spirit at the University of Kiel

a. The Danish coloring of town and gown

After the short spell abroad, *im Ausland*, Storm returned to his native Danish kingdom to study law at the University of Kiel. This institution of higher learning owed its existence to royal Danish decrees and, at the time of Storm's matriculation, received its funding from the coffers of Frederik VI, the monarch who was also the benefactor of Husum's Latin School. Kiel was the second oldest of the two universities (after the University of Copenhagen) located in the lands over which the Danish monarch ruled.

Storm began his academic studies at Kiel in the spring term of 1837. Just one year earlier, the bicultural Franco-German poet Adelbert von Chamisso had published his recollections of a visit to Kiel's university and recorded this observation: "Zu Kiel sind die Professoren deutsch, die Studenten dänisch gesinnt" (In Kiel the professors are German, the students Danish in their convictions).[74] Chamisso's observation was probably quite accurate. The students at this small university (there were only two hundred at the time)[75] had been, after all, raised in the Danish monarchy and knew little or nothing about life in lands not belonging to the Danish sovereign. The only connection many of the students had to German culture was their (often shaky) knowledge of the German language. Samuel

---

73   LL, IV, 445.
74   A. von Chamisso, *Werke*, I (Leipzig: Weidmann, 1836), 22.
75   According to Husum's *Wochenblatt* of June 8, 1845.

Laing, an early nineteenth-century Scottish traveler to Schleswig, had observed that only one-ninth of the population knew German well enough to pursue studies at a German-speaking university without first doing remedial work in the language:

> two thirds of the Sleswick population speak Danish only, and of the other third, speaking German in the Platt Deutsch form, one third only, it is reckoned, know the cultivated German language sufficiently to study at a German university without beginning to learn the language grammatically before attending the lectures.[76]

There can be little cause for wonder, then, that the students at the University of Kiel were particularly vocal, when the Congress of Vienna met in 1815, in insisting that the duchy of Schleswig should not follow Holstein's example in becoming a member of the newly created Confederation of German States. Whatever historical or social connections the duchy may have had to neighboring Holstein, the language of the students was overwhelmingly Danish, and these students had no desire, we are told by another observer, to loosen Schleswig's ancient ties to Denmark and politically realign the duchy to the German-speaking regions of Europe.[77]

If the students at Kiel were, as Chamisso claimed, far more attuned to Danish than to German culture, the professors, as Chamisso also understood, differed from their students. Because of their more advanced academic training, which had often included travel to German universities and firsthand knowledge of the scholarship of their colleagues in Germany, they had come to share German educational values. Doubtless, the temper of the more cosmopolitan German-speaking universities must have seemed more congenial to their academic interests than the more limited and uniform academic environment in Denmark, which had only one major university.

---

76 Samuel Laing, *Observations on the Social and Political State of Denmark and the Duchies of Sleswick and Holstein in 1851* (London: Longman, Brown, Green, Longmans, 1852), 61.

77 Johann Runge, *Christian Paulsens politische Entwicklung* (Neumünster: Wachholtz, 1969), 57.

But it would be a mistake to interpret Chamisso's comment to mean that Kiel's professors lacked any Danish cultural orientation. The circumstance of these professors at this second Danish university was, after all, quite different than that of faculty members at universities in Germany. They were beholden to the Danish king for their appointments as well as for their promotions. Most of them were also, like their students, brought up in lands belonging to the Danish crown. They were loyal subjects of the crown. At this small university where professors and students knew each other in close personal relationships, even those who felt most drawn to German academic life and scholarship could not avoid some adaptation to the Danish orientation of the university where they were employed. Nor could they be unreceptive to the Danish sentiments and assumptions of their students. All of this gave the university at Kiel, in Storm's time, a Danish tinge that made it fundamentally different from any other university where the German language was used. The Danish flag flying at the top of the main university building had genuine symbolic significance.

Most obviously, of course, the university's Danish coloring would be apparent at those festive times when the monarch himself visited Kiel. These were occasions of much patriotic pomp and ceremony. King Frederik VI came to Kiel in June 1839, and King Christian VIII arrived in September 1840. The report in Kiel's newspaper, the *Correspondenz-Blatt* of June 15, 1839, covering King Frederik's arrival gives us an idea of what Storm must have witnessed each time. With all the fanfare befitting such a royal visit, the important dignitaries of town and gown gathered at the waterfront to greet the sovereign when his paddle steamer sailed into Kiel's spacious harbor and moored at the pier just below the castle where he would reside. The colorful welcoming ceremonies, with magniloquent speeches, festive trumpet blasts, and all the red and white Danish flags flying from the numerous flagpoles erected for the arrival, took place only a few yards away from the foot of the *Flämische Straße* (Flemish Street), the little street on which Storm had his student lodging. We can well imagine that Storm would be nearby to experience firsthand the clamor of the monarch's arrival, especially because the university, located just two blocks away, quite probably suspended its normal functions in order that everyone could witness the king's auspicious arrival. Who would have wanted to miss all the excitement and pageantry?

At nightfall it was the students' turn to extend the welcome to their sovereign. They did so, as reported in Kiel's *Correspondenz-Blatt* of June 15, 1839, with an impressive torchlight procession from the university to the castle, where the king listened to the addresses of the student representatives and, doubtless, smiled in appreciation of the flattering words. He must have been even more pleased when the huge gathering sang into the night its loud "Hail to the King." As the newspaper report also informs us, the Danish sovereign then invited the students into the castle, where long tables of gourmet foods and beverages, hardly affordable for students in everyday life, awaited them.

Since the castle was just around the corner from Storm's abode in the *Flämische Straße*, it is hard to imagine that he would have been absent from the lavish festivities. With typically meager funds at his disposal, only an extremely diligent student would pass up such a royal feast so close by. That Storm was not that sort of serious student, we know from his absorbing love life at the time with Emma Kühl and Bertha von Buchan, which Storm biographers have taken such delight in detailing. His lack of seriousness as a student is also apparent from the quite unimpressive grades he received in his final examinations.[78]

Storm did not, of course, have to wait for the arrival of the monarch from Copenhagen in order to be aware of the strong presence of the Danish crown in Kiel. King Frederik VI's daughter Wilhelmine and her princely husband Carl lived all year round in the castle where the monarch stayed when visiting Kiel. Storm had to walk past the castle every day on his way to and from his student quarters and the university. Appropriately, the street on which he

---

78   These have been duly recorded by v. Fisenne, 12.

strolled with his books and papers was called the *Dänische Straße* (Danish Street). The street still bears that name today. Daily — or, more often, several times a day — Storm, walking down Danish Street, could see the bright red and white Danish flag flying in front of the castle, or he could stop to watch the colorfully dressed Danish sentries standing at attention in front of the castle's main entrance. This was the best display of Danish national pride next to the changing of the guard at the majestic Christiansborg Palace in Copenhagen.

All year round, too, Frederik VI's daughter Wilhelmine, together with her dashing husband Carl, saw to it that the splendor of the royal palace in Copenhagen radiated out from their "Little Christiansborg" in Kiel. Rudolph Schleiden, one of the students at the Law School whom Storm quite possibly knew well (there were only seventy or eighty students in the School at the time,[79] and Schleiden, like Storm, came from an old patrician family in Husum, which gave the two young men more in common), has given us in his memoirs an intriguing picture of the colorful court life at this "Little Christiansborg."[80] The glamorous court balls to which the students were invited, Schleiden tells us, continued all winter long, often night after night, usually for eight days in succession. The students danced until late into the night, well aware that these festive nights would not have been possible if the daughter of the king of Denmark had not established her royal residence in Kiel. Storm, living just around the corner and known among his fellow students as a man with strong romantic interests,[81] could not have delighted less than Rudolph Schleiden in dancing until late into the night at these Danish balls. If Storm's academic grades were less than what could have been expected from him, he may well have spent more time in this Danish ballroom than with his books.

Further conspicuous reminders of the university's Danish *mise-en-scène* were those many occasions when the entire academic com-

---

79 According to Husum's *Wochenblatt*, June 8, 1845.
80 Rudolph Schleiden, *Jugenderinnerungen eines Schleswig-Holsteiners* (Wiesbaden: Bergmann, 1886), 253, 298.
81 *Storm–Mommsen*, 45.

munity observed important events at the Danish court in Copenhagen. No royal birthday, wedding, or funeral was allowed to pass without the university taking advantage of the opportunity to proclaim anew its patriotic association with the Danish crown.[82] We can be confident that all regular teaching schedules were suspended in order that the entire student body, the teaching faculty, and other staff could attend the special convocations that were convened in the great *Auditorio*.

Storm was almost certainly present at these patriotic convocations. For one thing, attendance was in all likelihood mandatory. But he also had another reason for taking his seat in the auditorium. As long as he had studied at Kiel, the main address at such a convocation was always delivered by a faculty member from Storm's own small Law School. Danish patriotism must have been strong at the Law School, indeed stronger than at any of the other university faculties; otherwise it would be difficult to explain why one of the law professors was always chosen for such demonstrations of patriotism. Because the honor of giving the address always fell on a law professor, conversation among Storm and his fellow law students and friends, later on in the evening or the next day, surely revolved around what one of their own professors had said. Storm, never known to be an introvert, would not have wanted to miss these lively conversations of the day.

One such important convocation took place on January 16, 1840. On that day the professors and students (including, quite probably, Storm) attended the well-planned memorial service for King Frederik VI, who had died a month earlier. The eulogy was given by Nicolaus Falck, the distinguished professor at the Law School whom

---

82   Much unpublished documentation concerning the Danish patriotic activities at the University of Kiel during the years when Storm was a member of the student body is today in the possession of the Schleswig-Holsteinisches Landesarchiv in the town of Schleswig. I am obliged to the authorities for generously placing the extensive folios of Abt. 47 at my disposal. Many of my remarks are based on information gathered from these documents.

Storm had met on his very first day at the university. Falck, as dean of the Law School, had officially matriculated the new student.

It would be hard to imagine a more dutiful homage to the king of Denmark than the address Falck delivered on that solemn occasion, when the entire university community gathered to pay its respects to its departed sovereign. The university press quickly printed the eulogy so that it could be distributed to the widest possible audience as a permanent reminder of the esteem in which the university held its dead king.[83] The university book store then managed the sales of the printed eulogy. Storm, who, like other students, regularly visited the book store to purchase his texts and other supplies for his studies, quite likely picked up a copy because Falck was his revered mentor. It is also likely that he may have purchased the copy (or perhaps even an additional one) to forward to his father, who was a friend of Falck.

The following are a few of the eloquent words with which Falck, on behalf of the university community, eulogized its deceased Danish sovereign. Falck calls King Frederik "den Beschützer und Pfleger dieser Hochschule" (the protector and guardian of this institution of higher learning).[84] "Sein Andenken bleibet im Segen bei uns" (His memory will remain sacred with us).[85] "Ruhe denn sanft, theurer dahingeschiedener König" (Rest in peace, beloved departed king).[86]

After the period of official mourning at the royal court in Copenhagen and at the university in Kiel was over, preparations began for the university's participation in the coronation ceremonies for the new king, Christian VIII. The deans of all four academic faculties, according to the acts of the university (located today in the *Landesarchiv* in Schleswig), comprised the official delegation representing the university on June 28, 1840, at Frederiksborg Slot, the palace

---

83 N. Falck, *Gedächtnißrede bei der Todtenfeier Seiner Majestät König Frederik des Sechsten am 16ten Januar 1840 im großen academischen Hörsaale zu Kiel* (Kiel: Universitäts-Buchhandlung, 1840).
84 Ibid., 1.
85 Ibid., 23.
86 Ibid.

north of Copenhagen that would later play an important role in Theodor Fontane's novel *Unwiederbringlich* (Beyond Recall).

On the same day, a special academic convocation in honor of the new Danish king was convened in the great *Auditorio* in Kiel. The festival address was given by another of Storm's law professors, Georg Christian Burchardi. Storm had every right to attend and even to take a front seat, for the new king, concomitantly with his coronation, had just raised Storm's father, Johann Casimir Storm, to the rank of a knight of the coveted Royal Danish *Dannebrog* order. Since the son was a student in Kiel, this made news there. Kiel's *Correspondenz-Blatt* announced in its next issue (July 1, 1840) the high honor that had been bestowed on the elder Storm. The son must indeed have been tremendously proud of his father and no less impressed with the new Danish monarch who had honored the Storm family in such an exceptional way.

Burchardi concluded his festive oration with this panegyric flourish:

> Heil Sr. Majestät unserem Allergnädigsten König und Herzog Christian VIII., der sein Volk nicht bloß gerecht und gütig zu regieren, sondern auch zu großartiger Entwicklung zu führen versteht.[87]

> (Hail to His Majesty, our most gracious king and duke, Christian VIII, who not only governs his subjects justly and benevolently, but who also will lead the entire nation into a glorious future.)

We can be fairly sure that Storm joined in the vigorous applause that must have resonated across the entire auditorium when Burchardi stepped down from the podium. We can also be fairly sure that Storm observed the colorful parade through Kiel's streets on the same day in honor of the new king, about which Kiel's *Correspondenz-Blatt* further reported on July 1, 1840. Storm could see the Danish flag flying in every part of the parade and from the houses all along the parade's route as well, and be reminded that day many times over of the patriotic fervor that had gripped the town and its citizenry.

---

87   G. C. Burchardi, *Festrede gehalten bei der Krönungs-Feier den 28ten Juni 1840 in der Akademischen Aula zu Kiel* (Kiel: Universitäts-Buchhandlung, 1840), 25.

On many other ceremonious occasions Storm could also be reminded of Kiel's happy association with the Danish crown. On June 14, 1841, for instance, the university announced to its students and faculty that it would send a delegation of its four deans again to Copenhagen, this time in order that Kiel could be appropriately represented at the wedding of the Crown Prince, the future King Frederik VII.[88] On September 18, 1842, only a few weeks before Storm presented himself for his final examinations, the university again celebrated the birthday of its reigning monarch with a special academic convocation, as had been the annual custom during the entire period of Storm's study at Kiel.[89] Once more a faculty member of Storm's Law School delivered a lengthy oration proclaiming the university's affiliation with the Danish Royal House, and once more Storm could rise from his seat with the entire audience, as the speaker concluded his convocational address with the echoing words everyone in attendance was waiting to hear: "Gott erhalte den König!" (God save the king!). Promptly, as usual, the university printed the address in order that it could be distributed far and wide beyond the walls of its ivory towers.[90]

b. Two influential university teachers

No discussion of Storm's exposure to the Danish spirit at the University of Kiel would be complete without mention of two professors with whom he had a particularly close academic contact: Christian Paulsen and Nicolaus Falck. The latter's Danish patriotism has already been referred to in the eulogy he delivered at the university's memorial

---

88 Acts of the university: Abt. 471, document 78. In Schleswig-Holsteinisches Landesarchiv, Schleswig.

89 Kiel's *Correspondenz-Blatt* regularly reported to its readers an announcement similar to the one published in its September 19, 1840 issue: "im großen academischen Auditorio feiert heute die Universität den Geburtstag des Königs" (in the main academic auditorium the university will celebrate today the birthday of the king).

90 Emil Herrmann, *Rede bei der academischen Feier des Geburtsfestes Seiner Majestät des Königs Christian VIII. am 18. September 1842 im großen Hörsaale der Universität* (Kiel: Mohr, 1842), 22.

service for King Frederik VI. But more can be said about Falck's Danish patriotism and the impact he made on Storm. For he was the most significant figure in the community of scholars at Kiel during Storm's time; the influence he exerted on students and colleagues was considerable. Paulsen, too, played a role in the shaping of Storm's mind that should no longer be overlooked.

These two educators shared much in common. Both took an academic interest in the same subject matter: the legal history of Denmark, Schleswig, and Holstein. Both were prominent teaching members of Kiel's Law School. They alternated as dean of the Law Faculty. Both were natives of the duchy of Schleswig. Both frequently visited Copenhagen. Both had enviable connections to important officials at the Danish royal court. Both spoke Danish and German with equal ease (Falck, whose native tongue was Danish, learned German early in life; Paulsen, a native speaker of German, learned Danish early in life). Both had an abiding affection and a deep sense of loyalty to the Danish crown. Both had been knighted by the Danish king in recognition of their meritorious patriotic services. Both had been elected to membership in the Royal Danish Historical Society.[91] Not unsymbolically, both had stately residences on Kiel's *Dänische Straße* (Danish Street), close to each other and only two city blocks away from where Storm lived as a student. Crowning everything else the two mentors had in common, they were related through marriage; at family gatherings they could regularly affirm their shared patriotic convictions.

Little has been said in Storm criticism about the impact these two pro-Danish teachers made on Storm during several of the most impressionable years of his early manhood. Falck's name has been mentioned occasionally in passing, but with little or no attention to what Storm may have learned from him. The cursory treatment of this important teacher becomes perhaps most apparent in the lengthy Storm biography written by Franz Stuckert. In that work, Nicolaus Falck's name is passed over so hastily that it turns up on the printed

---

91   *Historisk Tidskrift*, I (Copenhagen 1840): 575.

page as Nikolaus Falk.[92] It speaks even worse for Storm criticism that the name of Storm's other important academic mentor, Christian Paulsen, has gone completely unrecorded. It is high time, therefore, that all those interested in Storm should take note of Paulsen, and that they should also become aware of the deception which, unfortunately, caused his name to be blotted out and replaced by a fictitious Professor Deller.

c. The fictitious Professor Deller in Storm criticism

The deception began when Storm's daughter Gertrud wrote in her biography of her father that he had studied Danish law in Kiel with a "Professor Deller"[93] (instead of with Christian Paulsen). But no Professor Deller had ever taught at Kiel University's Law School or at any faculty of that university when Storm studied there. The *Index Scholarum in academia regia Christiana Albertina* (Kiel's equivalent of the catalogue of courses at American universities, or the counterpart of the *Vorlesungsverzeichnis* at German universities of the twentieth century) lists for each of the terms Storm studied in Kiel no course whatsoever given by a Professor Deller.[94]

The name, hence, is completely fabricated. Yet, on the assumption that the poet's daughter must have known best, the name "Professor Deller" has stuck in Storm criticism, with critic after critic repeating her false statement, and invariably referring to her biography as the source for the information, with no attempt to check its accuracy. Not one critic has ever taken the trouble to find out the

---

92 Stuckert, 34.
93 Gertrud Storm, I, 131.
94 There is also no mention of a "Professor Deller" in three other works which duly record the names of faculty members on the university's roster: (1) Erich Döhring, *Geschichte der Christian-Albrechts-Universität Kiel 1665–1965, III: Geschichte der juristischen Fakultät* (Neumünster: Wachholtz, 1965); (2) H. Ratjen: *Geschichte der Universität zu Kiel* (Kiel: Schwers, 1870); (3) Friedrich Volbehr, *Professoren und Dozenten der Christian-Albrechts-Universität zu Kiel 1665 bis 1887* (Kiel: Universitätsbuchhandlung, 1887).

first name of this alleged teacher of Storm.[95] Of course, if they had done this, by looking at any one of a number of faculty rosters compiled at the University of Kiel, they would have discovered that no such professor had existed.

Why did the poet's daughter fabricate the name? Only one explanation seems plausible. With her instinctive business sense, and probably with additional prodding from her sales-oriented Prussian publisher, Karl Curtius, she realized that in the aftermath of the bigoted, but highly effective crusade by Ernst Matthias von Köller (the Prussian Governor General in Schleswig 1897–1901) to stamp out Danish culture in Schleswig,[96] her biography (begun in 1903),[97] might not sell as well in the newly established Prussian province of Schleswig-Holstein if it were to become known that Storm had studied under such a dedicated spokesman for the Danish cultural cause as Paulsen had been. Any mention of Paulsen's role in Storm's life would also have been inadvisable because the bellicose anti-Danish von Köller had figured so conspicuously in the unveiling ceremony of the Storm monument in Husum in 1898.[98] Gertrud Storm had, therefore, to suppress Paulsen's name, and to do so, she did not shrink from deception and forgery. She invented the fictitious "Professor Deller" with a non-Danish sounding name to substitute for the Danophile Paulsen. Nobody, she must have thought, would be able to chal-

---

95   See, for instance, Robert Pitrou, *La Vie et l'Oeuvre de Theodor Storm* (Paris: Alcan, 1920), 49; Stuckert, 34; v. Fisenne, 10.
96   See Sievers, 46–160; Troels Fink, *Ustabil balance: dansk udenrigs- og forsvarspolitik 1894–1905* (Aarhus: Universitetsforlaget, 1961), 66–83.
97   According to Wooley, "Gertrud Storm," 248.
98   Details in the *Husumer Nachrichten*, September 15, 1898 & *Husumer Wochenblatt*, September 19, 1898. Extensive documentation available in the Kreisarchiv Nordfriesland: Abt. D2, Nr. 4429.

lenge her statement with any authority as long as she remained the sole guardian of her father's literary legacy.[99]

d. Christian Paulsen

It is high time that Storm biographers recognize that the professor of Danish law in Kiel whose name has been omitted from Storm criticism in favor of the fabricated Professor Deller is Christian Paulsen. We know this from Paulsen's diaries, which were published in Denmark in 1946. In that dark postwar year there was no currency available in Germany to purchase books from abroad, and so Paulsen's diaries never became known to German critics of Storm. Elsewhere in the world, where Danish books could be purchased, Storm critics never took note of anything written in Danish. All of this is unfortunate, for Paulsen had recorded in his diaries that Storm was one of his outstanding students.[100] It is not hard to imagine why Paulsen was impressed with his student: the teacher must have perceived that Storm understood well what he sought to convey to his students in his lectures.

What were the factors which had shaped Paulsen's teaching? They were those of a highly educated and most assertive spokesman for the Danish way of life. Indeed, this teacher's affection for everything Danish was so great that, although he came from a German-speaking family in the duchy of Schleswig, he preferred more and more in the course of his life to use Danish as his primary language of communication. In early manhood he had fallen in love with the culture and advantages of Copenhagen. It was there that he completed his education. It was in Copenhagen, too, that he acquired enviable connections to important officials of the Danish State, including the monarch himself, which was no small achievement. His

---

99 Gertrud Storm's questionable scholarly behavior in this instance is, of course, altogether consistent with the manner in which she corrupted the texts of Storm's letters when she published them. See Franz Stuckert, "Der handschriftliche Nachlaß Theodor Storms und seine Bedeutung für die Forschung," STSG 1 (1952): 45.
100 *Flensborgeren, Professor Christian Paulsens Dagbøger*, 293.

Christian Paulsen's Danish gravestone in Flensburg.

friendship with Poul Martin Møller, the father of Danish Poetic Realism, brought him, furthermore, into close contact with the hub of literary activity in the nation's capital at the time. Thus, with all his heart, Paulsen came to embrace Danish cultural values. Frederik VI could hardly have found a more pliant candidate to represent the crown at the southern outpost of Danish learning in Kiel than when he appointed Paulsen to teach Danish law there in 1826.[101]

Storm, intent upon entering the practice of law in his native Schleswig, must have been eager to learn as much as possible from this authority about the complicated system of Danish laws governing various aspects of life in the duchy. In his first term at the university, Storm signed up for a lecture course given by Paulsen. In subsequent terms he enrolled in other courses with Paulsen and broadened further his knowledge of the historical factors that had contributed to making Schleswig essentially Danish in law, tradition, and custom. This view had always weighed heavily in Paulsen's lectures and publications.[102]

Much of what Paulsen expounded from his academic podium and in his writings proved to be contentious. This must have made what he said all the more interesting for his pupil Storm, who could observe the critical discourse that his professor's ideas provoked in academic and public circles. Here was a pedagogue who brought both a prodigious amount of learning and passionate patriotism to the discussion of the Danish tradition in Schleswig, but whose patriotic reasoning was frequently so open to challenge that his students — including, of course, Storm — could not help but become more aware of their mentor's pro-Danish convictions.

Storm's interest must have been particularly sparked, for instance, when Paulsen published a book on the use of the Danish language in

---

101 This discussion of Paulsen's life, ideals, and accomplishments owes much to the absorbing account of Johan Runge, *Sønderjyden Christian Paulsen. Et slesvigsk levnedsløb* (Flensburg: Studieafdelingen ved Dansk Centralbibliotek for Sydslesvig, 1981).

102 This is the major thesis of Paulsen's study *Om Slesvigs indre Forbindelse med Danmark* (Copenhagen: Reitzel, 1848).

Schleswig during the first thousand years of its history,[103] during the second term of his studies. The work added so much fuel to the campaign for the further advancement of the Danish cultural cause in Schleswig that it immediately became the subject of an extensive debate in Kiel's newspaper.[104] Paulsen's students, including Storm, must have avidly read this debate in their local newspaper, and discussed it when they gathered in front of their professor's lecture hall and when they sat together in the coffee houses and taverns of the city after classes were over. Whatever aspect of Paulsen's lectures and writings these students discussed, and whatever opinions they may have held about his views, of one thing we can be certain: Storm, in his association with Paulsen and his circle of students, was once more given the opportunity — this time on a higher educational level than ever before — to deepen his knowledge of the Danish cultural tradition in his native Schleswig.

e. Nicolaus Falck

With this influential professor, too, Storm began to study in his very first semester at Kiel. He enrolled in Falck's course on *Historium juris patrii* (The History of Law in the Danish Nation). The contact between the pedagogue from Schleswig and the student from Schleswig must have been quite close. Falck had once taught at Husum's Latin School and was, moreover, a personal friend of Storm's father. When Storm met with Falck in the latter's office for the first time, conversation surely must have touched on such topics as the town of Husum, the learning atmosphere of its Latin School, and the recent and past activities of the elder Storm. Each time young Storm and Falck met in the halls of academia and elsewhere in Kiel would underscore the cordial relationship that must have begun on the first day the two became acquainted. The personal relationship, in turn, could only have made the young Storm more receptive

---

103   C. Paulsen, *Det danske Sprog i Hertugdømmet Slesvig* (Copenhagen: Qvist, 1834).
104   "Deutsch und Dänisch im Herzogthum Schleswig," *Kieler Correspondenz-Blatt*, Jan. 13, 1838; Feb. 17, 1838; Feb. 21, 1838.

to what Falck taught in the lecture hall as well as in his scholarly writings.

What did Storm learn from Falck?[105] Certainly, as with Paulsen, a deeper appreciation of Denmark's cultural heritage, once again from the vantage point of a high level of education. Falck, born and raised in the northern, overwhelmingly Danish region of Schleswig, had deep roots in the Danish language. He was the son of Danish-speaking parents and had received his secondary education at the Latin School at Haderslev, the most Danish-oriented institution of learning in the duchy. Like Falck himself, most boys who attended school in Haderslev came from Danish-speaking homes and communicated with one another in Danish. Early on Falck felt himself drawn to the allure of the Danish capital city. He spent three years in Copenhagen, performing legal work in various governmental offices, and acquiring thereby an intimate knowledge of Danish institutions as well as an abiding sense of loyalty to the Danish crown. This patriotism, he came to realize, constituted the invaluable bridge that linked the duchy of Schleswig with all parts of the culturally rich Danish monarchy. Schleswig's ties to the kingdom as a whole, he always felt, were essential for the life of the duchy; without those ties, he believed, his native duchy could easily wither away into cultural impoverishment.

While in Copenhagen, Falck had acquired a remarkable familiarity with Danish literature. The few biographical sketches of Falck written in recent years have all stressed the unusual interest that the

---

105 Scholarship lacks a good biographical study of this teacher of Storm. Although many essays have been written on various aspects of Falck's career in law, there is no comprehensive account of his life that could compare with Johan Runge's biography of Storm's other influential university teacher, Christian Paulsen. My discussion of Falck's importance for Storm's development owes much to information recorded in the Falck papers deposited in the Royal Library at Copenhagen.

Nicolaus Falck wearing the Silver Cross and the Breast Cross of a Commander of the Royal Danish *Dannebrog* order.

jurist took in Danish literature;[106] indeed, the catalogue of books from Falck's own personal library, compiled for an auction after his death, shows that works of Danish literature comprised a substantial portion of that library.[107] He possessed approximately twice as many works of Danish literature than German literature, even though he could read German just as well as Danish. That, too, speaks for his strong interest in the literature of Denmark.

When Frederik VI appointed Falck to Kiel's Law Faculty, the king must have known that Falck would be an ideal emissary of Danish culture at the university in the German-speaking part of his kingdom. Falck's years at Kiel confirmed how Danish he always remained at heart. He was, as an impartial British historian informs us, "a local patriot inherently suspicious of the great [German] world south of the Elbe."[108] Only twice in his life did he visit that German world, and then only briefly.[109]

Because of the remarkable erudition Falck displayed in his publications (written in German in order to reach a larger audience), his name became so well-known in German academic circles that he received offers to join the teaching faculties of such prestigious German universities as Berlin, Bonn, and Göttingen. Yet he always refused such offers, preferring to remain in Kiel, at a university over which the king of Denmark presided as its chief patron. He did not feel comfortable *im Ausland* (in a foreign country).

Storm had studied for many years under the tutelage of his Danophile teachers Falck and Paulsen, at the Law School in Kiel that was so strongly infected by the Danish spirit. Nowhere else at the time, except of course in Copenhagen, did Danish cultural values

---

106 Ingwer E. Momsen, "Nikolaus Falck. Vor 200 Jahren wurde der große schleswig-holsteinische Jurist geboren," *Zwischen Eider und Wiedau. Heimatkalender für Nordfriesland* (1984): 177; Eckardt Opitz, *Die unser Schatz und Reichtum sind. 60 Portraits aus Schleswig-Holstein* (Hamburg: Christians, 1990), 114.
107 *Verzeichniß von Büchern und Handschriften aus dem Nachlaß des Professors N. Falck* (Kiel: Schulbuchdruckerei, 1851).
108 Carr, 77.
109 H. Ratjen, *Zur Erinnerung an Nicolaus Falck* (Kiel: Akademische Buchhandlung, 1851), 26.

permeate the learning process to the extent that they did in Kiel, where these two teachers exerted their considerable patriotic influence on the Law School. Not surprisingly, Storm, when he presented himself for his comprehensive examinations at the conclusion of his studies at Kiel, scored the best grades in the subject matter of Danish law, which he had studied with Paulsen and Falck.[110]

Before Storm left the university, however, he had one more contact with Falck that offers further proof of how successfully he immersed himself in the Danish cultural context of Kiel. He asked Falck to certify for the representatives of the crown in Copenhagen that he had acquired a competence in Danish at a level of attainment that could only follow from a study of the great masters of Danish literature. Such a certification was necessary before graduates of the Law School could be admitted to the bar in the Danish monarchy.

Storm made this request at a moment when the Danish patriotic spirit in Kiel had reached a high point in the annals of that university. Falck, whom the Danish king had honored shortly before with both the Silver Cross and the Breast Cross of a Commander of the Royal *Dannebrog* order (two of the highest honors the monarch could bestow on his subjects),[111] was now being considered for the post of *Rector magnificus* (the equivalent of President of an American university). The Danish halo surrounding the university thus gained a luster that shone brighter than it ever had before. One might expect that a candidate for this exalted administrative post might have been so busy with all sorts of university obligations that he would have asked another colleague to substitute for him at an examination certifying competency in Danish. In the case of Storm, however, Falck acted contrarily to this apparent expectation. He had come to know Storm personally quite well and was also well acquainted with his student's competence in Danish. Because of Falck's own Danish bias, moreover, it must have meant much to him that a

---

110 v. Fisenne, 12.
111 I am indebted to Nils G. Bartholdy, the archivist of the State Archives in Copenhagen, for identifying the decorations bestowed on Falck by the king.

student very proficient in Danish should receive the certification from a university official who had been so highly decorated by the king, which would give the recommendation the greatest possible weight. On November 29, 1842, Falck certified in writing that:

> Herr Candidat Storm nicht nur das Dänische mit guter Aussprache liest, sondern auch sowohl poetische als prosaische Stücke mit vollkommener Sicherheit richtig und fertig übersetzen kann.[112]

(Candidate Storm can not only read Danish aloud with good pronunciation, but can also translate [Danish] poetry and prose accurately and skillfully, with fluent ease.)

112　A photo of this certification is reproduced in Karl Ernst Laage, *Theodor Storms Welt in Bildern* (Heide: Boyens, 1988), 62.

The Poems

1. Storm's calling to poetry

On December 2, 1842, after Storm had successfully completed his examinations in (1) jurisprudence and (2) the Danish language and literature, he made a formal application to his sovereign, King Christian VIII of Denmark, requesting permission to practice law in the duchy of Schleswig.[113] The royal approval followed early in the next year. By April 20, 1843, Storm could open up a law practice in Husum. He was twenty-five years old and had reached what normally might be considered the threshold of maturity and the beginning of a successful career.

Not so with Storm. Settling down to earn a living in his native Husum, following in his father's footsteps as a respected local attorney, Storm's life would now be regulated by the timetables of bureaucratic work, office appointments, and social responsibility. All this signaled only a dull life ahead for him, one that could constrain him in a straitjacket of facts, duties, and practicalities. This was a life, he quickly realized, that offered him "wenig Befriedigung" (little satisfaction).[114]

To make matters worse, he became engaged to be married in January of 1844, in deference to family wishes and a society that deemed marriage to be essential for a man aspiring to a position of service in the community. The young woman, whom he married in September of 1846, was his cousin Constanze Esmarch, the daughter of his mother's sister. It was not a love match, as Storm often admitted.[115] Yet others in his family and circle of friends,

---

113 Storm's application to his Danish sovereign is printed in: v. Fisenne, 13.
114 *Storm–Constanze Esmarch*, I, 281.
115 See, for instance, *Storm-Brinkmann*, 146.

especially the two mothers, seemed pleased with the direction his new, mature life had now taken — except, of course, Storm himself.

As a result, the itch to write poetry, the art form to which he had been exposed so much during his schooling in the Danish Golden Age, more and more became a means to find relief from the tedium of both his personal life and of earning a meager living as a young small-town attorney.

Hence, it was in poetry, not in law, that he was to find his true calling in life. In 1868, in a statement of remarkable self-revelation, he wrote:

> Ich bin . . . wesentlich Lyriker, und meine ganze dichterische und menschliche Persönlichkeit, alles was von Charakter, Leidenschaft und Humor in mir ist, findet sich nur in den Gedichten.[116]
>
> (I am essentially a lyric poet, and my entire personality as a writer and as a human being, everything of character, passion and humor within me is solely to be found in my poems.)

With his poetic vocation, Storm would earn the right to take his seat among those lyricists of all ages who had come to occupy only the highest places on the Parnassus of the Muses. He would be able to climb to heights unreached by any other literary realist composing in the nineteenth century, in any language, anywhere in Europe, except in the Danish kingdom. Neither in English, nor in French, nor in Russian literary realism, for instance, do we find any of the major writers composing noteworthy verse. If England did produce some memorable poetry while the school of Victorian realism flourished, it did not partake of the most celebrated realism, in the fiction of Dickens and Thackeray. Poets like Swinburne, Tennyson, and Browning were thoroughly at odds with Victorian realism, and Hardy's canonical poems were written largely after the Victorian Age had passed.

---

116 *Storm. Briefe an Dorothea Jensen und an Georg Westermann*, ed. E. Lüpke (Braunschweig: Westermann, 1942), 30.

A similar situation existed in France. The realism that flourished with the novels of Balzac, Stendhal, and Flaubert found no counterpart in the lyric; it only provoked poets, such as Baudelaire, Verlaine, and Mallarmé, to compose strikingly anti-realistic verse. And Russia, in the age known for the realism of Turgenev, Tolstoy, and Dostoyevsky, conspicuously lacked any lyrical impulses. "Don't ask the reason," Turgenev wrote in 1869, "why there are no poets [in Russia]. There aren't any because there aren't any."[117]

In German Poetic Realism there were, we know, several poets of considerable stature, and among these no lesser talents than Gottfried Keller and Conrad Ferdinand Meyer. Yet Storm towered above these, primarily because he had accomplished something truly unique in the history of German-language poetry: he had taken, so to speak, a flourishing branch from Danish verse and grafted it onto the tree of the German language, from which a profusion of great poetry would then bloom forth with a new freshness.

The bilingual Storm must have been touched more by the steady poetic currents flowing from Denmark into his native Schleswig than by the German poems he read while briefly attending school in Lübeck as a *Schuckelmeyer* (again, a pejorative term for "Dane"), or while occasionally discussing German verse with amateur student friends at the University of Kiel. A poet from Schleswig in Storm's time would have to draw his creative inspiration, first and foremost, from the impressive flowering of the lyric in Denmark. Poetry had been, after all, the purest distillation of Denmark's Golden Age literature. The Danish historian Troels Lund once described Danish poetry at the time as "the light of everyone's life, everybody's darling."[118]

---

117   I. S. Turgenev, *Works and Letters* [title in Russian], Section Letters, 8 (Leningrad & Moscow: Nauka, 1964), 20.
118   Quoted in: *The Golden Age Revisited. Art and Culture in Denmark 1800–1850*, 13.

2. Storm's poetry in the judgment of Theodor Fontane and Thomas Mann

Of all those who have called attention to the radiant dimension that Storm added to German poetry, few have understood better his particular achievement, and his debt to the Danish muse, than Theodor Fontane and Thomas Mann. "Zehn Zeilen Storm," Fontane said in 1883, "wiegen den ganzen Jahresertrag aller jetzt regierenden lyrischen Machthaber auf" (Ten lines of Storm outweigh the entire annual production of all those who rule supreme today as champions of the lyric).[119] In 1888 Fontane praised Storm's verse with these words: "die nachgoethische Zeit hat keine feinere [Lyrik] gesehen" (the post-Goethean age has seen no finer poetry).[120] This superlative praise is as surprising as it is strong, for in the interval of the fifty-six years between the deaths of Goethe (1832) and Storm (1888), the *ars poetica* in German-speaking lands had produced several of its best practitioners, including gifted lyricists like Eichendorff, Heine, Mörike, Keller, and Meyer. But Fontane now claimed a higher place for Storm in the roster of German poets than for any of these talents. One year later, in 1889, he paid a further tribute to Storm's poetry when he said that everything Storm had produced belongs to the best that literature has to offer; but most especially, he added, this holds true for Storm's lyrics, for they are "dem besten ebenbürtig, das wir haben" (equal to the best we have).[121] This is high praise for Storm's poetry; coming from a critic of Fontane's stature, it is exceedingly high praise.

In the twentieth century, no less a successor to Fontane than Thomas Mann corroborated this judgment. Speaking of Storm's poetry, Mann wrote:

> In dieser zehnmal gesichteten und geseihten Lyrik steht Perle fast neben Perle, und es ist darin auf Schritt und Tritt eine bebende Konzentrationskraft der Lebens- und Empfindungsaussage, eine Kunst der Formung

---

119 NFA, XXI/2, 246.
120 Ibid., 86.
121 Ibid., XXI/1, 498.

zum Einfachen, die in bestimmten Fällen unfehlbar immer wieder, so alt man wird und sooft man etwas davon wieder liest oder sich vorspricht, dies Sichzusammenziehen der Kehle, dies Angepacktwerden von unerbittlich süß und wehem Lebensgefühl bewirkt . . . eine Kulturlyrik persönlichen und unvergeßlichen Klanges, von der wenigstens ein halbes Dutzend Stücke würdig ist, neben dem Höchsten und Reinsten seinen Platz zu nehmen, was Gefühl und Sprache hervorgebracht haben, und vollkommmenen Unsterblickeitscharakter besitzt.[122]

(In this ten times sorted and sifted lyrical treasure, gem stands almost next to gem. There is a constant, thrilling, concentrated power of expression about life and the emotions, a skill at shaping in the simplest form, which in certain poems — however old you are, however often you read them — unfailingly bring the catch in the throat as you are seized by that sweet and ruthless and woeful sense of life . . . at least half a dozen pieces are worthy to stand beside the best and highest in feeling and language and possess the unmistakable traits of immortality.)

Translated by H. T. Lowe-Porter[123]

Again, this is high praise for Storm as a lyric poet. Coming from the pen of Thomas Mann, it is the highest praise possible.

Fontane and Mann were able to detect the lasting brilliance Storm had bequeathed to German poetry because they possessed a most uncommon fascination for the Danish-speaking world and, hence, were able to detect the extent to which Storm had succeeded in grafting the gifts of the Danish muse onto German poetry.

Fontane, we know, had crisscrossed the Dano-German language frontier; he had visited Storm on the one side and had studied the charms of Danish life and letters on the other. If we interpret his own words correctly, the book he found most interesting in his lifetime of reading was Ludvig Holberg's *Dänische Reichs-Historie* (History of the Kingdom of Denmark).[124] Culminating his lifelong fascination with Denmark, Fontane wrote his great monument to Danish culture, the novel *Unwiederbringlich* (Beyond Recall). Its

---

122 Mann *Essay*, 16–18.
123 Mann *Essays*, 272–273.
124 NFA, XXI/1, 499.

plot unfolds against the background of a maze of Danish historical, political, and social conditions. Its hero, Count Holk, who lived in Storm's time and was also from the duchy of Schleswig, is a notorious Danish sympathizer. Indeed, it would be hard to find any fictional character in all German literature who had been more infected by the Danish spirit.

Mann also expressed on many occasions his indebtedness to Danish literature. His fondness for Denmark becomes apparent, perhaps most of all, when we notice how much the Danish world intrudes into the fictional design of *Tonio Kröger*. Almost one-third of the narrative description is taken up with the hero's journey to Denmark, his visit to Copenhagen, and his sojourn in the northern part of the Isle of Zealand. The Danish landscape is so lovingly portrayed that the reader feels as much enchanted by it as Mann himself must have been when he wrote the novella.

Fontane and Mann had been, thus, so finely attuned to the Danish spirit that they could not possibly have missed its echoing strains in Storm's poetry. For Mann's work, in particular, the topics of Denmark and the influence of Storm's poetry had obviously mingled. In *Tonio Kröger* references to Storm belong as much to the novella's structure and theme as does the attention given to Denmark. Strikingly, Storm's poem "Hyazinthen" (Hyacinths) is woven into the narrative. Twice the title hero cites it, and once, significantly, when he is vacationing in Denmark; the poem articulates a conflict between art and ordinary life that both Storm, the poet, and the hero of *Tonio Kröger* experienced. Storm's novella *Immensee* (Bee's Lake) also constitutes an integral part of the composition of *Tonio Kröger*. The bearded image of Theodor Storm himself emerges in Mann's novella, as Karl Ernst Laage has astutely observed,[125] when we hear of the "Vatergestalt des langen, wehmütig sinnenden Weißbartes mit der Feldblume im Knopfloch" (the father-image of the tall, dreamy graybeard with the wildflower in his buttonhole). Mann clearly had in mind the famous portrait of Storm in old age.

---

125 Mann *Essay*, 13.

3. Danish verse melody as the source of Storm's poetry

a. The verse of Hans Christian Andersen

If we look to Danish poetry as the source for the inspiration Storm needed in order to embark on those flights of fantasy that reached their haven in his verse, there is no Danish poet who offers more telling evidence of what Storm learned from the Danish muse than Hans Christian Andersen. Wilhelm Bernhardt, a German-American literary historian of a century ago, once tried to illuminate Storm's and Andersen's poetic achievements by referring to them as products of the same Danish chorus in German literature.[126] He was speaking of Andersen's verse in German, but what he said holds equally true for his verse in Danish. Bernhardt's comparative approach to the understanding of Andersen and Storm has been largely forgotten by subsequent literary criticism, which is a pity. It is worth bringing it to light again.

We have no specific facts of relationship, either personal or literary, between Storm and Andersen. Although they were contemporaries (Andersen 1805–1875, Storm 1817–1888), there is no record of a meeting between them. Yet, their paths certainly could have crossed on the many occasions when Andersen visited the duchies of Schleswig and Holstein, or particularly when he visited the small university town of Kiel during two of the years when Storm was living there as a student. Regardless, however, of whether there was actual personal contact between the two poets, their lyrics reveal definite affinities. A comparative study of these two poets can and should occur, therefore, in terms of lyric affinity, analogy, and tradition, rather than with reference to any specific personal influence. Comparative literature, René Wellek has taught us, need not be studied "in terms of nineteenth-century factualism;" it may also be studied as "an act of the imagination, like art itself."[127]

---

126 Wilhelm Bernhardt, *Hauptfakta aus der Geschichte der deutschen Litteratur / A Short History of the Poetical Literature of Germany* (New York, Cincinnati, Chicago: American Book Co., 1892), 57.

127 René Wellek, *Concepts of Criticism* (New Haven & London: Yale University Press, 1969), 285, 295.

Storm and Andersen shared, as poets, much in common. Each had received his poetic baptism in the currents pervading Danish literature of their time in the kingdom of Greater Denmark. Each was fluent in Danish and German. Each had a lifelong love of music that left its indelible mark on their poetry. Like few other poets, Andersen and Storm composed both poetry and music.

Johan de Mylius, the director of the Hans Christian Andersen-Centret in Odense, informs us that Andersen had fused poetry and music from the very start.[128] Music had been pivotal to his poetic self-realization, and it became the chief characteristic of his use of language. His lyrical poems are carried essentially by their tonal power, their sound effects, and their rhythmical qualities.

b. Andersen's "Gurre"

The remarkable musical effects Andersen used in his verse are displayed especially well in the poem "Gurre," which he composed in 1842. Adolf Strodtmann, the famous biographer of Heinrich Heine and a critic with an intimate knowledge of Danish letters,[129] once described this poem as a piece not only extremely typical of Andersen, but of the entire Golden Age of Danish poetry as well.[130] This is the first of the poem's three stanzas:

> Hvor Nilen vander Ægypternes Jord
> I Africas brændende Lande,
> Der mødtes to Fugle, de kom fra Nord,
> De talte om Danmarks Strande:

---

128 I am grateful for the assistance I received on my visit to the Andersen-Centret. My remarks here owe much to de Mylius's study on "Hans Christian Andersen and the Music World" in S. H. Rossel (ed.), *Hans Christian Andersen. Danish Writer and Citizen of the World* (Amsterdam: Rodopi, 1994), 176–208.
129 Alken Bruns, *Übersetzung als Rezeption: Deutsche Übersetzer skandinavischer Literatur von 1860 bis 1900* (Neumünster: Wachholtz, 1977), 106–149, esp. 115–116.
130 Adolf Strodtmann, *Das geistige Leben in Dänemark* (Berlin: Paetel, 1873), 90–91.

"O husker Du Sjølund, den deilige Ø,
Hvor de vilde Skovduer kurre,
De duftende Bøge, den stille Sø,
Husker Du Gurre!"
— "Ja, der har jeg bygget en Sommer-Dag."
Saa talte den lille Svale,
"Jeg havde min Rede ved Bondens Tag,
Jeg hørte ham synge og tale:
Jeg troer der er skjønnest i Danmark!"

Chor
Jeg troer der er skjønnest i Danmark!

Echo
— Skjønnest i Danmark![131]

(Where Nile floods wander through Egypt's sands
In Africa's burning hot deserts,
Two birds came together from northern lands
And sang there of Denmark's pleasures:
"Oh, remember Zealand, the heavenly isle
With the sound of turtledoves purring;
How fragrant the beech trees, the lake so still;
Remember Gurre!"
— "Yes, that's where I built for my summer's rest,"
The wee swallow sweetly tweeted,
"The farmer's roof gave me a place to nest,
I heard as he sang and repeated:
I find it most beauteous in Denmark!"

Chorus
I find it most beauteous in Denmark!

Echo
— Beauteous in Denmark!)

Translated by Richard D. Hacken

---

131 Text taken from *H. C. Andersens samlede skrifter*, XII (Copenhagen: Reitzel, ²1879), 188.

Essentially, the poem is characterized by the fantastic element of opera. Two swallows are singing in an enchanted world along Egypt's Nile River, intoxicated by a nostalgic yearning for the summer landscape surrounding Lake Gurre in faraway Denmark. In the background even the Nile itself seems to join in their song, as gentle waves rustle in the ever-flowing stream. The sense of operatic enchantment is so powerful that the visual images of such essential elements of the Egyptian landscape as the sphinxes and pyramids are sacrificed to the orchestral coloration. In further operatic effect at the end of the stanza, and at the end of the other stanzas as well, a chorus echoes the verbal melody of the swallows. The choruses alternate with the bird-soloists in glib imitation of the tonal dialogue of opera. This dialogue is then musically underscored by the steady alternation of feminine and masculine rhyme and by the lilting accompaniment of recurrent iambic and anapestic beats. It is hardly an exaggeration to say that Andersen in this exemplary composition shows how his mind is like a reed through which all thoughts turn into music. He demonstrates acute skill in arranging words and sentences to fit the musical phrases.

The musical quality that is so clearly exhibited here, which may also be found in the entire corpus of Danish Golden Age poetry, was not a general characteristic of German poetry at the time. No one perceived this more than the *pontifex maximus* of Denmark's literary world in the early half of the nineteenth century, Johan Ludvig Heiberg. He had been sent by King Frederik VI to the University of Kiel in 1822 to promote a greater interest in the study of Danish literature among students from German-speaking Holstein. The following year he published in Altona, then the southernmost outpost of the Kingdom of Greater Denmark, his *Formenlehre der dänischen Sprache* (Morphology of the Danish Language) so that German-speaking students could acquire, as he said in the preface, a sensitivity for the melodiousness of the Danish language and of Danish literature.[132]

---

132 Johan Ludvig Heiberg, *Formenlehre der dänischen Sprache* (Altona: Hammerich, 1823), xxiii.

This quality, he felt, some students had not yet learned to appreciate, having received instruction only in Latin, Greek, or German literature.

Turning from Andersen and Denmark's Golden Age poetry to Storm, we notice that he also, from the beginning, found his vocation in poetry by composing in the same manner of the Danish verse-melody. He, like Andersen and other poets of the time who had been raised in the Kingdom of Greater Denmark, had absorbed the musical artistry that prevailed in early nineteenth-century Danish verse.

The central statement of Storm's own poetic declaration of faith — his *poetisches Glaubensbekenntnis*, as he called it[133] — confirms this succinctly:

> . . . diese Worte [of a poem] müssen auch durch die rhythmische Bewegung und die Klangfarbe des Verses gleichsam in Musik gesetzt und solcherweise wieder in die Empfindung aufgelöst sein, aus der sie entsprungen sind.[134]

> (The words of a poem must be set to music by the rhythmic cadence and tone quality of the verse, thereby allowing them to dissolve back into the sensibility from which they arose.)

Few Danish poets of the Golden Age would have formulated a theory of poetry differently. The only thing that sets Storm apart from his fellow Danish poets is that he composed his "Danish" poetry in the German language. This made Storm unique in comparison with his Danish colleagues (except Andersen, who had tried his hand at writing German verse),[135] but this also gave him his particular claim to fame. With the echoing sound of the skylark's *Tirili*, a term he stubbornly sought to propagate among those unfamiliar with the Danish lyric,[136] he had no equal in German poetry.

---

[133] Curt Corrinth, "Ein unbekannter Bekenntnisbrief Storms," *Deutsche Allgemeine Zeitung*, 29. Juni 1942.
[134] LL, IV, 393–394.
[135] See Ivy York Möller-Christensen, *Den gyldne trekant. H. C. Andersens gennembrud i Tyskland 1831–1850* (Odense: Universitetsforlag, 1992).
[136] *Storm–Heyse*, II, 89; III, 28; *Storm–Schmidt*, II, 25; *Storm–Keller*, 86.

4. Early verse: "Der Entfernten"

One of the earliest of Storm's poems to appear in print (it was, in fact, his second poem) is "Der Entfernten" (For the Girl Far Away). Only recently, in 1992, has the poem come to light, thanks to the research efforts of Gerd Eversberg, the indefatigable Secretary of the Theodor Storm Society, who discovered it in the November 6, 1836 edition of Husum's weekly newspaper, the *Königlich privilegirtes Wochenblatt*. Storm was nineteen years old when he composed the poem, perhaps only eighteen if he had written it two or more months before it appeared in print. He was quite young. But the newspaper's editor, Heinrich August Meyler, must have thought it would appeal to the paper's readership. Meyler, who had been editor of the paper for twenty-three years when he agreed to publish the poem, probably knew, from his years of experience, that his staid local readers would hardly appreciate a poem if it did not move them with the sort of musical effects they were accustomed to in the literature popular in their Danish duchy of Schleswig.

> Eilende Winde
> Wieget euch linde,
> Säuselt mein Liedchen der Lieblichen vor;
> Vögelein singet,
> Vögelein bringet
> Töne der Lust an ihr lauschendes Ohr.
>
> Oeffne dich, Rose,
> Schwellet, ihr Moose,
> Reiht euch, ihr Blumen, zum duftigen Kranz;
> Weilt ihr am Herzen,
> Horcht ihren Schmerzen,
> Scheuchet den nagenden Kummer hinaus.
>
> Schimmernde Sterne,
> Strahlt aus der Ferne
> Himmlischer Höhen mir Freude und Lust
> Freundliche Sterne,
> Wärt ihr nicht ferne,
> Leuchtet ihr tröstend der trauernden Brust.[137]

(Hurrying winds
Cradle gently
Whisper this song to my beloved;
Birds sing
Birds bring
Sounds of pleasure to her listening ear.

Open yourself, rose,
Rise up, you mosses,
Gather yourselves, flowers, into a sweet-smelling wreath.
Linger at her heart,
Listen to her jests,
Banish the aching sorrow.

Shimmering stars,
Shine down joy and delight upon me
From afar off on heavenly heights,
Cheerful stars
If you weren't so far away
You could give light, comfortingly, to my sobbing breast.)

Translated by Richard D. Hacken

This is a love-song addressed to Storm's first love, the Frisian girl Emma Kühl, whom he knew from 1830 to 1837. Little has been written in Storm criticism about this love affair, and there has been little interest in it. But this newly discovered poem should compel us to become acquainted with the role that this era in his love life played in the development of his poetry.

This much we know: when Theodor and Emma first met as children, it was love at first sight. Eventually his feeling for her deepened into real sensuous love. By the time he turned twenty and she seventeen, he had fallen so madly in love with her that, in a moment of unbridled passion, as he later confessed,[138] he formally asked her to be engaged; she, feeling similarly, accepted the proposal immediately.

---

137   This text reproduces the original printing in the *Königlich privilegirtes Wochenblatt*. Gerd Eversberg has made a photocopy available in his article "Storms erste Gedichtveröffentlichungen," STSG 41 (1992): 46.
138   *Storm–Constanze Esmarch*, I, 106–107.

The poem reflects the agitated state of his emotions approximately one year before the betrothal. Is he singing for joy in thinking about her? Or is he sobbing with sadness at being so far away from her? We sense the music of exhilaration when the birds sing to the beloved's listening ear. And joy rings out with the lilting rhythms of the dactyls at the beginning of every verse, and when, especially, the same sound pattern is powerfully compounded by the dazzling choruses of triple dactylic feet in the third and sixth lines of each stanza. Yet, the ear attuned to such musical resonances will also notice that Storm balances these dactyls with a falling trochaic rhythm. In the first, second, fourth, and fifth lines of each stanza, the initial dactylic line is followed by the falling rhythm of trochaic meter. The sudden tonal change, ending on one lonely unstressed syllable in a short line of dimeter verse, stands out in sharp contrast to the echoing series of uplifting dactyls heard in the extended tetrameter of the third and sixth lines.

The interplay of the long uplifting lines dominated by the animated dactyls, on the one hand, and of the shorter lines ending with the falling trochees, on the other, gives us the alternating rhythm that mimics the conflict of joy and sorrow inherent in this love poem. But Storm, the musical poet, does not stop there. He embellishes the dactylo-trochaic structure with carefully constructed feminine and masculine rhyme schemes. They are closely interwoven (the first, second, fourth, and fifth lines end on a feminine rhyme; the third and sixth lines have a masculine rhyme). There is only one exception, which seems quite deliberate: the noun *Kranz* in the third line of the second stanza, a central position in the poem, lacks another noun to rhyme with it. According to the poem's structure, it should rhyme with *hinaus*; but the sounds do not match, and so *Kranz* receives a stress that is unnatural, according to the poem's strict rhyme scheme.

Thus the word stands out, and we become more conscious of its emphasis when we realize that in an earlier handwritten version of the poem, "An die Enfernte M . . . " (To M., Who is Far Away),

Storm had a good rhyme-word in place: *Strauß*.[139] Why did Storm decide to give *Kranz* such undue emphasis? Presumably, he had in mind a *Totenkranz* (funeral wreath). He had already used this image with considerable effect in the very first poem he had written.[140] Did Storm sense even then, in fearful anguish, that the happy love affair with Emma might come to an untimely end, which, as we know, is what did happen, when he withdrew his affection for her soon after their engagement? The strong shadow of death could sustain such a conclusion. And the reference to the sobbing breast, structurally aligned with the funeral wreath by virtue of the fact that *Kranz* comes at the end of the poem's first half and *trauernde Brust* at the end of the second half, could reinforce this conclusion.

What emerges with this poem, then, is a little opera of conflicting feeling, with joy and sorrow in rhythmic counterpoint. This is a poem written in glib imitation of Danish verse-melody in the Golden Age. Noticeably absent is any realistic description of the two lovers; nothing in the poem helps us to imagine how either of them really looked. Nor are there any particular details of the love affair. Realistic description is abandoned in favor of the appeal and demands of melody. The one blatant exception of *Kranz* (*Totenkranz?*) only confirms our overall impression in this poem that Storm is essentially a poet concerned with sound. Inner life becomes articulate as it is put into musical form. Storm was quite an effective composer of musical verse, as we hear in this poem, at a young age.

5. Reaping the benefit of a poetic apprenticeship: *Liederbuch dreier Freunde*

After Storm published "Der Entfernten" in November 1836, he spent four quite happy years at the University of Kiel in the company of inspiring teachers and intelligent students. His second year as a student, 1838–1839, was a lonely one in Germany, where he enrolled at

---

139 Eversberg, 47.
140 Gertrud Storm, I, 56.

the University of Berlin. The years 1839–1842, following his return to Kiel from Berlin, were doubtless the most important ones for the development of his poetry.

For one thing, he received from his mentors in Kiel, as we noted earlier, a heightened appreciation for Denmark's cultural heritage, for its language, institutions, and literature, all of which would influence his own artistic endeavors. He also benefited in these years from a singularly valuable poetic apprenticeship under the tutelage of the great classical scholar Theodor Mommsen, who later received the Nobel Prize in literature for his monumental *Römische Geschichte* (A History of Rome).

Storm criticism has treated the importance of this poetic apprenticeship rather lightly. Often biographical accounts have passed over it, merely referring to the fact of a friendship between the two. But "friends" they were not, despite the use of the word in the title *Liederbuch dreier Freunde* (Songbook of Three Friends). Although they were the same age, knew each other for a number of years, and even lived for a time under one roof, they always addressed one another with the formal *Sie*, never with the informal *Du*. Nor did they ever use first names in speaking or writing to each other.[141] What sort of friends were these?

Storm, moreover, must have found Mommsen rather overbearing. The classicist's examination grades were much better than Storm's.[142] The quality of Mommsen's term papers, in the opinions of their professors, must have been far superior to anything Storm produced. His scholarly achievements probably gave Mommsen a domineering, condescending attitude toward his fellow students. He certainly was not the sort of person with whom Storm liked to be friends.

What brought the two students together was their mutual interest in writing poetry. They met regularly, often joined by

---

141   See *Storm–Mommsen*.
142   The transcript of Storm's grades at Kiel is reproduced in v. Fisenne, 12–13. Mommsen's grades are given in Lothar Wickert, *Theodor Mommsen. Eine Biographie*, I (Frankfurt am Main: Klostermann, 1959), 469–470.

Mommsen's erudite younger brother, Tycho, to give practical criticism of each other's poems. In this activity, we are told, they seldom agreed.[143] The Mommsen brothers had been heavily influenced by the rules and conventions of Latin poetry, whereas Storm had his poetic roots in the Danish tradition. Theodor Mommsen, we are informed, was utterly unmusical,[144] and so he could hardly appreciate the music of Storm's cadences. For the classicist, rhyme was unimportant;[145] poetry was meant to appeal to the eye and the mind. For Storm, rhyme was all-important; poetry had to appeal to the ear. With the noble experiments of the Roman poets (who never used rhyme) as their models, the Mommsen brothers shook their heads in dismay at what they thought were Storm's weak attempts in composing poetry and, at the end of Storm's readings, they would humiliate him with their scathing critique.[146]

Yet for Storm, the purgatorial fire of this acerbic critique offered excellent lessons in poetic technique. He learned to arrange syntax better, to be more precise with his diction and punctuation, and to avoid irrelevant sallies. Best of all, he somehow learned to trust his own capabilities, for in the constant crucible of critique and rebuttal,[147] he could temper and sharpen his own aesthetic judgment and develop more confidence in his gifts of musical expression. As a consequence, he began to compose poetry more easily and readily.

Forty poems Storm had composed during the time of the battle of wits in Kiel found their way, together with verse of the Mommsens imitating their august Roman forebears, into an anthology published in 1843: *Liederbuch dreier Freunde*. It is wise, however, not to attach too much importance to these poems, for Theodor Mommsen, as the volume's controlling editor, decided to give the anthology a more uniform appearance by altering many of Storm's poems to conform

---

143   Wickert, 191–213.
144   Ibid., 137.
145   Ibid., 214.
146   Ibid., 201.
147   Ibid., 201–202.

to his own poetic principles, *der rote Faden* (the red thread) that, as critics have said, runs through the volume.[148] Today, we are not sure which elements Storm composed and which are marked by the elder Mommsen's tinkering.

For Storm, therefore, what turned out to be important in this apprenticeship was not so much the poetry he produced in the company of these narrow minds, but the experience and confidence he acquired in trying to win the favor of a discriminating audience.

6. The breakthrough: "Nixen-Chor zur Begrüßung König Christians VIII. in Husum"

As might be expected after this trying but invaluable apprenticeship, Storm soon emerged, after his return to Husum, as a professional poet. Soon he came to be regarded as such by the town's citizenry. Husum now had a real poet in its midst. The dramatic transition from amateur to professional poet occurred when the town's magistrates asked Storm to compose the official poem of welcome for King Christian VIII, on the occasion of the monarch's visit to Husum on September 3, 1845. Although the Danish monarch regularly visited Husum every summer, and the local officials were accustomed to welcoming him with all the fanfare befitting a royal visit, this time they were more anxious than ever to extend to him a lavish welcome, for a particular reason.

Over the years Husum's harbor, which had once been a prosperous seaport, began to fill with the mud that flowed in with the tides. This had gradually made it difficult for ships to move in and out of the harbor. Commerce had to be rerouted to other ports, with the result that Husum's prosperity, which depended greatly on its shipping, declined. By 1845 all the officials of town and state agreed that the harbor had to be dredged and new installations built. But royal approval had to be obtained to procure the necessary funds for

---

148 Ibid., 210, 500.

the project. Senator Franz Rehder, speaking on behalf of the magistrates, presented the case clearly in a moving address to the monarch soon after his arrival; this address was printed four days after its delivery, on September 7, 1845, in Husum's *Wochenblatt*. In order that the king might give his consent more readily, Storm was asked to write a poem for the occasion to give the welcoming ceremonies even more of a reverential tone. Could greater recognition be given to a budding poet than to be asked to compose for the king?

Storm certainly must have been flattered by this recognition of his poetic skill, and he could hardly say no to the request. He must have felt especially pleased to honor Christian VIII because the monarch had, upon acceding to the Danish throne five years earlier, raised Storm's father to the rank of a knight of the Royal *Dannebrog* order, as mentioned above. Storm insisted that his welcoming composition be in the form of a symphonic poem, with accompanying instrumental, choral, and even operatic effects. He was going to make every effort to compose a poem in the Danish musical tradition, perhaps to offer the king a more impressive honor than he had received on his visits to other towns and cities across the Danish countryside. Neither Storm nor Husum would be outperformed by ceremonies elsewhere in the kingdom. The monarch would then more easily, the town's leaders hoped, favor Husum with the funding it desperately needed to restore its commercial prosperity.

This milestone poem has not received critical attention. Interpretative analyses are lacking, and in comprehensive studies of Storm's *œuvre* as a whole, invariably it has gone unmentioned. The reason for the neglect is as understandable as it is lamentable. Until 1987, when the most recent edition of Storm's Collected Works appeared, only a terribly corrupted version of the "Nixen-Chor" (Nymphs' Welcoming Chorus for King Christian VIII) had been available to critics.

The poet's daughter, Gertrud Storm, was the first to publish the poem, using a manuscript from her father as her source, in 1916.[149]

---

149   Storm. *Briefe an seine Braut*, 82–83.

Her tampering with the text turned it into a poor poem. To make matters worse, a long series of editors and critics since 1916 reprinted Gertrud Storm's corrupted version of the poem. This has prevented the poem from getting a fair reading. It was easy, after all, to find fault with the poem when Gertrud Storm's text showed that it was, indeed, inferior to Storm's other work.

Since 1987, however, Storm's original text is available:

> Heil dir, heil dir, hoher König,
> Nimm den Gruß der Meereswogen!
> Dir entgegen silbertönig
> Sind wir rauschend hergezogen.
>
> Lustge Träume, Zukunftschatten
> Gleiten über unsre Wellen,
> Schlanke wuchtige Fregatten,
> Die im Flug vorüberschwellen.
>
> Gellend aus den schwanken Tauen
> Klingen wunderbare Lieder,
> Und von ihren Borden schauen
> Helle Augen zu uns nieder.
>
> Mähneschüttelnd, silberrändig
> Tauchen auf die Wellenrosse,
> Drunten wieder frisch lebendig
> Wird es im kristallnen Schlosse.
>
> Frohes, ahnungsvolles Leben,
> An der Krone Glanz entzündet,
> Freude hast du uns gegeben
> Und aufs Neu das Reich gegründet.
>
> Rauschend sind wir hergezogen,
> Dir entgegen, silbertönig.
> Nimm den Gruß der Meereswogen,
> Heil dir, heil dir, Meereskönig![150]

---

150 Text taken from LL, I, 242.

(Hail, all hail, oh lofty monarch,
From the ocean's depths we greet you!
Tinged with silver, we've swum onward
Through the roaring surf to meet you.

Joy-dreams of the future, flighty
O'er our waves like shadows gliding,
Slender frigates flying, mighty,
On the foamy crests are riding.

Loudly from the ship we're nearing
Wondrous songs are overflowing,
From on board bright eyes are peering
Towards us in the depths below them.

Brine-steeds of the waves, emerging
Shake their manes like silver tassels,
Down below comes fresh resurgent
Life within the crystal castle.

Happy life, so full of promise,
By your glorious crown has found us,
Joy it is you've brought upon us
And rebuilt the empire round us.

Through the roaring surf to meet you,
Tinged with silver, we've swum onward.
From the ocean's depths we greet you,
Hail, all hail, oh ocean monarch!)

Translated by Richard D. Hacken

In this symphonic poem, Storm serenades the Danish king with operatic effects that glibly imitate the opera performances the king often heard at the Royal Theater in Copenhagen. Twelve young women from Husum's Choral Society worked hard to prepare for the performance. To create the impression of grand opera, insofar as this was possible in a small provincial town, the singers were colorfully costumed as sea nymphs. Instrumental music was provided by two flutists and a bassoonist. Over this small opera of verses, voices, and instruments, Storm presided as the grand conductor.[151]

As soon as His Majesty arrived at eight o'clock in the evening, the serenade began. To court the exalted guest with appropriate solemnity, Storm composed regular lines in trochaic tetrameter; the pattern of one stressed syllable followed by one unstressed syllable repeats four times in each line. The auspicious repetitive rhythm of emphasis at the beginning of each metrical foot, sustained throughout the poem, gives the poem an incantatory quality, altogether appropriate in a song of ritual welcome for a king.

Yet the versatile poet, composer, and conductor also took care that the slow, unerring, measured trochaic music never sounds stilted or relentless. He divided the poem into six quatrains, so that five times there is a pause for breath. Each quatrain, moreover, has two pairs of lilting feminine rhymes. This adds a playful echo to the poem's overall trochaic pattern.

In the form of a musical flourish, furthermore, the opening and closing quatrains are interlocked in counterpoint fashion. The lines that echo in descending order at the beginning are inverted so that they appear in an ascending arrangement in the finale. Here it seems quite plausible that Storm was imitating the contrapuntal scores characteristic of the Baroque concerts performed before the king at Christiansborg Palace in Copenhagen.

Compounding the interplay of meter and rhyme, this song enchants us as a song of songs. There is the song of the nymphs from below the waves, the song of the ship's ropes creaking in the wind above the waves, the song of the frigates moving to and fro between the waves, and, perhaps most powerful of all, the song of the waves themselves roaring in their unabating rhythm, cresting and falling on the horizon.

Storm's musical accomplishment on the night of this performance before the king is all the more impressive because he conducted

---

151 Storm describes the preparations for the performance in *Storm–Constanze Esmarch*, I, 242, 253.

A typical welcome for King Christian VIII of Denmark when he regularly visited his subjects on Schleswig's West Coast. For one such visit Storm composed his "Nixen-Chor zur Begrüßung König Christians VIII. in Husum."

this serenade under great emotional stress. In January of 1844, as we know, he had become formally engaged to the daughter of his mother's sister, Constanze Esmarch. Six months later, however, he became involved with Doris Jensen, a lovely young blonde girl who was only fifteen years old.[152] In her he found, as he wrote to his friends Hartmuth and Laura Brinkmann, "jene berauschende Atmosphäre, der ich nicht widerstehen konnte" (that intoxicating atmosphere which I could not resist).[153] She felt much the same way.[154] But as luck would have it, he happened to be formally engaged to his cousin, and that match enjoyed the blessings of family and community.

It was difficult, therefore, for the two new lovers to meet without scandal. Yet there was one way they could meet: she could join the Choral Society he directed, and then they could see each other at rehearsals and performances. This is exactly what happened. The result, naturally, was that the more they saw each other, the more their passions were enflamed. What should he do? Breaking off the engagement to his cousin would cause enormous problems within his family. Yet not doing so constituted an insufferable act of violence against the hearts of the two lovers.

It must have been in the grip of this emotional torment that Storm conducted his grand serenade of welcome to the Danish monarch. The young woman for whom he felt such rapturous passion was one of the singers he directed.[155] Costumed in silver veiling with a sparkling array of pearls embroidered on it,[156] she must have looked more beautiful to him than ever before. To her, Storm must have seemed more handsome than ever before. He was dressed in his elegant *Schmiepel*, the impressive swallow-tailed coat he would wear on special occasions at that time in his life.[157] How she must have

---

152 "Theodor Storm und Dorothea geb. Jensen. Ein unveröffentlichter Briefwechsel," ed. G. Ranft, STSG 28 (1979): 34–35.
153 *Storm–Brinkmann*, 146.
154 Ibid.
155 *Storm–Constanze Esmarch*, I, 255.
156 Ibid., 242.
157 Ibid., II, 390.

stared at the maestro she loved! And when their eyes met, how the passion they felt for each other must have blazed!

Not surprisingly, given the passion raging within him, he lost control of both himself and his baton, right at the beginning of the serenade. The serenade got off to a wretched start, as he, to his intense chagrin, immediately realized.[158] As a result, the performance did not turn out to be the success he had hoped for. But it could not have been as bad as he feared, for in the newspaper account of the performance in Husum's *Wochenblatt* of September 7, 1845, there is no mention of anything having gone wrong. Still, if this poem set to music was not the great public triumph he had wanted, that was certainly not the fault of the poem. For Storm had produced here an exemplary composition and transformed it into a musical performance. Hans Christian Andersen, we can well imagine, would have heartily approved of the poem if it had come to his attention.

7. The immortal poem: "Oktoberlied"

a. The poem's importance

"Ich habe eben ein unsterbliches Gedicht geschrieben" (I have just written an immortal poem), Storm said after he put the finishing touches on the manuscript of his "Oktoberlied" (October Song); he beamed, we are told, when he uttered these words.[159] Rarely has a poet been as proud of one of his poems as Storm was of this "Oktoberlied." In all the various editions of his poetry published in his lifetime, he always made sure that "Oktoberlied" was printed as the first poem in the volume. Even when he published the multi-volume edition of his *Collected Works* (both poetry and prose), the "Oktoberlied" was the first composition to which his readers were introduced.

---

158   Ibid., I, 255.
159   Gertrud Storm, I, 191.

His pride in this poem never waned. In a letter to the Swiss poet Gottfried Keller he averred that he would not trade it for the entire verse production of Germany's poet laureate Emanuel Geibel.[160] To the Austrian poet Ada Christen he wrote, many years later, that "Oktoberlied" represented his lyrical talents at their peak.[161] Twice he went so far as to claim that, even among the best poets, verse of this quality was rare.[162]

A reader may be inclined to dismiss such intemperate self-admiration, but it must be remembered that Storm did not praise all of his compositions with such superlatives. Indeed, he lavished such praise on only a very few of his works. The poet's words must be taken, then, seriously.

We have more reason to do so given the enthusiasm that the greatest literary critic of the age in Germany, Theodor Fontane, had for this unique pearl of German literature. When Fontane read the poem for the first time, he said he felt ecstatic.[163] On another occasion he stated that the "Oktoberlied" was a poem of such high caliber that very few others had succeeded in producing anything of comparable merit.[164] Similar to the salutary importance Storm had accorded the poem in all editions of his poetry, Fontane in every edition of his anthology of German verse, *Deutsches Dichteralbum* (first published in Berlin in 1852), also placed this poem first.

Fontane, however, took this a step further than Storm, for the author only gave "Oktoberlied" primacy among his own poems, whereas Fontane gave it precedence over all the poems from all the poets he anthologized. Storm's gratification at seeing the pre-eminent position assigned to his poem must have been intensified when he heard from one of his brothers, Otto, who had just returned to Husum from a visit to Copenhagen, that a bookshop in the Danish capital had a copy of Fontane's *Album* on display, and

---

160   *Storm–Keller*, 118.
161   *Storm–Christen*, 44.
162   *Storm–Brinkmann*, 66; *Theodor Storm. Briefe*, ed. P. Goldammer, I, 163.
163   NFA, XXI/2, 95.
164   Ibid., XXI/1, 142.

"Schenk' ein den Wein, den holden! / Wir wollen uns den grauen Tag / Vergolden, ja vergolden!" (Pour wine of seasons olden! / And we will turn the gloomy days / To golden days, aye golden!) — "Oktoberlied."

that some Danish purchasers would make their first acquaintance with German poetry by looking at the "Oktoberlied" on the opening page.[165]

Storm must have also been overjoyed when he heard from Tycho Mommsen that the latter's brother, Theodor, had deemed "Oktoberlied" to be "recht sehr gut" (really very good).[166] This was an extraordinarily flattering comment from a classicist who had never seemed capable of saying anything complimentary about the poetry of his contemporaries.

b. The political context

Storm composed this poem on October 28 and 29, 1848. The date is highly significant, as it reveals the contemporary context in which the poet and his first readers held the poem in their hands.

Early in 1848, in February and March, insurrections against autocratic monarchs had broken out in Europe. With the exception of France, where the king was overthrown, the ferment of revolution usually died down as soon as the monarchs met the demands of the insurgents by promising democratic constitutions. This was what happened in Copenhagen on March 21 and 22.

Normally, this propitiatory action taken by the Danish sovereign would have been just as binding in the duchy of Schleswig as in the rest of Greater Denmark; the revolution would have then ended in Schleswig as quickly as it did in Copenhagen. A thorny dynastic problem, however, prevented this quick resolution.[167] Frederik VII, who had acceded to the Danish throne on January 20, 1848, was childless, which meant, according to Danish law, that his father's niece would succeed him upon his death. It was anticipated that Denmark would then have a queen and Schleswig a duchess as their next heads of state.

---

165 *Storm–Brinkmann*, 52.
166 Wickert, 203.
167 Succinctly explained in English by the Danish historian Holger Hjelholt, *British Mediation in the Danish-German Conflict 1848–1850*, 14–15.

In the duchy of Holstein, however, this would not have been possible, for according to Holstein law, only male succession could prevail. As a consequence, the nearest representative of the male royal line, Duke Christian August of Augustenborg, claimed the throne of Holstein, which, of course, he had every legal right to do. But since Holstein and Schleswig had ancient ties to each other owing to their *nexus socialis,* and since, more importantly, the duke's residences and sumptuous estates on the Isle of Als and at Augustenborg and Gråsten were all located within the duchy of Schleswig, he claimed that duchy for himself and his male descendants as well.

In his plan to wrest Schleswig from the Danish crown, the duke marshaled sufficient sympathy and support for an armed rebellion that erupted "in the most unblushing and flagrant manner," as Disraeli said in a moving speech before the House of Commons on April 19.[168] For five months, from March 24 until a truce was reached on August 26, the revolutionary Augustenborgian forces, under the command of Christian August's brother, clashed with Frederik VII's troops in fierce fighting up and down the Schleswig countryside. Large sections of the duchy were tainted with the smoke of cannons and the stain of spilled blood.

The galloping string of armed hostilities ended in that turbulent year of 1848 only after the great powers of Europe (England, France, and Russia) reminded supporters of the Augustenborgian cause that international treaties guaranteed that the duchy of Schleswig would always remain inseparably united with the crown of Denmark, and that further rebel action would thus be in vain. By September 8, the Augustenborgian troops realized that they had no choice but to disband. Duke Christian August, who served as the rallying point of the rebellion from the beginning, was banished from his imposing seat of power in Augustenborg Castle.

By October 21 the last vestiges of the insurgent government were dissolved. The dark clouds of armed rebellion now appeared to have blown over, as the bells of peace rang out from church steeples

---

168 Printed in *Hansard's Parliamentary Debates,* 98 (1848): 514.

all over Schleswig. This was a time of rejoicing for the duchy's citizenry. Laughter filled the air once more. The Huber theatrical troupe, according to Husum's *Wochenblatt* of October 8, 1848, resumed its business of performing farcical comedies in town after town throughout the duchy, much to the delight and mirth of the townspeople, who were anxious to forget the horrors of the recent war. We do not know whether Storm himself had taken a seat among Husum's laughing theater-goers, but certainly some acquaintances of his must have attended, and when they told him about the performances, he must have shared their laughter and relief after the months of political tension and war that had threatened to destroy the world in which he had grown up. This tone of merriment combined with relief is certainly present in "Oktoberlied."

Much else must have also lifted Storm's spirits at the time, and found an echo in the poem. Surely, he must have been relieved not only that the fighting of 1848 had ceased, but also that the western districts of Schleswig, including his native Husum, had been spared the worst of the war horrors.[169] The fiercest military battles had all been fought in eastern Schleswig.

Storm must have been even more cheered when he heard that his sovereign had issued, on September 22, an Emancipation Proclamation declaring that all slaves in the Danish colonies of the Caribbean had been set free. Frederik VII had gone even further, declaring that he would not tolerate any mistreatment of those who had been freed from bondage but could not yet cope with their freedom. This Proclamation of September 22, 1848, is one of the great documents on Human Rights in history. It boldly affirmed the dignity of human life, regardless of race or color.[170] The timing of the document made it particularly significant: Frederik VII had abolished

---

169 Felix Schmeisser, *Eine westschleswigsche Stadt in den Jahren 1848–51* (Husum: Delff, 1914), 1–24, has admirably described how fortunate Husum had been in 1848.
170 An English translation of this historic document is given in Carlo Christensen, *Peter von Scholten. A Chapter of the History of the Virgin Islands* (Lemvig: Nielsen, 1955), 30–31.

slavery and prohibited mistreatment of former slaves in the Danish colonies fourteen years before Abraham Lincoln earned acclaim for his Emancipation Proclamation. Not only had the Danish monarch's document come earlier, it also extended greater freedom. Storm's sovereign freed all slaves in his realm, while Lincoln's document applied only to slaves in the American states of the Union which were rebelling against federal authority. In other southern states, like Kentucky and Maryland, Lincoln did not abolish slavery.

The British scholar David A. Jackson has presented a compelling argument for recognizing that Storm was one of the great humanitarians of the nineteenth century.[171] Given his humanitarianism, Storm must have felt exhilarated when Frederik VII's Proclamation was announced in the fall of 1848. Although Storm criticism has not taken note of this, the poet must have been particularly well aware of the evils of the slave trade that had dehumanized life in the Danish colonies in the Caribbean. Several members of his mother's tightly knit family, the Woldsens, were living at the time in the Danish colony on St. Thomas.[172] Storm had always intensely enjoyed close relationships with his uncles Ingwer Woldsen and August Friedrich Woldsen,[173] brothers of Christian Albrecht Woldsen, who had gone to St. Thomas and raised a family there. Christian Albrecht's colorful experiences in such an exotic place must have come up often in conversation at the frequent Woldsen family gatherings in Husum. In the twilight of 1848, such conversations must have centered on the remarkable event of the abolition of slavery in St. Thomas.

For any number of reasons, then, Storm felt optimistic and hopeful in the fall of 1848 in Husum. Our knowledge that he would soon enough experience further tragedy in the world around him

---

171 This is the central thesis of David A. Jackson's book: *Theodor Storm. The Life and Works of a Democratic Humanitarian* (New York & Oxford: Berg, 1992).
172 Details are given in Johan Frederik Woldsen, *Stamtavle over Slægten Woldsen* (Copenhagen: Mayland, 1932), 18–19, 26–27.
173 For the poet's happy relationship with his uncle Ingwer Woldsen see *Storm. Briefe in die Heimat*, 123. We learn of the happy times Storm spent in August Friedrich's home in *Storm–Constanze Esmarch*, I, 243.

should not prevent us from recognizing that, at that time in that place, the poet was relieved and hopeful. It was this mood that gave rise to the jubilant song "Oktoberlied," the title of which refers, of course, to that happy month of Storm's life in 1848.

c. The poem as a drinking song

Essentially, "Oktoberlied" is an artfully composed drinking song. In it the speaker exhorts his friend, again and again, to drink wine with him, in a spirit of cheer and festivity. And the two merry friends do share the pleasures of drinking wine and of clinking their glasses. Antithesis is also central to the poem, however, as its cheerful tone admits of recent sorrows and apprehensions about the future:

> Der Nebel steigt, es fällt das Laub;
> Schenk' ein den Wein, den holden!
> Wir wollen uns den grauen Tag
> Vergolden, ja vergolden!
>
> Und geht es draußen noch so toll,
> Unchristlich oder christlich,
> Ist doch die Welt, die schöne Welt,
> So gänzlich unverwüstlich!
>
> Und wimmert auch einmal das Herz, —
> Stoß an, und laß es klingen!
> Wir wissen's doch, ein rechtes Herz
> Ist gar nicht umzubringen.
>
> Der Nebel steigt, es fällt das Laub;
> Schenk' ein den Wein, den holden!
> Wir wollen uns den grauen Tag
> Vergolden, ja vergolden!
>
> Wohl ist es Herbst; doch warte nur,
> Doch warte nur ein Weilchen!
> Der Frühling kommt, der Himmel lacht,
> Es steht die Welt in Veilchen.

Die blauen Tage brechen an;
Und ehe sie verfließen,
Wir wollen sie, mein wackrer Freund,
Genießen, ja genießen![174]

(The mist arises, the leaves fall,
Pour wine of seasons olden!
And we will turn the gloomy days
To golden days, aye golden!

Outside let things run madly on,
Kindly or unkindly;
Yet is the world, the lovely world
To be relied on blindly!

And though once more the heart laments,
Touch glasses, set them ringing!
We know full well a sturdy heart
Will live and keep on singing.

The mist arises, the leaves fall,
Pour wine of seasons olden!
And we will turn the gloomy days
To golden days, aye golden!

Well, it is Autumn. Only wait,
Wait a little while! Let's
Bide Spring's coming; the sky laughs
The world is full of violets.

The blue fall days are dawning now;
Before the Fates destroy them,
Let us then, old friend of mine,
Enjoy them, aye enjoy them!)

Translated by Carlyle F. MacIntyre[175]

---

174 Text taken from LL, I, 11.
175 Translation taken from *Oktoberlied by Theodor Storm*. With an English translation by C. F. MacIntyre (Los Angeles: Ward Ritchie Press, 1945).

d. The double structure in form and theme

One of the most obvious formal features of the poem is its division in two halves. Quatrains one, two, and three are juxtaposed against quatrains four, five, and six. The first quatrain, which introduces the first half of the poem, is repeated exactly in the fourth quatrain, which introduces the second half. The first half of the poem is dominated by the gloom of autumn and the falling of leaves, foreboding the barrenness of winter, while in the poem's second, echoing half, the gloom of autumn arises again in the repeated quatrain, but laughter anticipates the far-off coming of spring, suddenly brought into the present as a blanket of violets covers the earth, presumably with divine blessing ("der Himmel lacht").

This structure may mirror the two halves of the year 1848 in Schleswig: the gathering clouds and eruption of armed rebellion, which cast its gloom over so much of the first half of the year, and the passing of these ominous clouds when peace was restored in the latter half of the year. At the same time, "der Nebel steigt" indicates an uncertain future. This interpretation makes sense of the slightly curious way that the poem freely manipulates time and seems to conflate spring and autumn: "Es steht die Welt in Veilchen" describes "Der Frühling kommt" in the present tense, though spring is in the future, and the very next line, opening the final quatrain, reverts to autumn yet maintains the present tense: "Die blauen Tage brechen an; / Und ehe sie verfließen, / Wir wollen sie, mein wackrer Freund, / Genießen, ja genießen!"

Conventionally, poetry celebrates spring as a fleeting time of beauty, as in the famous lines of the seventeenth-century English poet Robert Herrick:

> Gather ye rosebuds while ye may,
> Old Time is still a-flying,
> And this same flower that smiles today
> Tomorrow will be dying.[176]

---

[176] Robert Herrick, "To the Virgins, to Make Much of Time," *The Norton Anthology of Poetry*, ed. A. W. Allison et al. (New York & London: Norton, ³1983), 246.

The Poems

Yet in "Oktoberlied," a spring-like autumn becomes the time to cherish. Again, this makes sense if we keep in mind the events of 1848. That year, spring and summer were indeed a gloomy time for Schleswig, as the Augustenborgian forces tried to wrest the duchy away from Denmark, bringing havoc in their train, while autumn brought peace and feelings of hope that are usually associated with spring. Significantly, with the coming of autumn and international pressure, the vitality of the rebellion weakened.

As much division and doubling as there is in the poem, as conflicting feelings of joy and sorrow are formally and thematically balanced, and as divided as the year 1848 appeared to be in the poet's perception, the poem is, in the final analysis, uplifting. As "Oktoberlied" depicts a tense balance between present peace against recent strife and fears of future conflicts, between autumn and spring, and between inside and outside, the dominant feeling alternates, but cheer and hope are continually emphasized and finally prevail. In the twenty-four lines of the poem, fourteen lines are indisputably affirmative or hopeful (2, 4, 7, 10, 11, 12, 14, 16, 18, 19, 20, 21, 23, 24), while the other ten lines express more doubt, ambivalence, sadness, and apprehension. Quite noticeably, the affirmative lines occur more frequently in the latter half of the poem.

Each quatrain admits, in its opening, the bleakness of life, but all that is gray, bleak or foreboding is overcome, however temporarily, by various saving graces: the wine and memories of former days that have the power to transform the gloomy present (quatrains one and four); the persistence of the lovely world (quatrain two); the strength and endurance of a good heart (quatrain three); the beauty and hope of spring (quatrain five); the pleasures of beautiful autumn days (quatrain six). *Weltschmerz* is always displaced by the will to feel joy, and the threats to happiness make its triumph all the more poignant.

The musical quality of this drinking song strengthens its theme of cheer triumphing over gloom. For despite the harrowing experience of the revolution, and despite the gloom of October foreboding the bleakness of winter, cheerful singing and the drinking of wine insistently prevail. This cheer is obvious in the singing of the two friends, and in the echoing chorus of the refrain. The refrain of the first quatrain in line four, at the beginning of the poem's first division, is repeated in the third quatrain in line twelve, at the beginning of the second division. This lends a tremendous quality of echo to the entire poem. Gloom and cheer, cheer and gloom echo throughout the drinking song, in much the same way as the repetition of the refrain makes the poem's dual structure resound. A similar echoing effect is also produced, rather obviously, with the abundance of internal rhymes and repetition of the same words in the poem (ein-Wein, Vergolden-vergolden, Unchristlich-christlich, Welt-Welt, gänzlich-unverwüstlich, Genießen-genießen). This emphasis on echo suggests both the insistence of the will to feel joy, and the need for such strength of will in the face of formidable gloom.

e. Meter and rhyme

The poet's exquisite use of meter and end rhyme adds further to the musical quality of the poem. The steady, regular rhythm of iambs in the first, third, and fourth lines of each quatrain contrast with the spondaic rhythm that opens the second line in each quatrain.

In five of the six quatrains, moreover, two lines (the first and the third) may disturb us with their lack of end rhyme, but this contrasts with the soothing fulfillment of soft feminine end rhyme in the second and fourth lines, which, coming last, echoes and lingers in our ears. This rhyme scheme, too, seems to articulate the tension between sorrow over the recent violence of the Augustenborgian rebellion and happiness at its resolution. That is, the first line of each quatrain begins in fear and worry, which is then emphasized by the jarring lack of end rhyme in the third line; but peace, order, and joy win out, as the perfect end rhyme of the second and lingering fourth lines affirms.

The exception to the above rhyme scheme occurs in the third quatrain. At that central turning point in the poem, there is no discordant end rhyme. "Herz" (heart) is rhymed with "Herz" to create a doubling that is even stronger than rhyme. Affirming, comforting sound occurs, hence, at the heart of this poem, reflecting Storm's positive outlook in October 1848, when he had every reason to feel heartened.

The poet constantly reminds us that in the background (or the foreground?) the two friends, whose hearts are joined in joy, keep making toasts to this happy month, clinking their wine glasses in continual, echoing accord. The ringing of the wine glasses seems to echo the church bells that rang out for peace throughout Schleswig in October 1848.

f. The echoing Danish tradition

Storm's buoyant song of cheer in the face of adversity is, as none of the critics of this poem have noticed,[177] altogether reminiscent of the singing tradition which had blossomed with the Danish poetry of the Golden Age in the early nineteenth century and which "took on epidemic proportions," as the Australian Scandinavianist Hans Kuhn has said,[178] in the large number of Danish drinking songs written during and about the Schleswig War of 1848. All the established Danish poets, Hans Kuhn informs us, contributed to the chorus of hope and triumph, anxiety and dejection, in the form of songs that follow military and political developments in Schleswig in 1848. Since drinking songs are usually joyous in tone,[179] the incentives to compose these Danish drinking songs of 1848 were likely sparked by the excitement and elation of the various royalist victories in battle, rather than by the defeats these troops suffered at times. When Frederik VII's soldiers did on occasion lose a battle, it was not despair over the

---

[177] Franz Werneke, "Theodor Storms Oktoberlied — Eine Interpretation," *Unsere Schule* 9 (1954): 223–228; Walter Silz, "Theodor Storm: Three Poems," *Germanic Review* 42 (1967): 296–298; Harro Müller, *Theodor Storms Lyrik* (Bonn: Bouvier, 1975), 31–43; Rolf Selbmann, "Vergoldeter Herbst. Storms 'Oktoberlied.' Emanuel Geibel und der Realismus in der Lyrik," STSG 45 (1996): 117–126. See, also, the passing observations on this poem in many general studies on Storm.

[178] Hans Kuhn, *Defining a Nation in Song. Danish Patriotic Songs in Songbooks of the Period 1832–1870* (Copenhagen: Reitzel, 1990), 18.

[179] Hans Ritte, *Das Trinklied in Deutschland und Schweden* (Munich: Fink, 1973), 7–8.

defeat that prevailed in the songs, but rather joy in the certainty that the Augustenborgian rebellion would eventually be overcome. The royalists and their supporters seemed assured of this outcome, for again, the great powers of Europe (England, France, and Russia), all concurred in their lack of sympathy for the rebellious Duke of Augustenborg.

The unusually high number of these drinking songs, to which Hans Kuhn has referred, indicates, of course, that literature breeds more literature. Each poet helped create an atmosphere that encouraged other poets to write in the same or a similar vein. Each poem that found its way into print became the catalyst for another poem. Danish poets competed in applying their lyrical skills to express cheer and hope at a time when pitched battles were capturing the imagination of every Danish citizen. Naturally, this held most true in that part of the united Danish kingdom which was feeling the brunt of the mutinous warfare: the duchy of Schleswig. Hence, it was in the Danish-language press of Schleswig that so many of these drinking songs first appeared. Newspaper editors knew what their readers wanted, and, just as well, what their monarch wanted.

Many of these popular compositions were quickly collected and reprinted in songbooks published in the various towns of the duchy. Three volumes, in particular, reveal the extent to which language and musical rhythm were combined in the duchy's political verse: (1) Peter Christian Koch, *Fædrelandsk Vise-Bog* (A Book of Native Melodies), published in Haderslev in 1850; (2) Kristen Karstensen, *Gamle og nye Sange til Brug for Skolen og Livet* (Old and New Songs for Use in Schools and Everyday Life), Sønderborg 1851; (3) Frederik Fischer, *Sangbog for Gamle og Unge* (A Songbook for Old and Young), Aabenraa 1852.[180] Looking through these volumes, a reader is hard put to say what is of greatest interest here: the opera of emotion set to music, or the war in Schleswig. Clearly, the language of most of the poems refers directly to the political scene of the moment, but

---

180 I am indebted to Jacob Thomsen of the Royal Library at Copenhagen for making these rare volumes available to me.

clearly, too, each poem exhibits real musical qualities. One of the anthologists, Peter Christian Koch, even adds to each printed poem a melody in one-part notation.

As a result of the wide circulation of these Danish convivial songs of 1848 in Schleswig's newspapers, Storm, who had already learned so much from Danish poetry, must have felt the desire to mold his own impressions of 1848 into a poem with musical form. The revolution which had inspired the Danish songs would have reminded him that no poetry in 1848 could be written in a vacuum, divorced from political events. The urgent need to offer cheerful declarations at a time darkened by war is something he must also have learned from his Danish contemporaries. Last but not least, the infectious musical quality that was so characteristic of Danish political verse in 1848 could not but help to encourage Storm to compose his poetry of the moment in a similar vein.

g. The contrast with German verse of 1848

We only need to reflect briefly on the nature of German poetry in the revolutionary year of 1848 to see the extent to which Storm, as a sort of Danish lyricist composing in German, must have been influenced by Danish verse of 1848 rather than by its German counterpart. Ferdinand Freiligrath was the most prominent of the German poets of 1848 who tended to support the uprising against the Danish monarch.

His most celebrated poem is "Die Toten an die Lebenden" (The Dead to the Living), composed in June 1848. Several verses addressed to the rebellion of the Duke of Augustenborg (Freiligrath refers to him as a prince) are typical:

> Wie Wellen braust' an uns heran, was sich begab im Lande:
> Der Aberwitz des Dänenkriegs, die letzte Polenschande;
> Das rüde Toben der Vendee in stockigen Provinzen;
> Der Soldateska Wiederkehr, die Wiederkehr des Prinzen;[181]

---

181 Ferdinand Freiligraths *Sämtliche Werke*, ed. L. Schröder, VI (Leipzig: Hesse, 1906), 34.

(All that on earth betides doth shake, like waves, our ghostly frame:
The folly of the Danish war and the latest Polish shame,
The rebels' outcry fierce and loud in the stubborn countryside,
The tramp of soldiers marching back, with the Prince in all his pride,)[182]

While these verses do not completely lack musical vitality, nobody would call the poem a "song," the label that Storm and the Danes had attached to their 1848 poems. The unwavering iambic beat throughout the very long poem (eighty-eight lines in total) is wearisome, to say the least, and simply provides a basic structure on which to hang a message of caustic satire. Its long lines could never be easily sung. The poem's forty-four rhymed couplets are likewise monotonous, and their form never seems to have much connection to what the verses wish to say, nor does the rhythm or rhyme vary to express different attitudes towards the theme, as these elements do in Storm's poem. Freiligrath gives vent to his indignation that the insurgent troops in Schleswig (as well as in Poland) had been turned back by the forces seeking to quell rebellion. He lapses into uninspiring propagandistic doggerel, inciting his readers to continue the fight of those warriors who had fallen in battle for the revolutionary cause. Yet Freiligrath offers no hope that further rebellion might succeed. For him, life in Schleswig (as in Poland) is dismal. Indeed, it threatens to become even more dismal.

In contrast, Storm's "Oktoberlied" of 1848, as well as the Danish poems of 1848, are essentially songs. Their short, lyrical lines could be and were sung, and their musical rhythms use repetition and variation to great expressive effect. The rhyme scheme in Storm's poem is also more complex and musical than that of Freiligrath's, which neatly ties up each caustic comment in a predictable couplet. In further contrast to Freiligrath, both Storm and the other Danes sing a song of hope and cheer, even when sorrow and despair remain in sight on the horizon.

But although Storm was obviously influenced by his fellow Danish songwriters, and apparently not by contemporary German

---

182   J. G. Legge, *Rhyme and Revolution in Germany* (London: Constable, 1918), 318.

poetry, that influence was not entirely overwhelming. Storm's poem still emerges with a distinct lyrical voice that expresses reactions to the political events of the time in a subtle, indirect way. The Danish drinking songs were overtly patriotic and they tended to focus on specific military and political events (just as Freiligrath's poem did), most frequently on the gains and losses of the despised Augustenborgian forces. These songwriters took undisguised pleasure in every possibility that the rebel Duke of Augustenborg would be defeated, just as they felt dismay on those occasions when his forces appeared to carry the banner of victory.

h. Storm's transfigured theme

Storm's "Oktoberlied," nourished as it had been by the creative mood of the Danish lyrics, leaves the arena of specific places and events in order to offer a transfigured, timeless theme. Despite the poem's obvious connection with the events of 1848 in Schleswig, evident from its context as well as some of its content ("Und geht es draußen noch so toll, / Unchristlich oder christlich"), this poem, playing out the heartfelt conflict between gloom and the will to joy, between hope and despair, creates a stirring message of hard-won triumph over adversity that both responds to and transcends the events in Schleswig that year. At the time of its publication, the poem must have touched the heart of any European who read it; the connection would have been obvious between the revolutionary events of 1848 and the universal human emotions of relief, joy, and apprehension which Storm felt in October of that year. The poem's description of autumn and spring scenes, and of the vaguely threatening world outside the room where the two friends drink wine, could describe many places and climates in Europe at that time. Anyone acquainted with Schleswig's landscape would not find details describing it in this poem. Indeed, the reference to drinking wine readily calls up a picture of the German Rhineland or of France, rather than of Schleswig, where the inhabitants in Storm's time preferred to drink rum, grog, or other strong spirits.

Local color, or detailed realistic description more typical of German poetry, hence, gives way to a more profound statement on the experience of Europe in 1848. And yet the poem also carries its more universal message easily into the twentieth and twenty-first centuries, when lack of knowledge of the historical context would do little to diminish the poem's emotional force. The poem records a lyrical affirmation of the will to hope and seek happiness, despite the persistence of horrors in the world which, as in Schleswig in 1848, encroach to defeat the human spirit. No poet writing in German since Goethe found it possible to achieve such a powerful affirmation. This helps us to understand why the critic Fontane could say, as quoted earlier, "the post-Goethean age has seen no finer poetry [than Storm's]."

We also understand why Storm called this poem "immortal." The poem has certainly lived well beyond his lifetime. The Danish songs of 1848, focusing more acutely on topical issues of the day, have lost their urgency and rarely appear in modern anthologies. As for Freiligrath's verses and other German political poems of 1848, the feather duster of an antiquarian barely keeps them from disappearing into oblivion. Storm's lyrical affirmation of the will to seek happiness, however, has remained to this day "a perennial favorite in anthologies."[183]

i. The divided opinion of modern critics

Curiously, not all critics, as Patricia Boswell has pointed out, have acclaimed this poem with enthusiasm.[184] Friedrich Sengle, for instance, gives an exceedingly complimentary evaluation of it,[185] whereas Walter Silz and Harro Müller have minced no words in criticizing it. Silz sums up his critique by claiming that the poem "is *unecht* [not genuine]. It abandons his [Storm's] characteristic restraint and under-

---

183   Silz, 296.
184   *Theodor Storm* (Leicester German Poets), ed. P.M. Boswell (Leicester: University Press, 1989), 74.
185   Friedrich Sengle, "Storms lyrische Eigenleistung. Abgrenzung von anderen großen Lyrikern des 19. Jahrhunderts," STSG 28 (1979): 17–18.

statement; it speaks loudly and confidently... its utterance is fulsome and its convivial optimism unsupported by inner substance."[186] Müller criticizes the poem even more vigorously. He considers its optimism to be hollow, and, referring to the poem as nothing but a drinking song, believes its aesthetic quality to be substandard.[187]

Protests must be raised against such disparaging statements. Silz's and Müller's cursory dismissals of "Oktoberlied" miss much of the pathos, subtlety, and lyricism of the poem. Growing out of the tumultuous experiences of observing revolution and rebellion in Schleswig and the whole of Europe in 1848, the poem cannot rightly be considered *unecht*. The poem also employs considerable restraint and understatement, as Storm distilled the diverse horrors of 1848 into apt, timeless images and metaphors of inevitable seasonal change and the cyclical nature of adversity: the grim spring of 1848 had passed and the peaceful but gloomy winter, and finally spring, lay ahead. Certainly "Oktoberlied" is much more subtle than Freiligrath's propagandistic verses. Nor does the poem speak loudly and confidently with unmeasured optimism. As shown above, "Oktoberlied" plays out a constant, close battle between hope and fear, cheer and gloom, with pathos that becomes especially obvious if we recognize that a feeling of hope usually associated with spring is strangely, perhaps desperately, associated with autumn. And the triumph of the will to seek happiness is threatened by apprehensions about the future in the poem's final quatrain: "Die blauen Tage brechen an; / *Und ehe sie verfließen,* / Wir wollen sie, mein wackrer Freund, / Genießen, ja genießen!" Müller's dismissal of the poem as nothing but a drinking song tainted by academic snobbery, which fails to honor the debt that lyric poetry has to oral folk traditions, also ignores, as Storm scholars tend to, the poet's debt to the Danish drinking song tradition.

We should also remember the words of Theodor Fontane, Theodor Mommsen, and Storm himself, all of whom rated the poem

---

186 Silz, 298.
187 Müller, 39, 43.

so highly. It does not seem to be mere vanity that made Storm value the poem so much; considering the tragedies that he experienced later, it is no wonder that he would cling to his one lyrical expression of hard-won optimism. We should also remember that numerous anthologists have deemed "Oktoberlied" worthy to be included among the best poems of the German language. In praising this poem, we should also honor the ancient tradition of the lyrical drinking song, which had flourished anew in Denmark during the first half of the nineteenth century, and whose musical appeal Storm brought into German literature. Not since Goethe's "Ergo Bibamus" of 1810 had the drinking song played any significant role in the German *ars poetica*. Last but not least, we should honor the marvelous testimony to the resilience of the human spirit that Storm, for the first time in German poetry since Goethe, created when he composed this immortal drinking song.

8. Poetry and life: "Hyazinthen"

a. Thomas Mann's fascination with "Hyazinthen"

In 1851 Storm composed the lyrical poem "Hyazinthen" (Hyacinths). It has become, justifiably, famous in world literature, not least of all because Thomas Mann wove its melancholic refrain "Ich möchte schlafen, aber du mußt tanzen" (I long to sleep, but you must dance) into the narrative of his novella *Tonio Kröger*, in which he turned the refrain into a poetic leitmotiv. Mann, the great "juge de Theodor Storm," as one French critic has called him,[188] bestowed further praise on "Hyazinthen" when he described the poem as "elegant, tender, rich like the notes of a cello with feeling."[189] With such an eloquent testimonial to the poem's musical and emotional richness, there can be no doubt about its importance in Storm's literary legacy.

---

188 Robert Pitrou, "Thomas Mann, juge de Theodor Storm," *Revue germanique* 22 (1931): 257–261.
189 Mann *Essays*, 273.

It is not difficult to discover why Mann was so powerfully attracted to "Hyazinthen" that he wanted to draw the attention of others to it. Storm had been, from early on, Mann's "literary idol."[190] He owed much of his early literary schooling to Storm's fiction. This poem, however, had the particular distinction of anticipating the theme that would remain close to Mann's heart for his entire literary career: the inescapable conflict between art and life, and the role of poet and citizen. Mann knew that by incorporating the conflict inherent in "Hyazinthen" into *Tonio Kröger*, he would increase and reinforce the same tension that he wanted his own work of fiction to emphasize.

b. Storm's Choral Society bridges the gulf between artistic inclinations and the demands of communal life

When Storm had taken up his pen to compose the cello-like notes of "Hyazinthen," he had long felt the difficulty of accommodating both the multifarious demands of communal life and the dictates of his artistic disposition. Ever since he had established himself as an attorney in Husum in 1843, he had experienced firsthand the conflict between his life as an artist and his distinctly unpoetic role in a provincial society regulated by both convention and the need to earn a living. The Danish historiographer Knud Fabricius, who was able to compare Storm with others who practiced law in the Danish monarchy, could clearly detect that Storm's heart was not in the law practice he began in 1843. Rather, Fabricius points out, "hans Hjerte var tidligt ved Digtningen" (his heart was from the start in poetry).[191]

For a while, however, Storm seemed to find a modest way to bridge this gap with the Choral Society he founded in 1843. In the performance of songs, both art and communal life could be brought together. The "power of song"[192] could make its emotional impact

---

190 Donald Prater, *Thomas Mann. A Life* (Oxford: University Press, 1995), 8.
191 Fabricius, *Sønderjyllands Historie*, IV, 458.
192 Storm was fascinated, we know, with Andreas Romberg's *Die Macht des Gesanges* (The Power of Song). See *Storm–Constanze Esmarch*, II, 241, 273.

on the lives of the citizens who heard Storm's choir, and the citizens who were choir members could find in it some respite from their provincial, rather mundane lives, embracing the inspirational creativity of musical performance. The presence of one choir member in particular, Doris Jensen (mentioned above in the discussion of "Nixen-Chor zur Begrüßung König Christians VIII. in Husum"), suggests that Storm also found romantic inspiration in the choir that he did not find in his marriage, just as he found artistic inspiration there that he did not find in his legal work. This association between romantic and artistic freedom, and the constraints of conventional society, will become important in our interpretation of "Hyazinthen." Storm, the well-known Husum lawyer, and Storm, the choir director, could bring two disparate worlds together. This happy arrangement might have continued had not disruptive political developments made it impossible.

The first upset came when Storm's Choral Society had to suspend its activities in 1848 due to the unnerving revolutionary events in Schleswig.[193] Although Husum was spared much of the rebellious havoc of 1848, the townspeople nevertheless could not go about business as usual. What occurred in other parts of the duchy, they knew, affected them too. Commerce suffered. Fear that the warfare would spread to Husum was always present. Men in and around Husum had left their homes and families to join the rebel forces. A number of them paid with their lives. No one, therefore, was in a mood to sing. The shortage of male voices, moreover, made performances, even rehearsals, out of the question.

c. The conflict between art and life in the revolutionary activity of 1849–1850

More upsetting for Storm was the spread of the revolution to Husum in 1849–1850. The peace that had been restored in Schleswig when the civil warfare ended in the fall of 1848 proved to be short-lived.

---

193   On the history of Storm's Choral Society, see Hans Jürgen Sievers, "Zur Geschichte von Theodor Storms 'Singverein,' " STSG 18 (1969): 89–105.

The rebel Duke Christian August, who refused to recognize the Danish king's claim to the duchy of Schleswig and who had been driven from the majestic seat of power at Augustenborg, now traveled far and wide, fanning the fires of revolution everywhere he went.

As long as this rebellious vassal of the Danish king persisted in his resistance to the sovereign's authority, he served as a rallying point for other insurgents who, the quelled rebellion of 1848 notwithstanding, continued to agitate for a severance of Schleswig's legal ties to the crown of Denmark. This was, of course, a thorn in the side of the Danish sovereign and all of his loyal subjects who wished to preserve the United Monarchy (the Danish *Helstat*).

Since the Augustenborgian menace to the status quo would not subside, the royalist government realized it would have to take further action. Universal military conscription was introduced in Denmark; the size of the army increased, and it was newly trained and newly equipped. By February 26, 1849, preparations for stamping out the smoldering embers of rebellion in Schleswig had advanced: the royalist government denounced the 1848 truce that had proven to be so tenuous. Once more the duchy found itself embroiled in civil war.

This time Husum was not spared. From 1849 to 1851, the town tottered between the exigencies of mutinous warfare and the tyranny of martial law. From conflicting Danish and German standpoints, both Holger Hjelholt and Felix Schmeisser, respectively, have provided detailed, gripping accounts of this turbulent period in Husum's history; the different viewpoints have made the chaos of the time seem even more bewildering.[194] Hjelholt, for instance, reports that mob rule on the rebel side often made it impossible for the royalist authorities to maintain law and order. But according to Schmeisser, on the other side, the pillaging of the marauding soldiers and sailors in the service of the king frightened the populace more than the rebel mob violence.

---

194   Holger Hjelholt, *Sønderjylland under Treårskrigen*, II (Copenhagen: Gad, 1961), 90–109; Schmeisser, 24–116.

Storm, as one of the town's respected attorneys, was kept busy counseling and consoling citizens who were alternately (and often arbitrarily) accused either of conspiring against or of collaborating with the agents of oppression on both sides of the conflict. In his defense of the many farmers and merchants who engaged his legal services, Storm then became involved in all sorts of endless quarrels with unsympathetic civil and military tribunals. The law cases he had to argue taxed his strength greatly.[195]

As a result, Storm felt that fulfilling these taxing obligations to the community now left him with less time than ever to pursue his imaginative impulses, and so he sought to curtail his activities in the public sector, trying as much as possible to do so without falling out of favor with his clients, on whom he depended for his living. His withdrawal from public life did not, of course, escape the attention of the civil authorities in Husum at the time. In 1851 they reported to Copenhagen that Storm, compared to many of his fellow citizens (and clients), had led a rather politically detached life in Husum during the civil war.[196]

---

195 *Storm–Brinkmann*, 31, 65.
196 It is to the abiding credit of the Danish historiographer Knud Fabricius that he discovered in the Danish National Archives in Copenhagen that Storm had made a noticeable effort to withdraw himself from public life at the time. See Fabricius, *Sønderjyllands Historie*, IV, 458–459. It is also to the great credit of the Danish Storm critic Anna Simonsen that she, taking note of Fabricius's discovery, decided to search further the docket in which he had found the report (Ministeriet for Slesvig, 1.Dpt.A: Sager om Advokater 1852–1862). Her perseverance paid off, for she discovered a second document, by another official, confirming Storm's choice to keep a low profile in public life at the time. See Anna Simonsen, "Theodor Storm og Danmark (med specielt Henblik paa hans Forhold under Krigen 1848–50)," *Sønderjydske Årbøger*, I (1950): 146–148. These two documents refute the opinions of generations of Storm scholars who, unaware of the archival evidence in Copenhagen, claimed that the poet had taken an active role in the rebellion.

d. Rendering the conflict in poetry

Storm had become acutely aware of the disjunction of his public life and the poet's life he longed for, and it was doubtless this awareness, along with conflicts between his private romantic life and his conventional marriage, discussed below, which provided him with the motivation to compose his ingenious poem "Hyazinthen," completed in 1851 and published in 1852:

> Fern hallt Musik; doch hier ist stille Nacht,
> Mit Schlummerduft anhauchen mich die Pflanzen;
> Ich habe immer, immer dein gedacht,
> Ich möchte schlafen; aber du mußt tanzen.
>
> Es hört nicht auf, es ras't ohn' Unterlaß;
> Die Kerzen brennen und die Geigen schreien,
> Es teilen und es schließen sich die Reihen,
> Und Alle glühen; aber du bist blaß.
>
> Und du mußt tanzen; fremde Arme schmiegen
> Sich an dein Herz; o leide nicht Gewalt!
> Ich seh' dein weißes Kleid vorüberfliegen
> Und deine leichte, zärtliche Gestalt. —
>
> Und süßer strömend quillt der Duft der Nacht
> Und träumerischer aus dem Kelch der Pflanzen.
> Ich habe immer, immer dein gedacht;
> Ich möchte schlafen; aber du mußt tanzen.[197]

> (Far music rings; here night is still and blue,
> Full of the slumbrous perfume of the plants.
> My thoughts have only, only been of you;
> I long to sleep, but you must dance and dance.
>
> It rages on, it does not cease or fail;
> The candles glisten and the viols shrill;
> They part and close again in the quadrille,
> And all are glowing, only you are pale.

---

197 Text taken from LL, I, 23.

And you must dance; and others' arms are lying
Close to your heart. — O do not suffer harm!
I see your white and gauzy gown go flying
And see your light and delicate young form. —

And sweeter night's sweet essence filters through
And still more dreamy from the dreaming plants.
My thoughts have only, only been of you;
I long to sleep, but you must dance and dance.)

Translated by Herman Salinger[198]

We hear music in this poem from the very start. Three powerful stresses on the first three words, terminating in "Musik," emphasize the word and music itself, and this emphasis receives more weight when the semi-colon following "Musik" provides a pause in which the phrase rings in our ears. The stillness of the night, described in the line's second phrase in a quieter, less emphatic sequence of soft iambs, contrasts with the strongly stressed first phrase and lets the initial explosive notes of music reverberate further. With the word "tanzen" at the end of the first quatrain, we know we are listening to the lively waltz rhythms of ballroom dancing.

The second quatrain continues to emphasize music. In lines six and seven, the shrill of "Geigen" (violins) rings particularly loudly against the sharp "ei" sounds of "schre*ei*en" and "R*ei*hen" (associated with "G*ei*gen" to vary the flatter "a" vowels of all the preceding rhyme words). To call more attention to the sounds of the string orchestra, he gives these two lines a recursive rhyme scheme (cddc) that sets them apart from the rest of the poem's rhyme scheme (abab–efef–abab), in the first, third and fourth quatrains. Storm thus stresses the importance of the violins resounding in this quatrain. Their sound is described as harsh and relentless, and the music, with the candles and the parting and closing quadrille (not closing and parting), all serve to contain the young woman dancing and constrain her to keep dancing.

---

198   Translation taken from *Lyrica Germanica*, I (1966): 1. Reprinted by permission of Marion C. Salinger.

In bold contrast to the poem's vibrant music and the scene of the ballroom stands the lonely figure of the lover who looks on and remains unimpressed, even annoyed by the lilting tunes that persistently fill the air. Jealously, he listens from outside the ballroom to the gaiety of the music from within. Two worlds are immediately juxtaposed. In the world of the candle-lit, festive ballroom, everyone moves to and is enchanted by the lively music of the violinists. In the other world, we have the sad figure of the frustrated lover; the intoxicating scent of hyacinths, of nature in bloom in the spring, has made him drowsy. And though he thinks of the woman dancing in the ballroom, he does not want to or cannot join her.

This contrast between art and life, between the starkly different circumstances of speaker and addressee, and perhaps between the public self and private poetic self, between the life of the solitary artist and the life of those who embrace and enjoy the human company of the dance, is brought out further with the description of how the dancing young woman is dressed: in a beautiful white dress with a swirling skirt, which would only be worn in the magical setting of a candle-lit ballroom. The solitary frustrated lover, somewhere outside the ballroom, made drowsy by the scent of hyacinths in spring, has no part in the magical realm resounding with lively music.

e. Compounding the conflict

If we have become aware of the conflict between art and life through the contrast between the magical waltzing and the frustrated lover who has no place in the ballroom, then we are made doubly aware of this dualism when the poet presents the same theme in reverse: the ballroom and its music become the world of real life, whereas the frustrated lover outside the ballroom, with whom we sympathize, now turns out to be an artist somehow removed from real life.

The ballroom dancers are, after all, lovers who may feel true love for one another as they move together with the steps of the waltz. Lovers dancing is an especially apt instance of the basic human experience from which the artist feels excluded and for which he feels some contempt. The "Ich" in the poem, as the frustrated lover, now becomes the poet, observing and describing the lovers and the dance instead of loving and dancing himself, a representative of the arts who is an outcast from the real world of life and love, separated from the community for which he writes. Certainly this is the way the poem was interpreted by Thomas Mann. The speaker is the "Bajazzo" about whom Mann — in a glib imitation of Storm — would later write.[199]

Yet, regardless of the angle from which we look at this poem, it is always the dualism of art and life, artifice and reality, imagination and fact, which obtrudes. We may be uncertain at any given moment which is which, but in the end we are sure that it is the pull between the two which constitutes the central conflict of the poem.

A series of other poetic effects strengthens this impression. Following the emphatic music of the poem's first three words, the poet formally affirms the dualism of the theme with an iambic beat of alternating stressed and unstressed syllables. The inherent dualism of this steady iambic beat is then compounded by the frequent alternation between the strict pentameter lines and lines containing an extra terminating syllable, corresponding to the alternating feminine and masculine end-rhymes that echo throughout the poem.

Storm also emphasizes the thematic conflict with frequent internal punctuation of commas and semicolons in individual lines, making us pause halfway through ten of the sixteen lines. This is a high proportion of punctuated pauses in individual lines. They doubtless mimic the rests in the music of waltzes, but the halting music of these divided lines also serves to emphasize once more the dualism of his two separate lives as a poet and as a citizen, and perhaps uncertainty as to how to resolve this conflict. It is with consummate delicacy that Storm uses punctuation to this effect, for a pause in every one of the sixteen lines, or too many consecutive pauses, would have

---

199 Mann, *Gesammelte Werke*, VII (Frankfurt am Main: Fischer, 1960), 106–140.

been overt and tedious; as it is, the ten broken lines gracefully reinforce the poem's dual melody and theme.

Storm also used several other ingenious poetic devices for the purpose of echoing his dual melody. For instance, the second and third quatrains, which emphasize the "Du" the poem addresses and the world from which the speaker is excluded, are juxtaposed to the first and fourth embracing quatrains, in which an opposing "Ich" presides. Similarly, in the third quatrain the heavy-sounding "U" of "Und" at the beginning of the first and fourth lines counterbalances the high-pitched "I"'s of "Sich" and "Ich" in the second and third lines. The fourth quatrain, in musical contrast, abandons this sequence of the "U" sound counterbalancing the "I" sound, in favor of a new doubling melody of a couplet of heavy "U" sounds followed by two successive high-pitched "I" sounds. Coming at the poem's conclusion, this rich orchestral interplay of light and heavy sounds, arranged in counterpoint fashion, reinforces the song of the conflict between real life and art, which lingers on long after we have read the poem.

f. A hidden confession

This interpretation of "Hyazinthen" could easily end here, but a particularly revealing confessional aspect of the poem is yet unexplored, which in turn reveals another source of the poem's grace and mysterious intensity.

The hidden confession begins to reveal itself in the lines of the refrain that echoes at the end of both the first and last quatrains:

> Ich möchte schlafen; aber du mußt tanzen.
> (I long to sleep; but you must dance.)

This was the line which so impressed Thomas Mann that he chose to immortalize it in his *Tonio Kröger*, as the perfect articulation of the conflict between art and life, particularly the hero's unrequited love for ordinary people who enjoy ordinary life — Hans Hansen and Ingeborg Holm — and his literary ambitions and pursuits. The refrain of "Hyazinthen" implies, if we think about it, some element of confession. But what did Storm have in mind when he wrote the line, and why should he have included a veiled confession in the poem? The reasons have indeed been hidden well, which explains why the secondary literature on "Hyazinthen" itself gives us no answers.

The analyses given by S. S. Prawer and Friedrich Ackermann, for instance, make no mention whatsoever of a confessional element in the poem.[200] Hans Bender, on the other hand, feels certain that a confessional element is present. He interprets the refrain as a reference to Storm's early, unrequited love for a young woman in Hamburg known to Storm biographers as Bertha von Buchan.[201] Dieter Lohmeier, the editor of the latest critical edition of Storm's poetry, likewise underscores the refrain's confessional tone. But in contrast to his predecessor Bender, Lohmeier thinks that the refrain refers not to Bertha but to Constanze Esmarch at the time of her engagement to Storm.[202]

All of these interpretations are inaccurate. If the confessional element constitutes an integral part of the poem's structure, as Bender and Lohmeier have noticed, we cannot be satisfied with any interpretation of the poem that neglects it. At the same time, however, an interpretation is not useful when identifications of the addressee miss their mark. The dancing woman is neither Bertha von Buchan nor Constanze Esmarch. When Storm composed "Hyazinthen" in 1851, his feelings for Bertha, whom he had known from 1836 to 1842, had long since faded. Incorporating them into a poem at a much later date would be anachronistic and emotionally unconvincing, which "Hyazinthen" is not. Much the same can be said against identifying the dancing woman in the poem as Constanze Esmarch. If such an identification could be made, Storm's observations about

---

200 S. S. Prawer, *German Lyric Poetry. A Critical Analysis of Selected Poems from Klopstock to Rilke* (London: Routledge & Kegan Paul, 1952), 177–181; Friedrich Ackermann, "Zum Rhythmusproblem: verdeutlicht an Storms Gedicht 'Hyazinthen,' " *Die Pädagogische Provinz* 19 (1965): 26–39.
201 Hans Bender, "Liebesmüdigkeit" in M. Reich-Ranicki (ed.), *Frankfurter Anthologie*, 5 (Frankfurt am Main: Insel, 1980), 114–116.
202 LL, I, 776, 966–967.

her dancing with another partner were also something of the past (Lohmeier gives the date 1846); they would hardly have stirred Storm in 1851 to write a poem of such longing and obsession.

Far more immediate in 1851 was his adulterous love affair with Doris Jensen, the young woman with whom he had first become involved in 1844, soon after his engagement to Constanze Esmarch, and whom he had directed in the Choral Society's performance of his poem for King Christian VIII, discussed above. It is specifically to Doris Jensen and their affair that he refers in "Hyazinthen." The American Storm biographer Elmer O. Wooley had discovered as early as 1933 that the copy of the fourth edition of Storm's poems, then in the possession of the poet's daughter Gertrud, contained the written letter "D" on the page on which "Hyazinthen" was printed. With careful research, Wooley also discovered that an effort had once been made to blot out the "D."[203] This clue, which has remained hidden from the various interpreters of "Hyazinthen," can open up our eyes to the significance of the confessional tone of the poem. The "D" makes it clear that "Hyazinthen" was a "Doris" poem, not a "Bertha" or a "Constanze" poem, and someone's (probably a family member's) subsequent attempt to cover up this fact by blotting out the "D" points us to the adulterous scandal that is obliquely referred to in the poem. The affair was to be hidden from the poem's readers.

By 1851 Storm's marriage to Constanze was in shambles. It had never been a love match. Hence, it was easy for Storm to become more and more infatuated with Doris Jensen. It was not long before the new lovers were sleeping together. A *ménage à trois* was set up.[204] Constanze, of course, longed to escape from the arrangement by fleeing to her parents' home in southeastern Holstein.[205] Yet that would only make matters worse, for then the two lovers could be

---

203 Elmer Otto Wooley, *Studies in Theodor Storm* (Bloomington, IN: Indiana University Press, 1943), 59–60.
204 Jackson, 44.
205 Ingrid Schuster, *"Ich habe niemals eine Zeile geschrieben, wenn sie mir fern war." Das Leben der Constanze Storm und vergleichende Studien zum Werk Theodor Storms* (Bern: Peter Lang, 1998), 40–41.

alone in the house in Husum, which would have been a source of scandal. A scandal would have risked, too, alienating many of Storm's law clients among the staid Protestant population of Husum, and that would have meant a loss of income the family of four could ill afford. (By January of 1851, Theodor and Constanze had become the parents of two sons.) Constanze had no choice, therefore, but to continue to share her husband with another woman.

Doris fully realized, of course, that she was destroying Storm's marriage, and this burdened her conscience. For years she struggled with the burden of guilt.[206] But she loved Theodor just as deeply as he loved her. In Doris, as mentioned earlier, Storm had found "jene berauschende Atmosphäre, der ich nicht widerstehen konnte" (that intoxicating atmosphere which I could not resist), and she, he realized, felt much the same way about him.[207] Each was irresistible to the other, and Doris had neither the will nor the courage to break out of the love triangle and leave the married couple to themselves.[208]

Yet an opportunity for her to break away did present itself when the townspeople of Husum were required to quarter Prussian soldiers (who had come to the aid of the Augustenborg forces) in their homes from September 1849 to July 1850. Perhaps surprisingly, this proved to be a happy time for both the civilian population and the soldiers, despite the raging civil war. The Prussian military band was, according to Felix Schmeisser's report, as delighted to enliven the spirits of the townspeople as they were to listen to its lively tunes.[209] And, as was the custom when dashing officers in colorful uniforms felt lonely in a town far from home, they were eager to escort the

---

206 See "Theodor Storm und Dorothea geb. Jensen. Ein unveröffentlichter Briefwechsel," 36, 46.
207 *Storm–Brinkmann*, 146.
208 Critics have occasionally claimed that Doris had opted out of the love triangle, even suggesting that this "probably" occurred early in 1848. A notable example of such a claim appears on page 55 of Franz Stuckert's Storm biography. Proof, however, was never cited. It was not until 1998 that the claim was found to have no basis in fact. See Schuster, 39 (her footnote 185).
209 Schmeisser, 66–67.

local belles to the military balls and to dance with them. One such Prussian officer, a Captain Gantzer, was housed with the Storms, and the twenty-one-year-old Doris must have caught his eye as she did Storm's.

It is not surprising that the officer should have asked her to go to a ball. The love affair between her and Storm was, after all, a well-kept secret. And why would she refuse his attention? He was an eligible bachelor and she an eligible young woman. If she had offered the only substantial reason she had to refuse his request, this might have brought her affair with Storm out into the open, which she would want to avoid. Of course, she accepted the dashing officer's invitation, and they both must have had a good time, which then led to further get-togethers and, finally, to his offer of marriage. This, naturally, she had to decline, unless she were to leave Storm's bed forever, which she could not bring herself to do.[210]

This all leads us to the understanding of "Hyazinthen" that has remained so hidden from the critics: Storm is referring to Doris waltzing at a ball in the arms of Captain Gantzer, while the poet, her true lover, must jealously look on from outside the ballroom and wait for her to return to him.

And now we know what the clue of the "D" reveals for the poem's interpretation. The imaginative portrayal of the dancing couple caught up in waltzes, in contrast to the frustrated lover outside — or, conversely, the portrayal of the dancing couple as representing the real world of love and life in the company of fellow members of society, in contrast to the artist who is separated from the community for which he writes — has a counterpart in the non-fictional, autobiographical account of Storm, the frustrated lover, and Storm, the poet, agonizing over his separation from Doris and

---

210 This becomes apparent from the content of a letter in *Storm–Brinkmann*, 146–147. In the notes to this correspondence, however, Captain Gantzer is wrongly identified as the latter's father, an aged clergyman (p. 225), which hinders our understanding of the love affair. See my review of the volume in *Journal of English and Germanic Philology* 88 (1989): 384.

the everyday life of the young townspeople so happily gathered in the ballroom.

The poem's musical lines and compelling theme seem even more impressive and authentic once we realize that they disguise this real life event. Our knowledge of what the frustrated poet and lover actually experienced when the smartly dressed captain of the Prussian militia intruded into Storm's illicit, passionate love affair with Doris reinforces in a powerful way, therefore, what we had already gathered from "Hyazinthen"'s ingenious composition.

This biographical knowledge also explains some aspects of the poem that may have seemed obscure in other interpretations. For instance, we can better understand why Storm describes the dancers thus: "Und Alle glühen; aber du bist blaß." If Doris was dancing with the captain in part to avoid drawing attention to her affair with Storm, she might indeed have been enjoying herself less than the other dancers; certainly Storm would have liked to think so. The repeated assertion that "Ich habe immer, immer dein gedacht" may also constitute a mild reproach to her, as she must also be thinking of the captain with whom she dances, while Storm only thinks of her. Perhaps, also, he was lying awake late at night, waiting for her to return home to him, unable to sleep while he heard the music of the ball and thought of her dancing there without him. Lastly, the refrain "Ich möchte schlafen; aber du mußt tanzen" may also refer to the difference in the ages of the lovers — in 1851, Storm would have been a married man of thirty-four, compared to Doris, a young woman of twenty-two, and thus going out to dances would be more appropriate behavior for her than for him.

This interpretation does not diminish the centrality of the conflict between art and life in "Hyazinthen." Rather, it reveals the conflict's specific genesis, and shows how the division between romantic love and married life, secret lover and public husband, may have paralleled the division between art and life, politics and privacy, for Storm, and, given his lively romantic life, thus provided him with a consistent source of poetic inspiration, somewhat like *Tonio Kröger*'s unrequited love for ordinary people gave life to his art.

g. The extension in Danish

Literary history has endowed "Hyazinthen" with further background that henceforth should become a part of its rich interpretation. Like the intruding figure of the dashing Prussian Captain Gantzer, whose presence in the poem has remained unknown to critics of "Hyazinthen," so too a frustrated Danish artist, who has also gone unrecognized by Storm critics, must be regarded as a figure who worked his way into the poem's evolving meaning.

His name is Alfred Ipsen (1852–1922).[211] He added an additional dimension to the living, immortal text of "Hyazinthen" when he translated the poem into Danish, endowing it thereby with an extended life in Danish letters.[212] Like Storm and so many Danish lyricists, Ipsen, too, was a musical poet. It was doubtless his penchant for melodious verse that had first aroused his interest in Storm's poetry. He felt drawn to "Hyazinthen" in particular, however, because in it he could recognize the cardinal predicament of his own life: the conflict between poet and citizen, between the dictates of his artistic disposition and the demands of his communal existence.

As a young lyric poet anxiously seeking public recognition, he had taken up his pen to combat every sort of artistic expression that was less inclined to align literature with music. His spirited journalistic writing soon won him the notoriety he desired to awaken the public's interest in his own poetry, but it also led to his polemical involvement in many disputes in Copenhagen's literary community. The unwanted success he achieved in journalism soon robbed him of his poetic energy. Writing at the center of a battle of wits in Denmark, he must have had only rare moments when his mind was free enough to allow the muses to enter. Yet the dream of writing poetry that could add to the tradition of Danish lyrics remained ever before his eyes.

---

211 Biographical information about Ipsen was obtained from (1) *Dansk biografisk leksikon*, 7 (Copenhagen: Gyldendal, 1981), 118–119 and (2) Oscar Geismar, *Nogle Digterprofiler* (Copenhagen: Gad, 1906), 57–75.
212 The translation was published in Alfred Ipsen, *Europæiske Digte* (Copenhagen: Schou, 1883), 34–35. As far as I know, this Danish version is the first translation of Storm's poem into any language.

How could Ipsen resolve the conflict between his public and poetic self? One small way was to translate Storm's poem into Danish, to transmute the experience of the lyrical I in "Hyazinthen" into his own experience as a frustrated artist, which he could then project back into a translated extension of Storm's poem in the Danish language. The two faces of Storm governing the compositional principle of the German poem "Hyazinthen" became now the two faces of Ipsen in the Danish poem "Hyazinther." The Danish reader, he felt, could be served with the translation of Storm's poem into the sounds of Danish, and his own creativity as an artist would gain new visibility once the public realized that he had both rendered and strengthened, in a Danish version, Storm's message about the dichotomy between art and life.

For the Storm critic, on the other hand, the knowledge that the frustrated artist Ipsen was so strongly drawn to "Hyazinthen" confirms once more (as with Thomas Mann's admiration for it) how much the conflict between poet and citizen, *Künstler und Bürger*, *kunstner og borger*, resounds in this powerful poem.

9. The *chef d'oeuvre*: "Meeresstrand"

a. The poem's fame

"Meeresstrand" (Seashore) is Storm's most famous poem. First published in 1856, in the second edition of his *Gedichte* (Poems), it has since appeared with more regularity, in one anthology of German poetry after another, than any other of his poems. When the noted Swedish poet Anders Österling once sought to win friends for Storm's verse in Sweden, this was the very first poem he chose to bring to the attention of his audience.[213] Manfred Hausmann, a prominent German poet of the twentieth century, felt that "Meeresstrand" was one of the ten most beautiful poems ever composed in the German lan-

---

213 Anders Österling, *Dagens gärning* (Stockholm: Bonnier, 1921), 169.

guage.[214] Thomas Mann ranked it among the half-dozen poems of Storm which he considered to "possess the unmistakable traits of immortality."[215]

The great appeal that "Meeresstrand" had for such influential men of letters has made it "the most consistently admired of Storm's poems,"[216] which, in turn, has given rise to a number of scholarly interpretations of its structure and content — professional criticism's highest form of flattery.[217]

b. Breaking out of the love triangle

Several conditioning factors have combined to make this poem Storm's *chef d'oeuvre*. These factors, in particular Storm's escape from the love triangle with Doris Jensen and his wife, have not been obvious to Storm scholars.

For some years in the late 1840s and early 1850s, as we know from our study of "Hyazinthen," the poet had been living the precarious life of an artist torn between his passionate affair with Doris Jensen and his marriage, between marital infidelity and the facade of

---

214 Manfred Hausmann, "Unendliches Gedicht. Bemerkungen anläßlich der Lyrik Theodor Storms," *Abhandlungen der Akademie der Wissenschaften und der Literatur in Mainz* (1962): 42.
215 Mann *Essays*, 273.
216 *Theodor Storm* (Leicester German Poets), ed. P. M. Boswell, 76.
217 Noteworthy analyses include: Paul Merker, "Theodor Storm: Meeresstrand," in *Gedicht und Gedanke*, ed. H. O. Burger (Halle: Niemeyer, 1942), 274–287; H. Müller, 78–82; Wilhelm Schneider, *Liebe zum deutschen Gedicht* (Freiburg i.B.: Herder, ⁵1963), 105–113; Franz Forster, "Theodor Storms 'Meeresstrand' und 'Die Stadt,'" *Jahrbuch der Grillparzer-Gesellschaft*, 3. Folge, 12 (1976): 27–37; Elfriede Stutz, "Verskundliche Notizen zu Storms Gedicht 'Meeresstrand'" in *In Search of the Poetic Real. Essays in Honor of Clifford Albrecht Bernd on the Occasion of his Sixtieth Birthday*, eds. J. F. Fetzer, R. Hoermann, W. McConnell (Stuttgart: Heinz, 1989), 243–253. An interesting Russian assessment of the poem is by Tamara Silman, "Theodor Storms Gedicht 'Meeresstrand,'" STSG 25 (1976): 48–52. I have interpreted this poem on several occasions, most recently in "The German Lyric in the Age of Poetic Realism" in *Life's Golden Tree. Essays in German Literature from the Renaissance to Rilke*, eds. T. Kerth & G. C. Schoolfield (Columbia, SC: Camden House, 1996), 174–176. The discussion that now follows is a revision and extension of my earlier readings.

respectability demanded of him by a society that insisted on a strict observance of the legal union between man and woman. Clearly, he saw that his illicit love life could not be concealed indefinitely in his closeknit provincial society. Bringing the affair out into the open would, of course, have meant the end of his legal career in the prudish town. It also would have had most embarrassing repercussions for his family, especially since his sister had just (in 1852) been forced into a hasty marriage after she had conceived a child out of wedlock.[218] One scandal was bad enough, but two scandals in rapid succession would have been a nightmare for the Storm family.

What to do? In this frustrating circumstance, a change in the political environment suddenly presented Storm with an out, and he was quick to take advantage of it. After the Augustenborgian rebellion had been quelled, the Danish government was anxious to restore law and order in the duchy of Schleswig. Storm, like many of his fellow attorneys, was asked to sign a declaration of unending loyalty to the Danish sovereign.[219] This he refused to do, and this decision led, predictably, to the withdrawal of the royal license to continue his law practice. That seems to be exactly what he hoped for; now he had the perfect alibi to move away from Husum, and the town's dour citizenry would never suspect that the real reason for his departure was to break out of the love triangle, whose tensions must have been consuming so much of his energy at the expense of his calling to poetry. As the Danish critic Anna Simonsen has said, the poet made it look as though he had been unjustly treated by the Danish government.[220] He even went so far as to fabricate stories in conversations and letters about a mutual hostility between the Danes and himself.

---

218 Storm himself gives the details in his letter of May 30, 1852, to his friend Hartmuth Brinkmann. See *Storm-Brinkmann*, 64.
219 Simonsen, "Theodor Storm og Danmark," 147, citing the report she discovered in the Danish National Archives in Copenhagen (= Ministeriet for Slesvig, 1. Dpt. A: Sager om Advokater 1852–1862).
220 Simonsen in her (unpublished) thesis *Theodor Storm og Hjemlandet* (University of Copenhagen, 1948), 38.

Much of German (as well as Anglo-American) critical tradition has taken these fabrications all too literally. Indeed, it has become almost *de rigueur* to speak about Storm's "anti-Danish stand"[221] and that he "suffered exile as a result of the Danish incursion of 1852."[222] But Georg Bollenbeck has now warned us not to be deceived by statements in Storm's letters.[223] And Danish critics have, of course, adamantly resisted all attempts to make Denmark the scapegoat for Storm's emigration.[224] Particularly on the strength of archival material in Copenhagen, the Danes have been at pains to show that Storm was not anti-Danish and that he was not forced to leave Husum with the return of Danish rule following the defeat of the Augustenborgian rebellion. Nothing, it has been said, would have prevented him from becoming a partner in his father's law firm and from retaining his clients in that way.

Danish scholarship is clear and compelling. No longer should it be believed, therefore, that contempt for Danish rule was the reason for Storm's desire to begin a new life elsewhere. It is far more plausible to believe that the burden of maintaining his consuming love life and the attendant burden of keeping it secret made him want to break away from Husum. Certainly, this stress must have weighed more heavily on the mind of the sensitive poet than any political attitude, especially since he was, as the literary historian Erich Schmidt said, "no politician, whichever way you looked at him,"[225] and hardly the sort of person who would be likely to take any active interest in the intricacies of Danish governance. This echoes, of course, what Danish criticism has maintained for a long time. "Han var en helt

---

221 G. Wallis Field, *A Literary History of Germany. The Nineteenth Century 1830–1890* (London: Benn; New York: Barnes & Noble, 1975), 114.
222 William F. Mainland, "Theodor Storm" in *German Men of Letters*, ed. A. Natan (Philadelphia: Dufour, 1962), 149.
223 Georg Bollenbeck, *Theodor Storm* (Frankfurt am Main: Insel, 1988), 118.
224 See especially Simonsen, "Theodor Storm og Danmark" and *Theodor Storm og Hjemlandet*; Morton Kamphövener, "Theodor Storm og Danmark," *Jyske Tidende*, 18 maj 1950: 4; Fabricius, *Sønderjyllands Historie*, IV, 458–460.
225 Quotation and translation in Mainland, 149, 166.

upolitisk Natur" (He was entirely unpolitical by nature), as Carl Roos stated in 1919.[226]

Given Storm's loveless marriage, it seems unlikely that Storm wanted to leave Doris, or that Doris wanted him to leave. But it was impossible to sustain the situation they found themselves in. At the same time, it would have been very hard, in those days, for the lovers to leave Husum together. Where could they have gone? How would Storm have supported them? Hence, they had to learn to live far apart. The force of their connection persisted, however; after the death of Storm's wife, years later, the pair was able to marry.

c. The elusiveness of escape

The relief from his troublesome love affair Storm hoped to find somewhere far away from Husum proved to be elusive. His training in the ancient laws of Schleswig and Holstein and in the Danish *Lex Regia* had not given him any particular familiarity with the laws prevailing in the various German states, and this put him at a competitive disadvantage when applying for an appointment in law in Germany. The applications he made in both Buxtehude and Gotha were rejected. In Prussia, however, he was more fortunate. He had acquired some knowledge of the Prussian legal system when he had studied for a year and a half at the Law School of the University of Berlin, which helped his application. He also benefited from the fact that, as Theodor Fontane said, Prussia looked favorably at this time on those who claimed to be victims of Danish oppression in the Augustenborgian rebellion.[227] Storm must have tried hard to portray himself as such a victim. At any rate, his application for a job in the Prussian judicial service was approved, though only after an exhausting series of negotiations, and then under humiliating conditions. It was not until shortly before Christmas in 1853 that he finally could begin his work, as an assistant judge, without salary, at the district court in

---

226 Carl Roos, "Slesvig, Holsten og den tyske Litteratur," *Ugens Tilskuer* 9 (1919): 152.
227 NFA, XV, 192.

Potsdam near Berlin. To support himself and his family, he had to beg for assistance from his father and other relatives.

Naturally, Storm would have felt despondent. To make matters worse, Potsdam was then the military citadel of the Prussian nation. In such an environment the poet felt uncomfortable. All too easily, his thoughts must have wandered back to the deliriously happy moments he had spent in Doris's loving arms, but the memory of the tensions created by the romantic triangle would have rivaled his reminiscence of passion, particularly because he felt that his life with Doris had become a thing of the past. Despite his unhappy existence in Potsdam, there seemed to be no turning back the clock.

d. Consolation in poetry

In poetry, however, Storm found the consolation he needed to cope with this hapless life. He quickly became a member of the Berlin literary club *Tunnel über der Spree* (Tunnel over the Spree) and its smaller side-group, the *Rütli* club, which some of the members of the former had set up. In a letter to his friends Hartmuth and Laura Brinkmann Storm states how refreshed he felt there.[228]

The *Tunnel über der Spree* took its name in part from the famous tunnel under the Thames completed in 1843; the name of the main river flowing through Berlin was substituted for its counterpart in London. The name itself signified an attempt to transplant a venerable institution from the Thames to the Spree, for the club was modeled on "The Club" of Samuel Johnson a century earlier in London. In each instance the membership comprised an association of highly civilized men, some of the best minds in the city. The group met regularly, once a week for several hours, in the smoke-filled room of a local tavern, and there applied its collective intelligence to the practical criticism of literature.

The Berlin club served, in particular, as a meeting place for individuals who believed that poetry was the highest form of literature.

---

228 *Storm–Brinkmann*, 100.

In this club, as well as in the *Rütli*, Storm could present new poems he wrote, and observe the other members nodding in approval over his successes or shaking their heads in dismay over his blunders. He could hear fellow authors read new poems, take part in the heated, incisive give-and-take of discussion of the works, and — after replenishing his glass of beer — he could cast his free vote of acceptance or rejection concerning the poems his rivals produced.

Regardless of whether he offered or received criticism, each session gave him inspiration and did much to sharpen his own verbal, rhythmic, and metrical facility. Best of all, he learned how to enlist the favor of even the most discriminating audiences, for nowhere in Europe at that time could the excellence of the schooling in poetry at the *Tunnel über der Spree* and the *Rütli* club be matched, except perhaps in the congregation of remarkable literati gathered around Hans Christian Andersen in Copenhagen.[229]

Theodor Fontane, who was also a member of the *Tunnel über der Spree* and the *Rütli* club, tells us in the autobiography of his youth, *Von Zwanzig bis Dreißig* (From Twenty to Thirty), how Storm, the singing master, had performed the musical recitation of his poetry one evening to a spellbound audience:

> [Er] ging dann auf die Tür zu, um diese zuzuriegeln . . . Dann schraubte er die Lampe . . . ganz erheblich herunter, und nun erst fing er an . . . Er war ganz bei der Sache, sang es mehr, als er es las, und während seine Augen . . . leuchteten, verfolgten sie uns doch zugleich, um in jedem Augenblicke . . . die Art der Wirkung bemessen zu können.[230]

> (He went to the door to bolt it shut. After that, he lowered the lamp, and only then did he begin his recital. He was completely absorbed in what he was doing, singing it more than reading it; and while his eyes sparkled, they were also carefully tracking us in order to measure our reactions at every moment.)

---

229 For a good picture of the poetry readings in the Copenhagen club see Wilhelm Marstrand's drawing included in Mitchell, *A History of Danish Literature*, between pp. 128 & 129.
230 NFA, XV, 205–206.

The Poems 141

Such tests of his abilities before a congenial but frank company of poets and subtle readers helped now to make poetry for Storm a more serious avocation than ever. He worked hard at improving his verse and increasing the amount he wrote, doubtless to the neglect of his work at the court house. His superiors at the court, at any rate, must not have been very impressed with his performance there, for each application he made for a better position in the judicial service in 1854 and 1855 was rejected.[231]

Storm's heart was in his poetry. The new flurry of poetic activity at Potsdam resulted in the publication of the second, enlarged edition of his poems in 1856, with the prominent Berlin publisher Heinrich Schindler. "Meeresstrand" was printed on the volume's opening pages. This poem had occupied him almost the whole time he lived in Potsdam. In a uniquely successful fashion, it expresses his deep sadness over the departure of Doris from his life, and his energetic turn to poetry to console himself.

> An's Haf nun fliegt die Möwe,
> Und Dämm'rung bricht herein;
> Über die feuchten Watten
> Spiegelt der Abendschein.
>
> Graues Geflügel huschet
> Neben dem Wasser her;
> Wie Träume liegen die Inseln
> Im Nebel auf dem Meer.
>
> Ich höre des gärenden Schlammes
> Geheimnisvollen Ton,
> Einsames Vogelrufen —
> So war es immer schon.
>
> Noch einmal schauert leise
> Und schweiget dann der Wind;
> Vernehmlich werden die Stimmen,
> Die über der Tiefe sind.[232]

---

231 v. Fisenne, 16.
232 Text taken from LL, I, 14–15.

(Lagoon-ward flies the seagull
As day gives way to night.
The wet-glazed flats at low tide
Reflect the evening light.

Gray fowl in flocks are darting
Close to the water's brim.
Like dreams appear the islands
In mist, remote, and dim.

I hear the eerie, seething ferment
In the ooze along the shore,
A seagull's lonely cry —
So it was evermore.

Again the wind wails softly,
Then slowly sinks to sleep,
And now are heard the voices
That hover over the deep.)

Translated by Gerd Gillhoff, revised by C. A. Bernd[233]

e. The commanding line

The line that attracts our attention most in this poem is the longest one, of nine syllables: "Ich höre des gärenden Schlammes." No other line compares with this length, which receives an added stress once we realize that the line also constitutes the ninth line of the poem. Its commanding importance is further emphasized by its central position in the middle of the poem. It is the only line, moreover, that contains an element of explicit personal involvement: the "Ich," which carries even more weight as it comes at the beginning of the central line. This single instance of the "Ich" does much to focus our attention on the line, but our sensitivity to it is also alerted by the lush tonal coloration it receives. The line's opening iambic syllables are followed by the beat of two melodiously rising anapests and, at the end, by a catalectic iamb. This rich rhythmic scheme is all the more

---

[233] The unrevised parts of this translation are reprinted, by permission of Johanna Gillhoff, from G. Gillhoff, *A Collection of German Poetry* (unpublished, 1973).

"Wie Träume liegen die Inseln / Im Nebel auf dem Meer" (Like dreams appear the islands / In mist, remote, and dim)
— "Meeresstrand."

striking in the context of its occurrence between the simpler rhythms of the lines that enclose it; both the eighth and the tenth lines convey considerably less elaborate melodies of three iambic beats.

What does the "Ich" hear in this ninth line to which the lyricist attaches such great importance? It is the seething ferment in the ooze along the shore, the bubbling of the water caused by decomposing organic life washed up on the shoreline by the flow of the tides. The departure of Doris from the poet's life has now been transfigured into an elegiac dirge on the ephemerality of life. Once we become aware of the transfigured message of transience at the heart of the poem, everything else in the poem falls, with the craftmanship of the poet, splendidly into place.

f. The quatrains

The somber script of man's short life cycle is presented to us when we see, from quatrain to quatrain, how our little "day" on earth ebbs steadily toward its appointed end. In the first quatrain the poet observes the seagull seeking evening refuge in the harbor, as the light of day departs with the setting of the sun. He observes, too, the eventide falling over the desolate expanse of mud flats made bare by the flow of the tide out to sea.

Darkness deepens in the second quatrain; the details of the scene grow dimmer to the eye. The seagull, which the poet had seen so clearly in the twilight of the first quatrain, is now replaced by more blurred, faded images: gray wings (presumably still of seagulls) scurry in the semi-darkness (as the three dark "u" vowels and three lighter "g" consonants in line five indicate), and the wavering contours of islands disappear from view in the gathering fog on the horizon.

In the third quatrain, the descending darkness has fully shrouded the earth and the sea. All things visible have disappeared from sight. The poet can only hear, and what he hears is the decomposing of life below him, and the last call of life uttered by the lonely seagull above him, still awake despite the late hour. A dash follows these lines, indicating, like a musical fermata, a hold or pause. The disturbing sound of decay and the haunting cry of the gull linger on in the darkness and, in the rest indicated by the dash, let the sting of death penetrate deeply into the reader's ear.

In the fourth antiphonal quatrain, the wind shudders before it, too, finally dies down after the hours have fully run, signaling both the end of the day and the end of man's brief stay on earth. Then comes the poem's grand finale: the ghostly foes ensconced in darkness, the sinister voices of nocturnal fear and fantasy, all join in one last chorus, only audible when the light and sounds of day have died out.

g. Imprisoned in transience

Amid this song of inescapable transience, indeed at its very center, is, as we said, the "Ich." Opening the poem's weightiest line, the "Ich" is trapped between the sad sights of descending darkness in the poem's imagistic first half, and the haunting sounds of death and annihilation in the poem's latter half, where aural emphasis prevails. The "Ich," a prisoner of transience, becomes, then, a tormented intelligence who sees the fading of life and feels the intrusion of impending death all around him.

Aural effects, in particular, constantly echo this, reminding us of all that Storm learned from Danish lyrical poetry. In the first line the vowel-melody begins at a low pitch *(An's Haf nun)* and then becomes high-pitched *(fliegt die Möwe)*. At the beginning of the second line, they strike a low pitch once more *(Und Dämm'rung)*; at the end of that line they ascend again to a high pitch *(bricht herein)*. In counterpoint, the subsequent two lines make the reverse sound-pattern audible: descending, the high vowels at the beginning of both lines *(Über die, Spiegelt)* contrast sharply with the vowel sounds at the end of the lines, where they first fall precipitously, then rise *(feuchten Watten, Abendschein)*.

The interweaving of life and death is also constantly reiterated in the music of the rhyme scheme. In each quatrain the first and third lines remain without a rhyme. There is no rhyme, or, to say this in another way, the rhyme is dead. The second and fourth lines, however, do have a rhyme. In them the rhyme is very much alive.

Few poems, I believe, contain such a rich coloration of metrics as can be found in "Meeresstrand." The poem is crowded with numerous mixtures of iambs, trochees, dactyls, and anapests. A huge orchestra with many instruments seems to be playing here. This considerable instrumentation transports the chilling message of transience down deep into the emotions, like the unabating rhythm of the roaring breakers along the shore.

Through the eye, too, transience and death are made to appear certain, although the incessantly flowing current of alternating seven and six syllabic lines trickling steadily down from the beginning to the end of the poem, racing ever downward until death brings the flow to a permanent halt, has, just as in life itself, various stops and changes in lifestyle along the way. Alternative routes, once this way and once that way, are as frequent as the alternating seven and six syllabic lines. Other temporary brakes upon the tempo occur in the seventh and fifteenth lines when, in two eight syllabic verses, we are reminded once more of the interlock of life and death as the life on the islands (line 7) is paired with the ghostly voices audible after death (line 15). Deviations from the normal pattern of seven and six syllabic lines also intrude in the ninth and sixteenth verses. The nine syllabic ninth line with its heavy emphasis on decay and dissolution warns us of the death that awaits us at the end of life's trail. The final line also receives an extra stress because there are now seven syllables instead of the six which have regularly occurred in the final lines of each preceding quatrain. This presents us with the haunting conclusion that the final sleep of death, which comes at the end of life's journey, is always longer.

The poet had indeed learned much about perfecting his verse when he attended the sessions of the *Tunnel über der Spree* and the *Rütli* club. The carefully constructed "Meeresstrand" conveys a most powerful message which is as shattering as Storm's own disquieting realization that his love for Doris, and her love for him, had become things of the past. We, no less than Storm himself, now discover ourselves to be helpless victims of transience.

10. From poetry to the novella

On the foregoing pages it was my desire to show how Storm came into his strength as a lyric poet. The task of chronicling all that he accomplished in poetry would be an almost endless one. Instead of going further into Storm's poetry, we turn now to the literary genre which, as Storm himself said, grew out of his lyrics.[234]

---

234 *Storm–Schmidt,* II, 57.

The Novellas

1. The Danish heritage

As with his poetry, the early schooling Storm received in Danish literature also taught him much that gave rise to his novellas. In his prose fiction, too, he stands on the shoulders of Danish predecessors.

In Denmark in the early nineteenth century, the novella led in quantity and quality as never before in European literature. Indeed, it had become a major form of prose fiction. The novellas of the Poetic Realists Thomasine Gyllembourg (1773–1856), Steen Steensen Blicher (1782–1848), Poul Martin Møller (1794–1838), and Carl Bernhard (1798–1865) were without equal anywhere in Europe at the time.

In the late 1840s and early 1850s Storm took up this high art of Danish fiction. He grafted it, just as he did the lilting strains of Danish poetry, onto German literature. In doing so, he was quite original, for prior to his work, the novella had only played a minor role in German literature. Despite occasional novellas of great merit by earlier German masters, such as Goethe, Kleist, Tieck, and others, this genre had never been, as with the Danes, a major class of fiction. But with Storm and his successors, especially Gottfried Keller (1819–1890), Conrad Ferdinand Meyer (1825–1898), and Paul Heyse (1830–1914), the novella now became the most distinctive genre of German literature.

When Storm took up his pen to raise the novella to such a high status, it seemed only natural that he should infuse it with notions which had contributed so much to its flowering in his native Greater Denmark. His concept of the novella was, at any rate, strikingly similar to the prescriptions of the leading Danish theorist of the genre at the time: Thomasine Gyllembourg.

Gyllembourg's theoretical pronouncements on the novella are scattered throughout a large body of critical commentary that was published from 1827 to 1830 in the literary journal *Kjøbenhavns flyvende Post* (Copenhagen's Flying Mail) as well as in the prefaces to the many novellas she continued to write until her death in 1856.

The central point of her theory was to demand that this form of prose fiction be pregnant with characteristics of drama.[235] Like drama, she pointed out, the dramatic novella should be filled with powerfully charged action. The novella, she wrote, ought to excite its readers as much as drama excites an audience, primarily through a sharply delineated or mathematically constructed plot, around which every detail should strictly revolve. Another important attribute of the novella leading to its dramatic excitement, she felt, is its limited scope, which allows it to jump right into the middle of things *(in medias res)* without forcing the reader to become acquainted with the entire lives of the characters in chronological order, from the cradle to the grave. The art of omission and economy was, then, important to Gyllembourg.

Another conviction was essential to the concept of the novella which she theorized and practiced. The genre was neither to be amusing, nor remote from everyday life, as, she thought, the hilarious comedies performed in the Royal Theater in Copenhagen tended to be. Rather, the novella should address itself to the salient problems haunting common human existence.

We do not know whether Storm, with his knowledge of Danish and Danish literature, acquired first-hand knowledge of Gyllembourg's theory of the novella, or whether he became acquainted with it through the novellas which had put that theory into practice. It is also possible that he learned about the theory from his schoolmasters in Husum, while reading and discussing Danish novellas in the various anthologies used for classroom instruction in Danish. Quite likely, too, is the possibility that he heard about the

---

235 The following summary of Gyllembourg's theory owes much to an account given by Elisabeth Hude, *Thomasine Gyllembourg og Hverdagshistorierne* (Copenhagen: Rosenkilde & Bagger, 1951), esp. 266 ff.

theory from his revered mentor at the university in Kiel, Nicolaus Falck, who possessed an intimate familiarity with Danish literature.

However Storm may have become aware of the Danish novella in early life, he certainly refashioned the traditional German genre along the lines of what he could only have learned from the Danish muse. With the advent of Storm, the German novella would no longer be the account of an unheard-of event, as Goethe had proposed. Nor would it deal with the strange, the unusual, or the extraordinary in far-away places, as had been the case with Kleist's sensational novellas. Neither would it distinguish itself, as Tieck had insisted, by its conspicuous *Wendepunkt*, the turning point that gave an unexpected twist to the plot and set it moving toward a conclusion that the reader would not have anticipated.

These bonds, which had hitherto limited the potential of the German novella, were now torn asunder by Storm.[236]

2. Early glory: *Immensee*

a. The enduring classic

Immensee (Bee's Lake), the novella with which Storm made his most impressive debut in prose fiction, was published, after many revisions, in its book-length form in 1852. It has since become an enduring classic.[237] Seldom has a story-teller's skill at making much out of little been more effective. Theodor Fontane attested that "'Immensee' gehört zu dem Meisterhaftesten, was wir jemals gelesen haben" (it is

---

236 The Hungarian critic György Lukács, in 1910, was the first to realize that Storm had refashioned the German novella. See the English translation by A. Bostock, *Soul and Form* (London: Merlin, 1974), 72. Despite Lukács's observation, however, the full magnitude of Storm's historical achievement has gone unnoticed, primarily because the model of the Danish novella has not received the attention it deserves.

237 As early as 1858 the Prussian government official Alexander von Wussow had prophesied that *Immensee* would become an enduring classic. See Storm, *Briefe an seine Frau*, 55.

one of the greatest masterpieces of prose fiction I have ever read).[238] Thomas Mann, in a letter to E. O. Wooley, commented that it had "always played a certain symbolic role in my life and writings."[239] Even his own *Tonio Kröger*, Mann said, is but an "ins Modern-Problematische fortgewandelter 'Immensee'" (a modern continuation of *Immensee*).[240]

Before the copyright of Storm's novella finally expired in 1918, no less than seventy-nine further editions of this classic appeared in Germany. Since *Immensee* entered the public domain, countless publishers have sought, and continue to seek, to profit from additional reprints. Other printings can be found in the many collections of Storm's works and in anthologies. Translations in a wide variety of languages have appeared the world over; in many countries numerous translations have competed to captivate the imaginations of readers.[241]

In 1927 a prominent Germanist in the United States, Bayard Quincy Morgan, could say that *"Immensee* has been, and will doubtless continue to be, more widely read by American High School and College students than any other single work in the German language."[242] Twenty-two years later another American Germanist, George Schulz-Behrend, made an even bolder claim: "It is probably safe to say that no other modern foreign language text has found [in the U.S.] wider use than *Immensee.*"[243]

The unusual fascination this unique piece of prose fiction has exercised on countless readers has led, not surprisingly, to a flood of

---

238 NFA, XXI/1, 148.
239 E. O. Wooley, "Four Letters from Thomas Mann to E.O. Wooley," *Monatshefte* 56 (1964): 16.
240 Mann, *Gesammelte Werke*, XII (Frankfurt am Main: Fischer, 1960), 106.
241 In the United States the best known translation is by C. W. Bell in *Great German Short Stories. An Anthology*, ed. V. Lange (New York: The Modern Library, 1952). The latest translation in Britain is by D. Jackson & A. Nauck, in T. Storm, *"Hans and Heinz Kirch" with "Immensee" and "Journey to a Hallig"* (London: Angel Classics, 1999).
242 Theodor Storm, *Immensee*, eds. B. Q. Morgan & E. O. Wooley (Boston: Heath, 1949), iii.
243 George Schulz-Behrend, "Forever Immensee," *The German Quarterly* 22 (1949): 159.

innovative scholarship about it. Wiebke Strehl has produced an absorbing overview of this criticism.[244] From generation to generation, we learn from her telling survey, battalions of eager critics have continued to revitalize this novella for their contemporaries, and such work has regularly served to open our eyes to new shades of meaning inherent in the novella's structure.

b. Invoking the theory of the Danish novella

One aspect of this inexhaustible classic that has not received the attention it deserves is the novella's reflection of what Storm learned from his upbringing in the Danish cultural and literary tradition. For over a hundred years, critics have kept so busy chasing and speculating about phantom German literary sources for *Immensee*[245] that little time or energy was left, it seems, to think about what Storm could have learned from the theory and practice of the novella in his native Greater Denmark. Here — not in Germany — is where the novella as a literary art flourished most, precisely at the time Storm was searching for originality in prose fiction and feeling grateful for models he could put to creative use.

It is first to the Danish novella, therefore, that we should look when we wish to find the doors that opened up the writer's workshop in which *Immensee* was created. Thomasine Gyllembourg, we noted, had demanded that the novella should have a sharply deline-

---

244 Wiebke Strehl, *Theodor Storm's "Immensee." A Critical Overview* (Columbia, SC: Camden House, 2000). I have addressed myself to this novella twice, in *German Poetic Realism* (Boston: Twayne, 1981), 32–34, and in *Poetic Realism in Scandinavia and Central Europe 1820–1895* (Columbia, SC: Camden House, 1995), 148–150. This new reading is an extension of the previous ones and represents my increased understanding of the novella.

245 J. M. Ritchie has given us an entertaining account of the astonishing number of curious German literary sources critics have come up with: Goethe's *Werther, Wilhelm Meisters Lehrjahre*, and *Faust I*; Novalis's *Hymnen an die Nacht* and *Heinrich von Ofterdingen*; E. T. A. Hoffmann's *Der Sandmann* and *Der Magnetiseur*; Heine's *Die Heimkehr*; Eichendorff's *Dichter und ihre Gesellen* and *Das Marmorbild*; Stifter's *Der Hagestolz*; Mörike's *Maler Nolten*. See the introduction to Ritchie's edition of *Immensee* (London: Harrap, 1969), 10–13.

ated dramatic structure which would address itself stringently to the salient problems haunting human existence. Storm, we observe, endowed *Immensee* with a dramatic conflict around which everything else in the novella revolves. That conflict is, according to Storm, the foremost struggle an individual must cope with: the struggle of the human being ever oscillating between (1) the fear of the destructive force of passing time and (2) the reassuring feeling that this anguish can be overcome with the counterweight of memory.

If we attend to the role of passing time in this novella, and turn to the part of *Immensee* coming chronologically earliest, we read of the narrator's childhood happiness that is gradually but steadily destroyed by the passing of time. While still young and in school together, the characters Reinhard and Elisabeth are happy. The changes of time, however, force them apart. Reinhard matures and leaves primary school, where he has been with Elisabeth, to go to a boys' secondary school. Now he can share only his after-school leisure with his childhood companion. After a gap of seven years in the narration (made visible by the art of omission that Gyllembourg had called for), Reinhard loses even his leisure hours with Elisabeth; his secondary education is completed and he moves away to a distant university.

When the subsequent six months have drifted by (again through the art of omission), the previous warmth of affection has faded into the forced chill of prolonged separation. The passing of more time only intensifies their estrangement. Two more years (omitted in the text) sever the ties between Reinhard and Elisabeth so decisively that Elisabeth agrees to marry someone else. "Wiederum waren Jahre vorüber" (again years had passed), we are told, without any indication of what may have occurred in this time span. They meet again. Several days pass and they realize that the enchantment of their youth is gone forever.

Thus, the reader of *Immensee* learns how human happiness erodes with time, but our feelings of sadness are then mitigated by a countervailing message. In spite of the narrator's sensitivity to the destructive effects of transience, he seems confident that the power

"'Elisabeth!' sagte der Alte leise; und wie er das Wort gesprochen, war die Zeit verwandelt; *er war in seiner Jugend*" ("Elizabeth!" said the old man softly; and as he uttered the word, time had changed: *he was young again*) — *Immensee*.

of memory can overcome his grim sense of temporality. The story of the loss of closeness between Reinhard and Elisabeth, the story of the passing of human happiness, is prefaced and followed by the thoughts of Reinhard as an old man (again the events of all the intervening years are explicitly omitted, in order to make the central conflict more apparent), as he relives in his memory the same joyful scenes he had once known. Through recollection, the aged Reinhard can detach himself from his immediate experience and surroundings, and recapture the lost happiness as though it had not been obliterated by time.

But not for long. For the dramatic tension between time and memory is compounded when we discover that the narrator's sensitivity to time's ravaging effects, and his apparent ease at escaping this haunting threat through memory, is also interwoven with an awareness that the power of memory will prove deceptive. In the closing chapter, just as earlier happiness had eroded, the power of memory, too, will be engulfed by time: the aged Reinhard's memory dwells in a fragile body that is prey to senility and final dissolution.

The narrative ends, thus, on a disquieting note. The drama between time and memory has developed into a tragedy. Yet, we take leave of this tragedy with another reassuring feeling, for the drama between the two conflicting forces is contained, of course, within the novella, which recalls the entire story of Reinhard and Elisabeth and preserves it for posterity. As long as the novella continues to be read, Reinhard's recollection will not have perished, but will live on in the memory of literature.

But an afterthought also intrudes. For how long will *Immensee* continue to be read? Five hundred years? One thousand years? Will the dust of time on our bookshelves eventually destroy it?

Thomasine Gyllembourg would have been intrigued by this dramatic novella. She would have been delighted with what the young writer from Schleswig had produced, and all the more so because she had spent much time traveling in that area of the Danish monarchy, trying to extend the influence of Danish literature. With *Immensee* she would have seen her efforts richly rewarded.

c. Another door to the workshop of Immensee: *Blicher's* En Landsbydegns Dagbog

Another door that could give us an insight into the workshop in which *Immensee* was created is Steen Steensen Blicher's Danish novella *En Landsbydegns Dagbog* (The Diary of a Parish Clerk). Following its initial publication in 1824, it quickly became the most widely read and most unreservedly acclaimed Danish novella of the nineteenth century.

With unusual speed, it traveled across Denmark's language frontier to the northern outposts of German-speaking Europe. A publisher in Lübeck commissioned a translation almost immediately after the initial Danish publication. It appeared in 1827.[246] In 1829 it was reprinted by a publisher in Hamburg,[247] who again reprinted it in 1833.[248] When the translation first appeared in Lübeck (only a few years before Storm visited that city's literary salons), doubtless it was as much talked about there as in Denmark. What affected Denmark also affected this port city at the southeastern tip of the Jutland peninsula, with its strong commercial ties to the island nation in such close geographical proximity.

It is not unreasonable to assume that Storm knew this novella and that he had it in mind when he took up his pen to write his own novellas. Critics, at any rate, have suggested this on several occasions.[249] In that case, it is also not unreasonable to believe that *En*

---

246 *Bruchstücke aus dem Tagebuche eines Dorfküsters, aufgefunden, durchgesehen und herausgegeben von S. S. Blicher,* trans. L. Kruse, in *Hemera, Taschenbuch auf das Jahr 1827,* ed. H. Asmus, I (Lübeck: Schmidt, 1827).
247 *Das Wiedersehen, Bruchstücke aus dem Tagebuche eines Küsters, Die Prinzessin mit den Rosen und die Kunstreiter-Familie,* trans. L. Kruse (Hamburg: Herold, 1829).
248 In L. Kruse's *Ausländische Romane und Erzählungen,* VI (Hamburg: Herold, 1833).
249 See Victor A. Schmitz in (1) *Dänische und norwegische Dichtungen* (Heidelberg: Kerle, 1949), 78, and in (2) *Dänische Dichter in ihrer Begegnung mit deutscher Klassik und Romantik* (Frankfurt am Main: Klostermann, 1974), 142; Stuckert, 447; Emanuel Hirsch in Søren Kierkegaard, *Gesammelte Werke,* XXX (Düsseldorf/Cologne: Diederich, 1960), 181; Roger Paulin in (1) *The Brief Compass. The Nineteenth-Century German Novelle* (Oxford: Clarendon, 1985), 118, and in (2) *Theodor Storm* (Munich: Beck, 1992), 93.

Landsbydegns Dagbog might harbor clues which could help to illuminate further the narrative fabric of *Immensee*.

What are some of the characteristic features of Blicher's novella which could sharpen our vision for what Storm sought to accomplish with *Immensee*? Certainly, the power of passing time, we notice, looms heavily with Blicher. Time puts in its appearance on the opening page when we read "den 1ste Januar 1708" (January 1, 1708), which is a logical way to begin a book that works within the convention of diary. Specific references to the passing of calendar time intrude again and again throughout the novella, often as frequently as two or three times on every page. No fewer than sixty-four dated entries occur in this short novella. At the end, chronological time appears in its most obtrusive form: the reader senses that it has destroyed all the dreams and aspirations of a lifetime.

But if Blicher seems to tell us that there is no escape from the destructive effects of passing time, we notice, too, that his disheartening story is constructed contrapuntally. The tale unfolds in the form of a diary, a quotidian record. The diary preserves for posterity what had fallen prey to transience. We have, therefore, again a dramatic tension between the obliterating forces of time and the soothing assurance that man has a power at his disposal to counteract these forces. After we close the book, we are not sure which feeling remains with us longer: the sting of certain death to our happiness and our very selves with the passing of time, or the consoling hope that we may not be as helplessly trapped in the sequence of events as we had at first believed.

The parallel between *En Landsbydegns Dagbog* and *Immensee* is strong. Reading the two novellas in relation with each other helps to alert us to the similar drama in each work.

d. The challenging question

If we accept the conclusion that *Immensee* is a drama of an everyday life, focused on the annihilating forces of passing time and the counteracting power of memory — a drama which the theory and practice of the Danish novella helps us to realize more sharply — then the question arises as to why such a young writer as Storm should have been so obsessed with the wish to combat the destruction and death that passing time inflicts. Storm was only in his early thirties when he composed *Immensee*, still far away from that stage in life when a person who is approaching his appointed end looks back at what has been destroyed by evanescence. Yet this is the story of an old man, as Reinhard is described at the beginning and end of the novella. Why should the young Storm have assumed the guise of an old man to tell his story?

Only one explanation seems possible, and it relates directly to events in Storm's life during 1849 and 1850, precisely at the time he was busy writing and revising *Immensee*. Simultaneously, he composed his poem "Hyazinthen." The genesis of each work is related to the other. In our earlier discussion of "Hyazinthen," we said that the love triangle between Storm, Doris Jensen, and the dashing Captain Gantzer was central for our understanding of that poem. This is no less the case, we submit, for *Immensee*. The affair with Doris Jensen was as much on Storm's mind when he wrote the novella as when he composed the poem, which could hardly be otherwise once we realize that both were written in the same years.

Storm, we learned from our analysis of "Hyazinthen," sought to cope with his despondency at having a rival in his love for Doris. The feelings he expressed are altogether similar to those the poet portrays in *Immensee*. The difference is that in "Hyazinthen" the poet fears the impressive suitor might succeed in permanently winning the affections of the woman they both love, whereas in *Immensee* he concedes in his heart that the suitor will have succeeded as time passes, and only with the power of memory can he then remain close to her. That is the way he could soothe his feeling of the loss he anticipates and that is why he fictionally transforms himself into an old man, looking back upon the lost love of his youth.

It is not unimportant to remind ourselves that Thomas Mann in his *Tonio Kröger* had immortalized both "Hyazinthen" and *Immensee*. Of all the works by Storm, these were the two which Mann chose to meld together in the design of his own novella. Did Mann sense the relationship of the two works better than anyone else? I think so.

3. A Danish novella in German disguise: *In St. Jürgen*

a. From Immensee *to* In St. Jürgen

Immensee quickly became an astonishing success. Year after year new printings were on display in the windows of bookshops. Basking in the sunshine of this success, Storm received, in the summer of 1856, a new judicial appointment in the picturesque town of Heiligenstadt in Prussian Saxony. The move to Heiligenstadt was particularly fortunate, for he found there little distraction from his calling as a writer. The work at the court, unlike that in Potsdam, was not very demanding. With the few new friends he made, he shared little in common; none of them could compare with the fastidious minds he had known in the Berlin literary clubs. His love life, too, was peaceful, for the first and perhaps the only time in his life. Years had now passed since he had last seen Doris. Constanze continued to live by his side, although inwardly she remained as estranged from him as ever.

With little else to interfere, a flurry of creative activity set in, as Storm worked to add to the success he had achieved as the author of *Immensee*. One new novella followed another in quick succession. Writing so much, he acquired more and more skill in prose fiction.

The finest fruit of this sustained effort to emulate the success of *Immensee* is the novella *In St. Jürgen* (St. George's Almshouse),[250] completed in the spring of 1867. Of all of Storm's early novellas,

---

250 It has been translated into English several times, most recently by (1) G. W. McKay in *The Penguin Book of German Stories*, ed. F. J. Lamport (Harmondsworth: Penguin Books, 1974) and (2) James Wright in *T. Storm, The Rider on the White Horse and Selected Stories* (New York: New American Library, 1964).

this one is the most dramatic. Its "strong dramatic flavor" was recognized long ago.[251] It was this characteristic that had doubtless moved Erich Schmidt, the bellwether of academic literary criticism in Germany a century ago who had an unrivaled knowledge of Lessing's theory and practice of drama, to say that *In St. Jürgen* belongs in every respect to Storm's best creations.[252]

b. The Danish dramatic heritage of In St. Jürgen

Like *Immensee*, *In St. Jürgen* took its vision in part from the Danish dramatic novella. Our awareness of this literary heritage can alert us to the especially strong sense of drama in the tale. A unique, telling incident that occurred early in the literary reception of *In St. Jürgen* helps to communicate just how "Danish" this novella is. In 1879 Georg Festersen, a bookseller and publisher living in Basel, Switzerland, submitted to Switzerland's most widely read newspaper, the *Neue Zürcher Zeitung*, what he claimed was a German translation of a Danish novella. Festersen hoped the newspaper would publish the novella in serial form. The editorial staff recognized, however, that the novella was not a translation from Danish, but was, in fact, word for word, Storm's *In St. Jürgen*. A response to Festersen was then printed in the *Neue Zürcher Zeitung* on April 24, 1879.[253]

What is interesting about this incident, which has hitherto gone unnoticed in criticism, is that a person as highly literate as Festersen could think that readers would believe *In St. Jürgen* to be a German translation of a Danish novella. The characteristics of the Danish novella must be strong indeed in *In St. Jürgen*, and Festersen was in a unique position to perceive this. He was born in 1839 in the town of Haderslev, in the northern, predominantly Danish-speaking part

---

251   By Frank Vogel in the introduction to his edition of *Geschichten aus der Tonne von Theodor Storm* (Boston: Heath, 1905), vi.
252   Erich Schmidt, *Charakteristiken*, I (Berlin: Weidmann, ²1902), 410.
253   The response is printed in *Storm–Keller*, 52–53.

of the duchy of Schleswig. His family background was Danish.[254] In his schooling in Haderslev he certainly must have become acquainted with the nineteenth-century Danish novella, particularly since he took a more than ordinary interest in literature, as indicated by his decision to become a bookseller and publisher of literary works.

In order to escape Bismarck's Prussification of Schleswig following the Dano-German War of 1864 and the politically motivated eradication of Danish culture in Haderslev, Festersen emigrated to Switzerland, where he became active in the book trade. In his bookshop in Basel he must have become acquainted with the German novellas of his time, particularly those of Keller and Meyer, which were selling so well in the German-speaking areas of Switzerland. Like few others, therefore, the bilingual Festersen was aware of the differences between the Danish and the German novella, and he could recognize, too, that *In St. Jürgen*, though written in German, had a distinctly Danish flavor and had its roots in the Danish literary tradition. It shared, he could easily tell, more with Blicher's dramatic novellas than with those of Keller and Meyer.

c. Storm's personal drama in the early 1860s

Yet if the strong sense of drama inherent in *In St. Jürgen* can be attributed, at least in part, to Storm's roots in the tradition of the Danish novella, then it must also be said that this tale acquired a particularly heightened dramatic quality because of the sudden drama in Storm's own personal life in the years immediately preceding *In St. Jürgen*'s completion. How did the personal drama come about?

In January of 1861 Wilhelm I acceded to the throne of Prussia. He was very beholden to the Augustenborgian cause. The Danes, fearing that the House of Augustenborg, with fresh Prussian sup-

---

254   His Danish baptismal certificate, preserved today in the Staatsarchiv of the city of Basel, clearly attests to this. The certificate and other documentation are located in the file Bürgerrecht HI 15: Bürgeraufnahmen von 1877, Nr. 58. I am grateful to the authorities of the Staatsarchiv Basel-Stadt for making me aware of this file and for generously placing it at my disposal. All of my remarks on Festersen are based on information from this file.

port, would energetically renew its claim to the duchies of Schleswig and Holstein, took an extraordinary step to try to prevent this. Their plan was to dissolve legally the duchy of Schleswig, and then incorporate its territory into Denmark proper. But before this plan could be accomplished, Prussia served notice that it would not tolerate such an arrangement. Throughout the early 1860s the fate of the duchy engaged the minds of almost everyone in Schleswig, Holstein, Denmark, and Prussia, including Storm, who, as a native of Schleswig and now a Prussian civil servant, was particularly caught up in the anxiety over the possible outcome. The proposals and counterproposals of statesmen added further fuel to the fires. In November 1863, finally, a new Danish constitution effectively abolished the duchy of Schleswig. Prussian troops then invaded Denmark in early 1864. Denmark sued for peace and was forced to sever all of her historic ties to Schleswig and Holstein.

In the turbulence, confusion, and crisis of that historic year of 1864, Husum suddenly found itself without its former Danish governing authorities. As a consequence, Storm, who had by now become Husum's favorite native son because of the fame of his poetry and novellas, was invited to return to the town of his birth and become the district's new chief magistrate. He was, of course, not well prepared for such a demanding administrative post, and surely he must have feared that the conflict between the roles of artist and citizen, which he had felt so often, would arise with greater force than ever. Yet the high honor and high salary left him little choice but to accept. In March of 1864 he was installed in his new position. Chaos and bewilderment remained, however, the order of the day when he assumed his duties. With the absence of the ancient legal order of the Danish monarchy, the political future of Schleswig was bewilderingly unsettled. No one knew from day to day what to expect, and least of all perhaps the politically inexperienced Storm, now playing the role of governing official. It was an absurd situation for a poet.

Yet the drama of his life at the time was compounded when, later in 1864, Doris re-entered his life. The flames of passion of former years were reignited. Several months later, early in 1865, Contanze died of puerperal fever, but not before telling him that he should marry Doris after her death. He did just that another year later, in June of 1866. The drama of events touching Storm's life had indeed escalated. To make his life more turbulent, the new marriage proved to be troublesome from the very beginning. His children from the first marriage, particularly his sons, could not adjust to their new stepmother, and never did, as revealed by the unpublished family correspondences in the Schleswig-Holsteinische Landesbibliothek in Kiel.

Before *In St. Jürgen* could be completed the following spring, however, the world around Storm would become more chaotic. Bismarck, as Prussia's prime minister, thwarted the Augustenborgian hope to govern Schleswig and Holstein when, in January of 1867, he annexed the duchies to Prussia. Most of the population, including Storm, was aghast, for now began a rapid and chilling Prussification of Schleswig and Holstein. This led, in turn, to the destruction of many ancient and venerable institutions in these lands, and also to a soaring exodus of hapless young men to the greener pastures of America and elsewhere around the globe. Thousands now hurried to emigrate, especially in order to escape the dreaded compulsory conscription into the Prussian army, which the new conqueror had introduced. This massive emigration had, of course, a highly disruptive effect on the economy, bringing a great deal of political instability in its wake. Storm, in his new administrative post, had to cope with both of these problems.

Such was the stirring set of circumstances which gave rise to *In St. Jürgen* and which can help us to understand how this novella took on a more obvious dramatic shape than *Immensee*.

d. Compounding the fictional drama of memory and temporality

The drama in this novella is, of course, the same conflict that we encountered in *Immensee*: the struggle between the narrator's fear of the obliterating action of passing time, and his reassuring feeling that the destructive effects of transience can be overcome with the power of memory. Only now, this drama is played out in a more intensive and more vexing way.[255]

Instead of one old man remembering his past, as in *Immensee*, *In St. Jürgen* is composed of the memories of five different characters: the primary character recounts what he remembers about two elderly people whom he had known in early youth; an old woman (Agnes) recapitulates her youth; an old man (Harre) recollects his past; his wife remembers an event from the past; and the old woman's father recalls former times. The memorializing structure of *Immensee* has now been compounded five-fold.

In St. Jürgen is similar to *Immensee* also in that the dominant note, aside from memory itself, is the disclosure of the narrator's sensitivity to passing time. Again, though, this sensitivity is portrayed far more elaborately than in *Immensee*, and thus it strikes the reader with greater intensity.

In the thirteen pages containing Harre's recollection in the Laage-Lohmeier edition of Storm's works, for instance, the narrator explicitly emphasizes on eleven occasions that he is highly aware of passing years, e.g.: "Jahr auf Jahr verging" (year after year went by), "So gingen die Jahre hin" (Thus the years passed by), "nach Jahresfrist" (after a year). He is also very much aware of the evanescent nature of the days, weeks, and months, e.g.: "Am dritten Tage" (On the third day), "In der letzten Woche" (In the previous week), "einige Monate später" (a few months later).

It is to the movements of the clock, however, that the narrator appears to be most sensitive, e.g.: "Aber die Zeit drängte; unter uns schlug dröhnend die Viertelglocke" (But time was pressing, beneath us the clock boomed out the quarter-hour); "Am andern Morgen hatte es eben fünf vom Turme geschlagen" (On the next morning the church clock had just struck five).

---

255 The following analysis of the drama in *In St. Jürgen* draws upon my earlier interpretation in my book *Theodor Storm's Craft of Fiction* (Chapel Hill, NC: University of North Carolina Press, 1963, ²1966), 57–73.

A profusion of indefinite references also conveys the narrator's sensitivity to time. Within the novella's forty pages (Laage-Lohmeier edition), for example, we find him using the word "dann" (then) no less than thirty-nine times, almost on every page.

Constant references to the aging and maturing of the characters constitute another way that we are made aware of this sensitivity to time. Agnes, for example, is described as a child and then as a young girl with blond hair; later we see her gray-haired and old, all in a short space of a few pages. In a parallel manner, her lover Harre develops from school boy, to apprentice, and then passes the age of forty; later he is depicted as a grandfather with white hair, again, all in a short span of pages.

e. The power of memory

As in *Immensee*, the reader finds that *In St. Jürgen*, while making its narrator's sensitivity to passing time apparent, also shows very clearly his determination to counteract this feeling. This becomes perhaps most obvious when we observe that the primary character in this novella retells the tales remembered by other characters. Everything he recounts to his listeners has previously been recalled from the past by other characters. This constitutes a double, reinforced attempt to preserve the past from annihilation by fleeting time.

The more intensified effort in *In St. Jürgen* (in comparison with *Immensee*) to counteract the ravages of transience acquires even greater urgency when we notice that, in addition to using a plurality of memories and tying these memories together in an all-embracing memory, the narrator now also resorts to a host of other mnemonic devices to thwart the devastating effects of evanescence. In the description of the huge banquet hall in the almshouse, for instance, two ornaments are particularly conspicuous: an old-fashioned grandfather clock, the legacy of a deceased resident, and a life-size portrait of the institution's founder in a scarlet jacket. The clock points, of course, to the flux of time, not only because it registers the passing of time, minute by minute and hour by hour, but also because, as the legacy of a deceased person, it serves as a constant reminder of the passing of human life. On the other hand, in mentioning the life-like portrait of the founder, in vivid scarlet clothing, the narrator seems to fire his imagination with the thought of a deceased person who has not yet passed into oblivion. In contrast to the sensitivity to transience that is symbolized by the clock, therefore, the portrait seems to counteract the destructive forces of passing time, keeping the past alive with an image so graphic that the founder seems to live in the present.

The portrait of the founder, as well as two other portraits in the narrative, are not, however, the only mnemonic devices that reveal a more energetic attempt — in contrast to *Immensee* — to cling to the past as though it had not fallen prey to evanescence. We are told that memorial windows keep the past from being forgotten; that linden trees vividly retain the ideas of a former, historically important epoch; that chronicles prevent the past from becoming forgotten; and that old buildings, an old garden, and old-fashioned furnishings constantly recall past eras, customs, and events for posterity.

f. Calling into question the effectiveness of memory

As in *Immensee*, so too in *In St. Jürgen* the drama between evanescence and remembrance takes on an added dimension when the narrator calls into question the ability of memory to generate an enduring history. Memories, we are made to realize, will eventually fall prey to the very force they had seemingly conquered. Memories, we learn, become ever fainter through the years and thus gradually lose their ability to retain the past. All five characters whose memories perpetuate the past are aging quickly in the short pages of the novella. Before we reach the end of the story, two have already died of old age; the death of the third, also of old age, seems imminent. The others, doubtless, will soon follow. In each instance, the obliterating stream of time has already engulfed or will soon engulf the power of memory. Hence the need to have another framing memory of a younger person to preserve the memory of the older characters so that it does not die with them: "du mußt doch von mir wissen, wenn ich nicht mehr bin" (you must know about me when I am gone), Agnes tells her young listener.

g. The power of art to outwit death

As in *Immensee*, the premonition that the soothing effects of memory will prove deceptive is not the final note in this new drama between time and memory, for once again we realize that the lost battle is contained within a memorializing novella. The entire story lives on in the artistic memory that keeps it alive for as long as readers continue to read *In St. Jürgen*. Has memory become the final victor? The answer could be a resounding yes if the skepticism raised throughout this novella would not make us feel that perhaps at some distant date in the future *In St. Jürgen* might cease to be read.

h. The chorus of swallows: a literary borrowing from Hans Christian Andersen's Isjomfruen

Complementing the drama of time and memory, which unfolds here with greater intensity than in *Immensee*, is a chorus of swallows fluttering back and forth. The French critic Robert Pitrou felt long ago that this chorus constituted a literary borrowing from Hans Christian Andersen's *Isjomfruen* (The Ice Maiden),[256] and Georg Festersen may well have sensed the same connection when he said that *In St. Jürgen* was a Danish novella. If these assumptions are correct, and we have with the swallow chorus a conscious borrowing on Storm's part, then we must take particular notice of it.

The importance of this chorus becomes apparent, too, when we glance at the first book edition of *In St. Jürgen*, a rare copy of which is preserved in the archives of the Theodor-Storm-Gesellschaft in Husum. One of the most striking details of this edition is the gilt impressions of swallows on the cover, which an early Canadian trans-

---

256 Pitrou, *La Vie et l'Oeuvre de Theodor Storm*, 421.

The chorus of swallows at the almshouse — *In St. Jürgen.*

lator of the novella was anxious to emphasize, for he changed the title thus: *The Swallows of St. Jurgens.*[257]

Why are the swallows so visible and so audible throughout the novella? They add another emphasis, not yet known in *Immensee*, to the drama between the two forces that rival each other for domination of the narrator's thoughts. They echo his sensitivity to passing time; they echo, too, his joy at knowing that memory offers a means to overcome this sensitivity; and they make audible his anguished realization that even memory will fall prey to the passing of time.

It is especially his awareness of passing time that the swallows emphasize. When Agnes and Harre recognize, for instance, the warning bells of the quarter-hour, a swallow appears and pours forth a flood of rapturous sounds, underscoring the poignancy of the clock's threat. At the moment when their happy hours spent together come to an end, the same swallow appears again, this time illustrating the event by spreading its wings and flying away.

It is not by chance that the narrator tells his readers of the spectacular and clamorous arrival of a flock of swallows on Agnes's sixty-fifth birthday, that the swallows follow her when she becomes an inmate of the home for the aged, and that the scene depicting her bier is enhanced with the swallows flying off singing. By using the musical chorus of the swallows to focus more attention upon her aging and death, the narrator gives added stress to his awareness that a lifetime has ebbed away and has, at last, come to its appointed end.

In a similar manner, the swallows' chorus echoes the narrator's countervailing joy at knowing that memory offers a possibility for retrieving the past. We are repeatedly informed of this sentiment by the number of sunny, song-filled scenes of swallows that occasion and accompany the remembering of the past. The springtime return of the swallows and their twittering the song "Als ich Abschied nahm, als ich Abschied nahm" (When I went away, when I went away), the narrator tells us, cause the primary character, with his encompassing memory, to think of his youth. The song of the swallows also ac-

---

257 In *The Canadian Monthly*, II (1872): 323–344.

companies the recollections of Agnes; their sight provokes her to recall, as her sigh near the novella's beginning reveals, the happiness that she once enjoyed when swallows had fluttered about her. Similarly, it is the swallows' chorus in the spring that evokes, year after year, memories of the past in Harre.

But just as the swallows arrive in the spring to make the remembered renewal of the past audible in song, so they depart in the fall, to emphasize musically the eventual failure of memory to retain the past. In the final scene in which the narrator shows how the memories of Agnes and Harre succumb to the ravages of passing time, the swallows fly away singing: "Als ich wiederkam, als ich wiederkam/ War alles leer" (When I came again, when I came again / There was nothing there). They leave behind nothing but an empty nest. Significantly, this song constitutes the story's conclusion. The novella ends on this sad note, as does the drama of time and memory. Time, the chorus of swallows suggests, has carried the final victory, unless, of course, we could admit the possibility of the swallows' return the following spring, when their song might again revive old memories. Then the annihilating force of time in the drama would not have won the battle after all. Memory would have proved the stronger.

4. Painting in oils: *Aquis submersus*

a. Storm begins to paint in oils

A new period in Storm's novella-writing began in the 1870s. The author called it his "zweite Periode" (second period), but Paul Heyse, who became the third German to be awarded the Nobel Prize for literature, characterized this period better when he said that Storm had begun then "in Öl zu malen" (to paint in oils).[258] Heyse's distinction between Storm's earlier and later novellas as that between water color and oil painting describes more accurately, the Cambridge literary historian Edwin K. Bennett informs us, the difference

---

258   LL, IV, 510.

between the two styles. It is a difference of coloring; a greater depth and richness is apparent in the novellas "in oils."[259]

The subject matter in both the earlier and later novellas, the dramatic conflict between time and memory, persists essentially unchanged. Storm was far too obsessed with this theme to give it up. When he did try, on a few occasions, to experiment with other topics, he was not very successful, as he himself realized, and so he always returned to his art of tensely balancing a remembered past with a remembering present, the art for which he will forever be remembered.

b. C'est un jeu très compliqué

Certainly the most colorful of these narrative paintings "in oils" is *Aquis submersus*, which first appeared in 1876 in the prestigious monthly *Deutsche Rundschau*.[260]

In the story, Coz Ursel, a character painted so vividly that she seems to be a figure lifted almost directly out of comic opera, and who makes a lasting impression on the reader, refers to a game she plays by saying *c'est un jeu très compliqué*, and that is exactly what this novella is: a very complicated game. Its intricacy is what makes it so colorful, what gives it its depth, its richness, and its uniqueness. Owing to this artistic complexity, to which the French words standing out in the German text especially alert us, it can come as no surprise that this tale has elicited extravagant praise from many, foremost of all from Storm himself. I am convinced, he wrote on September 13, 1876, to his publisher Elwin Paetel, "daß ich Ihnen damit das Beste gebe, was an Prosa-Dichtung bisher aus meiner Feder aufs Papier gelangte" (that I am offering you herewith the best work in prose

---

259   E. K. Bennett, *A History of the German Novelle*, revised and continued by H. M. Waidson (Cambridge, England: University Press, ²1974), 171.
260   The most recent (and best) translation in English is by Jeffrey L. Sammons in *German Novellas of Realism II*. The German Library, Vol. 38. (New York: Continuum, 1989).

that has ever come from my pen).[261] He never used such lavish words for any other novella.

Many critics, too, have long felt that this novella ranked second to none in the author's literary legacy. The first such claim was made by the Danish critic R. Zachariae. In the obituary of Storm which he wrote for the Danish reading public, he stated unequivocally that *Aquis submersus* was Storm's "bedste (best) Novella."[262] Others have also felt that *Aquis submersus* is second to none in the author's literary legacy. In 1909 Calvin Thomas of Columbia University stated frankly that "the art of Storm culminated in *Aquis submersus*."[263] A decade later, in 1919, Albert Köster, Storm's faithful editor in Leipzig, echoed the same opinion, in even more emphatic language: "Der Gipfelpunkt aber war . . . mit der Novelle *Aquis submersus* erstiegen, die ohne alles Dingen und Feilschen Storms Meisterwerk geblieben ist" (the high point [of Storm's literary career] was reached with *Aquis submersus*, about which one can make the claim, without any haggling or bargaining, that it has remained Storm's masterpiece).[264]

How could Storm's drama of time and memory have assumed in this novella such an intricate artistic form that cognoscenti of literature felt that it was the author's supreme creation in prose? We need only to look at Storm's personal life at the time to better understand the reasons why the work has been so admired. It was a period filled with the utmost joy that any creative mind could have wished for, but it was also a period of excruciating grief. The drama of joy and sorrow in Storm's life had now become so consuming that it largely determined the intensity of the dramatic action in this novella.

Let us look first at the great joy he experienced. By the early 1870s, Storm had become, as noted by Rudolf Eucken, the second

---

261 This letter, still unpublished, is preserved today in the Schleswig-Holsteinische Landesbibliotek in Kiel.
262 R. Zachariae, "Theodor Storm," *Literatur og kritik* 1 (1889): 240.
263 Calvin Thomas, *A History of German Literature* (New York: Appleton, 1909), 377.
264 Storm, *Sämtliche Werke*, ed. A. Köster, I (Leipzig: Insel, 1919), 50.

German to receive the Nobel Prize for literature, the most famous and most important person living in Husum.[265] His poetry and his prose had made him a celebrity, both at home and abroad.

Immensee and *In St. Jürgen*, the two flagships of his early prose, had quickly been translated into English, the former as early as 1858 in *Colburn's New Monthly Magazine and Literary Journal*, the latter in 1872 in *The Canadian Monthly*. More translations, Storm surely knew, would soon follow, in English and in other languages.

In Germany, publishers were now vying with one another for contracts with Storm. Editors of literary journals, he took undisguised delight in saying in 1875, were "fast . . . auf den Knien" (almost on their knees) begging for contributions from his pen.[266] Perhaps the greatest flattery he could receive came as Julius Rodenberg, the erudite editor of the *Deutsche Rundschau*, informed him that he could expect to have everything he wrote published in the *Rundschau* immediately, without any further editorial approval.[267] This was indeed a rare tribute to an author. Far and wide Storm was becoming well-known to the reading public. In 1868 his Collected Works were published in a handsome edition of six volumes. It sold so well that by 1872 it had to be republished. Storm was a huge success as a writer, and his pride and joy in this fact must have been great.

But there was at the time also another force in Storm's life that did not let him bask for long in the sunshine of his success as a writer. By the 1870s his personal life was on the brink of disaster, compelling him to fight despondency at every turn.

First came his frustration over the Prussification of his native Schleswig, following its absorption into the Prussian State in 1867. With the establishment of every new Prussian institution in Schleswig, he saw the blows of the Prussian cultural whip strike again. "Es nagt an meinem Leben, daß ich Beamter dieser Regierung bin," he wrote in 1868 (It galls me that I have to serve in an official capacity in this

---

265 Rudolf Eucken, *Lebenserinnerungen* (Leipzig: Koehler, 1921), 42–43.
266 *Storm. Briefe*, ed. P. Goldammer, II, 101.
267 *Conrad Ferdinand Meyer und Julius Rodenberg. Ein Briefwechsel*, ed. A. Langmesser (Berlin: Paetel, 1918), 73.

[Prussian] State).[268] "Niemand kann das spezifisch preußiche Wesen mehr hassen, als ich," he said in 1870 (Nobody can hate the Prussian system more than I).[269] Particularly after the unification of Germany under Prussia's leadership in 1871, the Prussification of Schleswig gathered momentum. The tighter the knots were tied in the subjection of Schleswig to Prussia, the more Storm despaired.[270]

Next came the family problems that weighed heavily on him, and which grew worse from year to year. The troubles began with his marriage to his old lover, Doris Jensen, in 1866. His children from the first marriage found it hard to accept their new stepmother (as unpublished family letters preserved in the Schleswig-Holsteinische Landesbibliothek in Kiel inform us). Discord entered the family's life and never left. Storm was helplessly caught in the middle. The children's distrust remained even after the poet's death, when the matter of dividing the inheritance between stepmother and children had to be settled.

The family troubles were compounded immensely in the early 1870s when his three sons left Husum and the home over which their stepmother presided in order to study in Kiel and Leipzig. They took little interest in their studies and embarked, instead, on paths of self-destruction. Drinking problems, heavy debts, and even venereal disease soon took their toll on the sons, and caused father Storm no end of grief.[271]

He might have despaired completely without the buoying power of his enormous success as an author. Yet the gratification he experienced as a writer did not let him overlook his sorrow as paterfamilias, just as that sorrow did not let him forget his literary success. Two

---

268 *Storm–Brinkmann*, 154.
269 *Storm–Christen*, 37.
270 It is one of the salient characteristics of Danish criticism that it has vigorously called attention to Storm's despair over Prussian rule. See Roos, 153; Simonsen, "Theodor Storm og Danmark," 151.
271 The full magnitude of these sordid events in Storm's life has only recently come to light, through the efforts of David A. Jackson in his article "The Sound of Silence. Theodor Storm's Son Karl and the Novelle *Schweigen*," *German Life and Letters* 45 (1992): 33–49.

antipodal forces thus entrenched themselves in his breast. He felt constantly the unresolved intricate drama between his private and public lives, the pressing concerns of his home life and his happy flights of the imagination.

This acutely felt drama became, then, in the 1870s, the *jeu très compliqué* of Storm's existence, and it tells us why the fictional drama between time and memory, ever close to his heart, could now assume, beginning with *Aquis submersus*, a deeper and denser coloration than in his earlier novellas, written under less frustrating circumstances.

c. The novella's core

At the core of the novella, that part that comes chronologically earliest, the narrator tells about the happy boyhood of a portrait painter named Johannes. Remembering *Immensee* and *In St. Jürgen*, however, we immediately notice something else: that time plays havoc with the happiness of young Johannes.[272] First a rival appears on the scene to court the same girl, Katharina, he is fond of. Then, after seven years have passed, the colorful Coz Ursel begins to make him feel unwanted. Soon the time for his departure from his happy environment arrives. As the day begins to draw to a close, he has to take his leave, and at sunset he feels compelled to hasten his departure. Finally, the passing of five more years makes him lose all contact with the people and scenes associated with this happy early period in his life.

Of course, we also quickly realize that there is another thought on the narrator's mind while he tells this early part of the story. He appears to have the reassuring awareness that, despite his sensitivity to the destructive effects of passing time, his apprehension can be overcome by the power of memory. This is conveyed to us when, on the pages immediately preceding and following this earliest part of the story, he relates how the painter, five years after his happy boyhood ended, can relive in his memory the same joyful scenes he had once known. Through recollection the painter can absent himself

---

272 The following analysis of this novella is a reworking of the interpretation in my book *Theodor Storm's Craft of Fiction*, 11–53.

from his immediate surroundings, feel once more the warmth of his former patron, Gerhardus, and enjoy speaking again to Katharina. Even the carefree mood of this bygone period can be recaptured in memory. The way the narrator colors the image of the painter as he recollects the past makes this clear: it is a sunny May day; he is well-dressed and feels rather fortunate because of the money he has at his disposal. The gladdening song of birds echoes in his heart, and he believes a fruit tree is whispering to him. He is in such a cheerful mood, we further hear, that he brushes every care aside and likens the scene of the surrounding pine trees to delightful memories.

d. Subverting the pleasure of memory

Yet, as the tale progresses beyond its core scene and its chronological origins, the narrator describes the gradual but very distinct passing of a lengthy period of time in which the young painter's recollected joy becomes increasingly diminished.

We first become aware of this in the way the figure of the recollecting painter is introduced. We are told that he is walking briskly toward the manor house of his former patron. Immediately, we sense that the element of passing time is added to the picture that the narrator gives of his recollecting character: the steady strides forward mirror the regular movement of passing time like the relentless ticking of a clock. The passage of time during the walk is further illustrated in the change of the sun's position. At the beginning of the walk the sun has not yet climbed above the shadow of the forest; toward the end of the same walk, the painter goes out into the full sunshine of the later morning.

As far as Johannes's recollection is concerned, these additional time references have a negative significance. As the walk progresses, Johannes passes through one site of the past into the other, and in each, new interests attract his attention and rival with memories to dominate his thoughts. Changes in surroundings thus mirror changes in time in order to vivify the detrimental effects of the movement of time.

The first such point at which Johannes's recollected joy is interrupted occurs when he observes the hideous traces of a war which had recently raged. He becomes depressed when he sees that the houses, in which he was entertained in his boyhood, are now reduced to ashes. He is saddened, furthermore, when he notices that the fields he had formerly seen covered with blooming rye now lie desolate and overgrown with weeds. As he continues his walk, a dark forest brings another thought to disturb his joyous recollections: he cannot help but be haunted by the thought of his wolf-like adversary who bore the telling name: Junker Wulf. The continuity of pleasant memories is broken once more when the sight of two rows of gigantic oak trees causes, as he says, an uncanny feeling to overcome him.

By far the most penetrating interruption of Johannes's joyous recollections comes when he passes through the gateway of the estate on which he had spent the early happy vacations of his boyhood. The bright vision in his memory is overshadowed when he notices that the growth of foliage now conceals the manor. The joy Johannes feels in always being with Gerhardus in thought is shattered by the news that his patron had recently died. His memory of the warm welcome and friendship of his former patron is further diminished when he is now welcomed by the howl of savage bloodhounds rushing after him, and when he discovers that the study, which he has remembered as the place where he had received such understanding counsel, is now devoid of any human presence, as the conspicuously empty armchair indicates. The merriment associated with the memories of his friend Dieterich disappears when he discovers that his friend's hair has turned snow-white and that his eyes have become dull and troubled. Above all, Johannes is shocked to find that his former girlfriend is no longer happy as he remembers her, but instead, is now pale, tearful, terror-stricken, and overcome with wrath and pain.

Yet, the painter's steps, with their implicit movement forward in time, do not constitute the only way in which the narrator reveals his obsession with the thought that the joy which seemed to be preserved by memory has diminished with the further passage of time.

As soon as the walk is terminated, time starts to pass even more quickly for Johannes.

We are especially reminded of this when we are told how the hours of the clock go by: "Auf dem Tisch … war die Kerze fast herabgebrannt, und die … Schlaguhr hatte schon auf Eilf gewarnt" (On the table … the candle was almost burned down and the Dutch clock … had already struck eleven o'clock); "Es wurde Dämmerung, es wurde Nacht … ich fühlte die Glockenschläge durch das Holz der Bettstatt drönen, und ich zählete sie alle die ganze Nacht entlang" (Twilight came, and night fell … I felt the bell strokes droning through the wood of the bedstead, and I counted them all night long).

As the hours go by, so too, we read, the days pass: "in Ängsten sahe ich Tag um Tag vergehen" (anxiously I saw day after day pass by); "einen Morgen um den andern" (one morning after the other). The weeks also go by: "Es war manche Woche danach" (It was many weeks later). References to the seasons also mirror the flux of time. With regard to the year 1661 we are first informed of the time, in early spring, when the tulips were just breaking through the soil. Then we are told how, later on in the spring, the rye fields were already standing in silver-grey blossom. Soon it is the Monday before Midsummer Day (June 24). Summer has come and gone when we are told that the last leaves had fallen from the trees. The Christmas holidays begin. Finally the winter is over and once more (by now it is 1662) the trees were beginning to turn green. Thus we learn how an entire year, from spring 1661 to spring 1662, has passed.

No less revealing are the movements of the painter's brush to and fro. The more he paints, the more we are reminded that time is ticking away on his clock: "du sollst mein Bild ja malen" (you are to paint my picture), Katharina tells Johannes, "du wirst eine Zeitlang hier verweilen" (you will stay here a while). Yet, with each stroke of the brush, the time they have together runs out: "…wir hätten … die Zeit gern stille stehen lassen" (…we would gladly have let time stand still). It did not, however, stand still: the paint continually "floß … durch den Pinsel heimlich auf die Leinewand" (flowed secretly through the brush onto the canvas) and, as a result, the day arrives when the portait is just about finished and Katharina is no longer allowed to sit before him.

When we arrive at this point in the narrative, we know that young Johannes's joy at recollecting his childhood happiness has turned to sorrow. The passage of time has nullified even the pleasure of remembering.

e. The use of a memoir

The narrator of *Aquis submersus* is, we realize, as poignantly conscious of the evanescent nature of his main character's recollected joy as were the narrators of *Immensee* and *In St. Jürgen*. But this time he proves to be more resourceful, for he weaves into his narrative fabric another mnemonic instrument not known in earlier stories: a written memoir. The tale of the recollected joy of young Johannes is interwoven with another, superimposed narration informing us that the entire story of Johannes's recollection is being recalled again by Johannes, many decades later, this time in the more permanent, fixed form of a memoir that will outlast what he had recalled in his mind. Now, after Johannes dies, his memories will be preserved from extinction. The portrayal of Johannes, as an aged man, writing down his memories makes the narrator's intention clear. Johannes says that he must hasten to complete the written account of his life "ehbevor auch an meiner Uhr der Weiser stille steht" (before the hand stops on my clock).

Again, however, even though the narrator is aware of a capacity to counteract his consciousness of the evanescent nature of the once recollected joy — this time with the more permanent instrument of a memoir — he at the same time reveals a fear that even this mnemonic device will, in turn, fall prey to evanescence. The pages on which the memoir is written have become, we are told, "stark vergilbt" (heavily yellowed) with age. This means that, although the memoir can apparently keep the recollected joy from fading after Johannes's death, that device, too, is destined to fade and does fade.

Revealing, too, is the significance that the narrator ascribes to the Low German proverb that is mentioned twice and thus doubly emphasized: "Geliek as Rook un Stoof verswindt, / Also sind ock de Minschenkind" (Like smoke and dust upon the wind / Is every child of human kin). We are told that this proverb lingers in the mind of Johannes as he writes the memoir. We are told, too, that it stands out on the pages of the memoir; when one of the notebooks containing the memoir comes to light many years after the painter's death, the proverb is discovered as the heading on the very first page. We are told, moreover, that it serves as the key to the memoir's discovery: the finder of the memoir makes his discovery only after the proverb had caught his eye and motivated him to enter the house that holds the memoir. It is clear, then, that the proverb and its message are always in the foreground when the narrator thinks of the memoir, and that the words of the proverb apply directly to it.

Another artistic device revealing the narrator's apprehensions about the eventual failure of the memoir to retain the past is the description of the memoir as two separate notebooks, each containing only part of the story they jointly seek to preserve. The underlying reason for this, I believe, is to make us aware of how insubstantial the narrator considers the memoir to be. In individual notebooks, not bound together, the two parts of the memoir can and, according to the narrator's way of thinking, most likely will become separated over time. Detached from each other, they will eventually land in different places, and then be preserved only as fragments of the story, not the whole.

f. *The use of memorial portraits*

If the narrator in *Aquis submersus*, by introducing a memoir, seems to try harder than his fictional counterparts in *Immensee* and *In St. Jürgen* to take action against the unreliability of personal memory, then he must have been all the more frustrated when he realizes that even this more permanent means of preserving the past will become a victim of the ravaging brush of time. Disappointed as he must have been, however, he does not give up his fight against time. He resorts to another commemorative medium. This time he makes use of the most vivid means of recalling the past that he knows: painting.

We had already seen how the narrator in *In St. Jürgen* had focused on portraiture to appease his sensitivity to evanescence. Now, in *Aquis submersus*, painting is given a far more extensive function in the narrative design. The narrator seems to be placing great stock in the feeling of support he thinks he can get from this mnemonic device. Can it prove to be more lasting and reliable than the written memoir?

The importance the narrator in *Aquis submersus* attaches to the memorializing quality of painting becomes most immediately apparent when he tells us that his main character, Johannes, is a portrait painter and that all of the many pictures he paints are expressly made to serve as reminders of people or, as in the case of one painting, of a particular place.

Similarly, the narrator's confidence in the pictorial means of retaining the past comes to the fore when he weaves into the narrative design the names of two seventeenth-century painters: Bartholomeus van der Helst (1613–1670) and Jürgen Ovens (1623–1678). The Dutch artist van der Helst is noted for his skill in permanently rendering on canvas the likenesses of specific personages of his time. Ovens, who hailed from Storm's Schleswig but whose name has been invariably and curiously passed over in Storm criticism, is a painter who, specifically because of his strong religious belief in the transience of earthly things, sought to memorialize these for posterity.[273]

The greatest comfort that the narrator receives from painting, however, comes when he tries to show how it can counteract his own misgivings about the eventual disintegration of the memoir. He

---

273 See Harry Schmidt, *Jürgen Ovens. Sein Leben und seine Werke* (Heide: Westholsteinische Verlagsdruckerei, n.d. [1922]). This informative book by a Storm scholar deserves to be retrieved from the oblivion to which critics of *Aquis submersus* have consigned it.

tells us of a painting that was made in order to remind its viewer of the same story recorded in the memoir, but which, unlike that memoir, had not deteriorated over the years. "Es war noch wohl erhalten" (It was still well-preserved).

This is further brought out when he refers to the same painting as fortifying the memoir's capacity to recall the past. We are told that the painting hangs in such a way that it appears to keep faithful watch over the memoir. By mentioning this, he suggests that the painting may prevent the memoir from being forgotten. He tells us, too, that the painting appears to watch over the reader of the memoir, and that it even reminds the reader, when he interrupts his reading, to go on with it in order to recall all of the details of the past. This reveals that it is not just the memoir but rather the story contained therein that the painting protects. Furthermore, we are told — and this seems to be the strongest evidence that the painting is a means of securing the memoir's recapture of the past — that the memoir is brought to light again only because the painting arouses the viewer's curiosity enough to make him open the box in which the memoir is buried.

But again, even though the narrator makes us realize that he can counteract his fear of the memoir's disintegration by resorting to the commemorative medium of painting, he also does not fail to let us know that even this, his most vivid means of restoring the past, is not lasting.

The first clue we have of this is when he tells of a shadow that hangs over the painting designed to recall the story contained in the memoir. Since this "shadowing" takes place a century after the picture was painted, we are given to understand that the painting is no longer as vivid to its spectators as it once was. Such an admission, in turn, brings to light the narrator's doubt about whether the painting can continue to keep the past alive.

There are more indications of this doubt. A century later, we are told, the same painting is encircled by an atmosphere of death. Everything we learn about the room in which it hangs suggests this. Both the room's inhabitant and his descendant have died and, as a result, the room stands vacant and has been closed off for many years. In it there are antiquated furnishings, which have become meaningless to a later generation and are therefore referred to as "Siebensachen" (all kinds of odds and ends), and heavily yellowed sheets of paper with very old script.

This deathly atmosphere surrounding the painting is reinforced when we are further informed that the room is situated within a house over whose front door hangs the inscription which we mentioned earlier: Like smoke and dust upon the wind / Is every child of human kin. It is as if there were no escape for the painting from the closed-off, coffin-like room in which it hangs.

There seems to be little doubt that the narrator's faith in the painting as a lasting memorial is destined to crumble. Yet, he goes to a great deal of trouble to confirm his fear. He refers to a number of other paintings in a similar way. It is not, therefore, just this one painting that he feels will not last, but rather it is his faith in painting in general, as a preserving medium, about which he has persistent doubts.

The various pictures in the portrait gallery of the manor house are enveloped in an atmosphere so still that only the silent movement of the motes can be seen. The air is not only deathly still but it is also filled with lifeless particles that hover and — I should like to add — attempt to cover the surface of the paintings. In this dusty atmosphere the portraits appear as lost as the solitary spectator standing in the gallery. With the passing of time, we sense, they are destined to become so obscured by the gathering of dust that the faces they memorialize will hardly be discernible to the gaze of a future generation. Of course, interest in the portraits will then wane, and so also will their capacity to recall the past in the way that the artist intended.

More doubts about the permanence of painting surface when we learn about the fates of various individual paintings. The portrait of Katharina, for instance, was commissioned for the express purpose of perpetuating her memory in her ancestral home when, after marrying, she took up residence elsewhere. But Katharina's picture

"wenn eine adelige Tochter das Haus verläßt, so muß ihr Bild darin zurückbleiben"
(when a noble daughter leaves her house, her portrait must remain behind)
— *Aquis submersus.*

cannot do this for long. We learn that it was removed from the ancestral home after a time and then placed in the deathly atmosphere of a faraway house with large, almost empty rooms whose walls are whitewashed and bare, where another painting admonishes that everything turns to dust. This house, in turn, is situated between houses whose thatched roofs have become blackened by the passage of time. The entire landscape surrounding these houses has become desolate. It is, moreover, close by a rumbling sea, in whose waves, we are told, hundreds of people had perished, and which constantly threatens all life near the shoreline.

Perhaps the strongest proof of all for the narrator's fear that painting will not succeed as a commemorative device is what he tells us at the conclusion of his narrative. We learn that the painting of Lazarus, which had helped to perpetuate the memories of two different men, was sold and had then vanished. In a later century, the church in which it had hung was itself demolished. The restless waves of time, as the concluding words *Aquis submersus* reveal, had submerged it and its memories in the sea of oblivion.

Tellingly, the narrator uses Latin, the universal language, to inform us of this. It is the fate that is universal for all mankind that has destroyed the most vivid means he could think of for the purpose of outwitting ephemerality. It is significant, too, that Latin is a dead language, in the sense that it is no longer spoken.

g. The preserving vault of subjectivity

Yet, once more, the narrator does not let this renewed awareness of ephemerality triumph over his hope of outsmarting the ravages of time. He makes still another prodigious attempt to battle the impingement of time upon the pages of life. The means he employs this time, as we might expect, is again memory, but memory of a more powerful kind than we encountered in our discussions of *Immensee* and *In St. Jürgen*. A young man living some two hundred years later has collected and preserved in the vault of his subjectivity the contents of all the recollecting media we have referred to thus far. As a result of this all-embracing frame narrative, all the fears we felt concerning the inherent weakness of the other commemorative devices seem nullified. Everything we learned about the failed attempts to keep Johannes's memory alive are locked within another depository and presented to us from a further remove.

But not only that. The frame narrator, we know because of his use of the first person right at the beginning of the novella, is now trying to pass the story of Johannes on to us. Johannes and all the memories of him will, hence, find a new life in the individual minds of the audiences to whom the first-person narrator is speaking.

Of course, as it should by now be clear from this complicated mosaic of references to mnemonic devices and the quicksands of ephemerality, every mental depository within individuals can only preserve the past as long as the individuals themselves have not succumbed to time's cruel music. Will there always be another person at hand to catch, wholly and completely, what a previous narrator had kept stored in the vault of his subjectivity? Are there any assurances that subsequent rehandlings of the story will not alter its contents, eventually beyond recognition? We can only gather that the fictional narrator of *Aquis submersus*, who was present before the first-person frame narrator could be introduced, must have had his lingering doubts.

h. The preserving vault of art

That is why the fictional narrator incorporates all of these memories, and all of his misgivings about those memories, into the artistic structure of a memorializing novella. Our readings of *Immensee* and *In St. Jürgen* had already familiarized us with the role an enduring monument of fiction can play in man's battle against time. Now, in *Aquis submersus*, the immortality of a work of art again becomes the final rejoinder, the final answer to the challenge of time.

Can this preserving medium of art now succeed in giving us a lasting message of triumph over the enemy of time? Yes and no. Certainly, an enduring classic of literature, like *Aquis submersus*, which has found generations of readers all over the world, has outlived the test of time. Certainly, too, the objective form of literary art has more permanence than the subjective storehouse of memory, which is constantly in peril on the sea of life. The stress here falls, hence, entirely on the preserving power of art.

We could take leave of this artwork with a sigh of relief, but Storm, with greater insistence than in *Immensee* and *In St. Jürgen*, makes sure we do not do this. He places over the entire novella the title *Aquis submersus*. To be submerged in the aqueous grave of time must be the final destiny of this artwork, too. Storm knows this. Indeed, he knew it as soon as he had penned the title. But life, he also knows, is worth fighting for, and fight he indeed did when he composed this amazing *jeu très compliqué*.

i. The memory of criticism

Did Storm, despite *Aquis submersus*'s foreboding title, succeed in his battle to keep the memories in this novella alive? The living extension of it in the criticism that has developed around it, and which cannot now be separated from it, would seem to indicate that he had.

The Scottish Germanist William Mullan has reminded us that "almost as soon as the ink was dry on Storm's manuscript there began a controversy unresolved to the present day."[274] Indeed, more so than with any other work by Storm, critical opinion on this novella has remained sharply divided. This high incidence of diverging attempts to revitalize *Aquis submersus*, the memory of criticism, has kept this novella very much alive to the present day.

Interestingly, the center for the critical appeal of *Aquis submersus* has gravitated in modern times to the Anglo-American world. Ernst Feise had ushered in this new critical interest from the Anglo-American world when, in 1938, he published his magisterial analysis

---

274 W. N. B. Mullan, "Tragic Guilt and the Motivation of the Catastrophe in Storm's 'Aquis submersus,' " *Forum for Modern Language Studies* 18 (1982): 225.

of the novella's form.[275] As a student of Albert Köster, Storm's faithful editor in Leipzig, Feise had been, early in his scholarly life, influenced by Köster's claim, cited at the beginning of our discussion of this novella, that it [*Aquis submersus*] has remained Storm's masterpiece. Feise sought to prove that claim.

Owing to the conspicuous role Feise came to play in the promotion of German literature in the United States in the course of a long academic career, and the great influence he exerted on generations of students aspiring to careers in Germanics,[276] he was able to kindle an absorbing enthusiasm for this novella which, in turn, has given rise to a host of further challenging interpretations on this side of the Atlantic as well as in Britain.

My own interpretation of 1963 endeavored to come to another enlivened understanding of the novella by drawing attention to the fictional narrator, who, as I tried to show, is a tormented intelligence, ever oscillating between his fear of the all-consuming maw of passing time on the one hand, and a soothing knowledge of his ability to overcome this phobia on the other.[277]

One year later, in 1964, further fuel was added to the controversy surrounding *Aquis submersus* when E. Allen McCormick offered a greatly conflicting opinion on the functions of both the frame and painting in the novella.[278]

In 1971 Leonard L. Duroche compounded the enigma of portrait painting in the views of the interpreters by polemically stating

---

275 Ernst Feise, "Theodor Storms 'Aquis submersus.' Eine Formanalyse," *Monatshefte für Deutschen Unterricht* (Wisconsin) 30 (1938): 246–256. The analysis immediately invited challenge. See Feise, "Berichtigung zu meinem Aufsatz über Storms 'Aquis submersus,'" *Monatshefte* 30 (1938): 334–335. An updated version of the analysis appeared in Feise, *Xenion. Essays in the History of German Literature* (Baltimore: Johns Hopkins Press, 1950), 226–240.
276 See the obituary of Feise published in *Monatshefte für Deutschen Unterricht* 58 (1966): 353–354.
277 Bernd, *Theodor Storm's Craft of Fiction*, 11–53.
278 E. Allen McCormick, *Theodor Storm's Novellen* (Chapel Hill, NC: University of North Carolina Press, 1964): 99–107, 119–129. See my review in *The German Quarterly* 38 (1965): 223–225.

that "contrary to McCormick's opinion," paintings "rather than saving something from death, seem to destroy" what they intended to memorialize.[279]

Soon after Duroche had published his essay, the criticism of *Aquis submersus* took a further, exciting step forward when two eminent English scholars, David A. Jackson and William A. Coupe, clashed with one another on the question of guilt in the novella.[280] Brilliantly argued on both sides, this constituted literary criticism at its best, and it certainly went a long way toward keeping this tale at center stage.

More attention was focused on *Aquis submersus* when, also in the early 1970s, another English critic, Patricia M. Boswell, published a lengthy, inspiring commentary on its "formal excellence."[281] This study, well-written and addressed in particular to university students all across the English-speaking world, had a wide appeal.

If Patricia Boswell had sought to engage the minds of a new readership by offering a remarkably comprehensive account of the novella's artistry, several years later an American colleague, William Cunningham, concentrated his efforts on calling attention, more specifically, to the water symbolism that is so important to the novella's structure.[282]

The next decade, the 1980s, enlivened the Anglo-American discussion of the novella even more. The criticism of that decade began in a familiar tone when the Scottish critic William Mullan, whom we mentioned earlier, echoed once more the (by now) substantial body of critical opinion that had insisted on the fundamental im-

---

279 Leonard L. Duroche, "Like and Look Alike: Symmetry and Irony in Theodor Storm's *Aquis submersus*," *Seminar* 7 (1971): 1–13, esp. 12.
280 David A. Jackson, "Die Überwindung der Schuld in der Novelle 'Aquis submersus,'" STSG 21 (1972): 45–56; W.A. Coupe, "Zur Frage der Schuld in 'Aquis submersus,'" STSG 24 (1975): 57–72.
281 Patricia M. Boswell, ed., *Theodor Storm. Aquis submersus*. (Oxford: Blackwell, 1974), x–lviii, esp. xi.
282 Wm. L. Cunningham, "Zur Wassersymbolik in 'Aquis submersus,'" STSG 27 (1978): 40–49.

portance of the concept of transience for any understanding of the work.[283] The Scottish journal in which Mullan's essay appeared in print had hardly sufficient time to circulate when another Scottish colleague, Mark G. Ward, felt prompted to take issue with it. With much argumentative skill, Ward shows that Mullan (and the whole succession of critics in whose footsteps he followed) had reduced the text to a statement of transience that did not give sufficient consideration to the social stratification and religious ideology of the era in which Storm had lived.[284] This was tantamount to a declaration of war within the camp of *Aquis submersus* critics, and it could not help but raise many eyebrows, the net effect of which made, of course, the preoccupation with this novella more exciting than every before, and not only in Scotland.

The year 1985 also witnessed the publication of two other absorbing contributions to *Aquis submersus* criticism. They came from the pens of American critics. Both contributions elevated this novella to the status of one of the brightest stars of all German literature in the second half of the nineteenth century. *Aquis submersus* became now not only one of Storm's most outstanding achievements but, beyond that, an important showpiece for the illustration of what the entire literary movement of Poetic Realism in Germany was all about. Roy C. Cowen accorded it the status of one of the ten most significant works of the period.[285] Robert C. Holub highlighted *Aquis submersus* even further when he analyzed it as one of the three most representative "reflections" of Poetic Realism.[286]

---

283 Mullan, 225–246, esp. 238–241.
284 Mark G. Ward, "Narrative and Ideological Tension in the Works of Theodor Storm. A Comparative Study of *Aquis submersus* and *Pole Poppenspäler*," *Deutsche Vierteljahrsschrift für Literaturwissenschaft und Geistesgeschichte* 59 (1985): 461.
285 Roy C. Cowen, *Der Poetische Realismus. Kommenter zu einer Epoche* (Munich: Winkler, 1985), 235–247.
286 Robert C. Holub, "Realism and Recollection. The Commemoration of Art and the Aesthetics of Abnegation in *Aquis submersus*," *Colloquia Germanica* 18 (1985): 120–139. See, too, the inclusion of this analysis in Robert Holub's volume *Reflections of Realism: Paradox, Norm, and Ideology in Nineteenth-Century German Prose* (Detroit: Wayne State University Press, 1991), 132–151.

The high critical response to *Aquis submersus* did not slacken in the next decade, the 1990s. Indeed, as far as American criticism was concerned, the response even seems to have improved. With a remarkably good knowledge of the secondary literature on the novella, and with valuable insights garnered from Hans-Georg Gadamer's teachings on hermeneutics, John Pizer, in 1992, revisited the themes of temporality, memory, history, and historical framing in the novella, confirming once again their essential importance for any interpretation, while giving us, at the same time, a fresh and refreshing understanding of their significance.[287]

In the same year David L. Dysart renewed and heightened our awareness of the role of painting in this novella. His book is addressed to the significance of painting for so many of Storm's tales, but for none of these does his argument about painting's contribution to narrative structure come across as persuasively as with *Aquis submersus*.[288]

Crowning everything else written on *Aquis submersus* to date, came the book that was written by Gunter H. Hertling in 1995.[289] His purpose is to engross his reader's attention with his own irrepressible fascination for this novella and to convince the reader that it is truly *the* towering pinnacle of all that Storm had created in prose fiction.

One might ask now whether the extensive and continued critical revitalization of *Aquis submersus* by so many critics has given this novella the power to circumvent the obliterating effects of passing time. For if the living extension of this work in criticism has anything to tell us, it is, above all, that *Aquis submersus* is no piece of

---

287 John Pizer, "Guilt, Memory, and the Motif of the Double in Storm's *Aquis submersus* and *Ein Doppelgänger*," *The German Quarterly* 65 (1992): 177–191, esp. 178–184.

288 David L. Dysart, *The Role of the Painting in the Works of Theodor Storm*. North American Studies in Nineteenth-Century German Literature, Vol. 11 (New York: Peter Lang, 1992): 101–110, 128.

289 Gunter H. Hertling, *Theodor Storms 'Meisterschuß' "Aquis submersus." Der Künstler zwischen Determiniertheit und Selbstvollendung* (Würzburg: Königshausen & Neumann, 1995). See my review in *The German Quarterly* 70 (1997): 304–306.

fading fiction, subject to the ravages of evanescence. Even the apparent futility of art to withstand the test of time, about which the narrator speaks so stirringly, seems to be canceled out once we realize that the criticism of this novella's artistry has kept the persons, facts, and memories of *Aquis submersus* very much alive up to the present day, more than 125 years after its first publication. Has the memory of criticism carried the final victory?

5. Final triumph: *Der Schimmelreiter*

The success that Storm felt he had achieved with *Aquis submersus* encouraged him, quite naturally, to continue his effort to create novellas "in oils." One new novella quickly followed another. By 1888, the year of his death, there were seventeen new titles on the shelves of German bookshops.

The most celebrated of these is unquestionably *Der Schimmelreiter*,[290] the last work Storm was able to complete (1888). Thomas Mann, the great "juge de Theodor Storm,"[291] said this novella was not only "the masterpiece with which Storm crowned his life-work" but also "the finest and boldest thing he had ever ventured on."[292] Who would care to argue with Mann?

Many factors in the intervening years between *Aquis submersus* and *Der Schimmelreiter* had combined to make this final triumph possible. Above all, of course, the continued, intensified experience in writing novellas helped Storm to develop the skill he displayed with his final production.

---

290 Many English translations are available. The most recent ones are (1) *The Dykemaster*, trans. Denis Jackson (London: Angel Books, 1996) and (2) *The Rider on the White Horse*, trans. Stella Humphries, in J. L. Sammons, ed., *German Novellas of Realism II*. The German Library, Vol. 38 (New York: Continuum, 1989).
291 Pitrou, "Thomas Mann, juge de Theodor Storm," 257–261.
292 Mann *Essays*, 285–286.

a. The flowering of correspondences with critics

No less important for the further development of his mastery of the novella at this time was the flowering of his correspondences with important men and women of letters. Storm had always been a prolific letter writer. But now, in the wake of his success with *Aquis submersus*, he had become famous so far and wide that his correspondences mushroomed. In these correspondences he received others' comments about his novellas, and he also freely gave his own comments on others' novellas. As a result, he became a greater authority on the novella and a more skilled practitioner of its art than ever before.

Storm corresponded with many, many men and women of letters. The Storm Society in Husum has been kept very busy sponsoring elaborate critical editions of these correspondences. Naturally, some of these exchanges of letters offered Storm more criticism and encouragement for his growth as an artist than others. The most important correspondents at this stage were surely Gottfried Keller, Paul Heyse, Erich Schmidt, Theodor Fontane, and Johannes Magnussen, although a good case might also be made for including in this notable array of adviser-critics the Dano-Prussian privy councillor Wilhelm Petersen, a lover of the arts and friend of poets.[293]

b. Gottfried Keller

Foremost amongst these critics was Gottfried Keller, Storm's illustrious Swiss competitor in the art of the novella. The correspondence between these two writers began when Storm sent his contemporary a copy of *Aquis submersus*. That sparked a great interest on the part of both authors in each other's subsequent accomplishments. They also regularly confided to one another their opinions on the novellas of others. Fifty-nine letters were exchanged.

This constitutes literary criticism at its best, and the educated public has always found that to be the case: to meet the demand of

---

[293] See *Storm–Petersen*. See, too, C. A. Bernd, "Wilhelm Petersen," *Schleswig-Holsteinisches Biographisches Lexikon* 3 (1974): 208–210.

readers over the years, nine editions of this correspondence have been published.

For Storm the critical stimulus he received from this renowned "Shakespeare der Novelle" (Shakespeare of the novella)[294] must have been salutary. It inspired him to compete with this great genius of the novella, perhaps even to excel him. More than ever before Storm would now focus his creative insights on this art form. So intensely did he engross himself in the novella that by 1885, as he admitted to Keller, his new deep interest in this genre had "verschluckt" (swallowed up) his impulse to write lyric poetry.[295]

c. Paul Heyse

Keller was not the only important writer who gave Storm invaluable food for thought at the time. A literary correspondence with Paul Heyse also provided him with much useful encouragement and criticism. This correspondence had begun as early as 1853, but it intensified when Storm sent this friend a copy of *Aquis submersus* in 1876, asking for his candid opinion. Heyse's reply was quickly forthcoming. He said it was the best that Storm had written to date. From then on, until Heyse commented on *Der Schimmelreiter*, almost two hundred letters of stimulating discussion of each other's work and of their rivals' contributions to the art of the novella were exchanged.

Heyse was then at the zenith of his own literary career and had become something of an institution in *belles lettres*. He had passionately promoted their cause and was, in particular, a conspicuous visionary on the craft of the novella, not only in Germany but all over Europe. He was especially familiar with that craft as it had early emerged in Renaissance Italy; and as a result of his knowledge of the Italian novella, he had developed a theory of the genre which became as famous — or even more famous — than his own fast-selling novellas. Storm was fortunate, in his huge correspondence

---

294 *Storm–Schmidt*, I, 33.
295 *Storm–Keller*, 126.

with this singularly versatile practitioner and promoter of the novella, to receive an invaluable polishing of his own prowess as a writer of novellas.

What likely proved to be most rewarding for Storm's further development as a writer of novellas was the great interest he took in Heyse's multi-volumed anthologies of known and unknown examples of the genre from all over Europe: the *Deutscher Novellenschatz* (Treasury of German Novellas), published in twenty-four volumes between 1871 and 1876; the *Novellenschatz des Auslandes* (Treasury of Foreign Novellas), published in fourteen volumes in 1872 and 1873; and the *Neuer deutscher Novellenschatz* (New Treasury of German Novellas) which appeared in twenty-four volumes between 1884 and 1887. This was a mammoth undertaking. Never before had such an effort been made to acquaint readers with this genre, nor was it ever to be repeated.

Few readers could have learned more from these volumes than Storm. Energetically, he corresponded with Heyse about which novellas to include. Often the opinions of the two correspondents clashed. But whether Storm sought to convince Heyse to include a particular novella, or whether he expressed reservations about a novella Heyse had chosen to include, the intense indoctrination Storm received regarding the capabilities of the genre certainly must have expanded his ideas of what the novella could do. How many novellas Storm must have read! How many must he have read over and over again, because they fascinated him, or because he wanted to be sure that he had neither overrated nor underrated their qualities. From how many novellas must he have learned new possibilities, or even tricks, of the art of novella-writing. There could be no doubt about it: Storm had received, shortly before he was to write *Der Schimmelreiter*, a most valuable set of lessons on what constituted successful and less-than-successful novella-writing. Doubtless he had already advanced far enough in his career as the writer of novellas not to need these lessons. Nevertheless, he now became a greater authority on the genre.

d. Erich Schmidt

A third major critical influence that heightened Storm's awareness of the possibilities for the genre of the novella came as a result of his extensive correspondence with Erich Schmidt. Schmidt was one of Germany's leading literary critics, and after 1886, when he received the chair for German Literature at the Royal University in Berlin, he became the most prominent of all the nation's academic critics. The correspondence began in 1877, soon after the publication of *Aquis submersus*, and during the last decade of Storm's life it, too, provided him with an incalculable stimulus for his further novellistic production. A total of 146 letters were exchanged.

This time Storm corresponded with a critic in the ivory tower of German academia, where critical persuasions, assumptions, and tastes in literature were determined, almost exclusively, by the legacies of Lessing, Goethe, and Schiller, and that meant a heavy concentration on drama, the genre in which all three of these luminaries had particularly excelled. Schmidt's chief claim to fame had been a monumental two-volume book on the dramatist Lessing. It seemed only natural, therefore, that, in this critical correspondence, drama should become as much a point of interest as the novella, and that this should sharpen Storm's notions about the dramatic quality of the novella — notions which he surely had learned from Danish practitioners, as I have earlier tried to show.

In the ebb and flow of commentary by Storm and Schmidt on both drama and the novella, Storm suddenly formulated, in October 1879, a thought he had felt all along but now understood more clearly than ever: that the novella constituted "eine Parallel-Dichtung des Dramas" (a related form of the drama),[296] as he wrote to Schmidt. Less than two years later, in July 1881, he reformulated the definition with even more conviction, calling the novella "die Schwester des Dramas" (the sister of the drama).[297]

---

296 *Storm–Schmidt*, I, 120.
297 Ibid., II, 43–44.

e. Theodor Fontane

The criticism of Fontane also played an important role at this particular stage of Storm's development. Fontane was the greatest critic of the age in Germany, and he and Storm were long-time friends. He had always assigned to Storm's poetry a higher place than he was willing to grant to the novellas: "seine höchste Vorzüglichkeit," Fontane wrote after Storm had died and completed his life's work, "ruht nicht in seinen vergleichsweise viel gelesenen und bewunderten Novellen, sondern in seiner Lyrik" (his preeminence rests not in his much read and much admired novellas, but rather in his lyrics).[298]

Nevertheless, Fontane did find words of flattery for some of Storm's accomplishments in prose. In the period in which Storm wrote "in oils," for instance, Fontane singled out *Zur Chronik von Grieshuus* (A Chapter in the History of Grieshuus, 1884) for exceptionally high praise. It was the most beautiful thing Storm had created, he wrote to his friend on October 28, 1884.[299]

Storm, in his reply of November 2, 1884, said that although he was happy to hear that Fontane liked *Zur Chronik von Grieshuus*, he found it unfair that his correspondent thought less of the novellas he had written prior to it. These, Storm insisted, were every bit as good.[300]

Of course, Storm knew his critical friend well enough to guess why he had a higher opinion of *Zur Chronik von Grieshuus*. Fontane was the unsurpassed social novelist of the time in Germany. He had written, by 1884, a brilliant series of tersely composed novels which had described human beings interlocked in an existing social order and acting in response to their environmental circumstances. *Zur Chronik von Grieshuus* had to have been much to Fontane's liking, for in that novella the action focuses on the fate of a noble squire

---

298 NFA, XV, 207.
299 *Storm–Fontane*, 136.
300 Ibid., 137.

caught between his love for the daughter of a serf and the dictates of his aristocratic society, which forbade such a relationship.

This social dimension of fiction had undoubtedly entered Storm's consciousness through the energetic efforts of Helen Mary Mannhardt. Little is known about her in Storm criticism. Indeed, her name has been scarcely mentioned. Yet she was an active — perhaps the most active — participant in the literary gatherings that occurred every fortnight in Storm's home during the 1880s. A highly erudite Englishwoman with prominent literary forbears (according to her descendants), she was naturally well-acquainted with the English novel of her time and its concern for men and women whose lives were determined by the foibles and liabilities of Victorian society. The English social novel must have served, then, as the basis for the opinions she regularly voiced in Storm's gatherings, and it seems likely that he learned from her to think about trying his hand at a fiction of social forces.

Thus, doubtless, *Zur Chronik von Grieshuus* came into being, and for a while he seemed tempted to continue writing in the vein of that novella. In both *John Riew'* (1885) and *Der Doppelgänger* (The Double, 1886–1887), for instance, social issues loom large. Yet, however much Helen Mannhardt's spirited comments and Fontane's flattery may have encouraged him to write novellas of social awareness, he knew that this form of fiction was essentially alien to him. He would be trying to be someone other than he was. Nothing could have strengthened him more in this conviction than Fontane's belittling criticism of the novellas written prior to *Zur Chronik von Grieshuus*. That angered him. He could not — or would not — abandon for long the lesson of the Danish novella he had learned and adapted so well.

In *Der Schimmelreiter*, therefore, he would again embrace the tone in which he had matured, only this time, doubtless in part because of his lingering anger over Fontane's critique, with even more determination than before.

f. Johannes Magnussen

This Danish man of letters, whose name, alas, is rarely mentioned in Storm scholarship,[301] may not have been a literary critic in the strict sense of the term, but his importance for the course of Storm's literary career in the 1880s should not be overlooked. He was a professional translator of foreign literature into the Danish language and, as such, had translated eleven novellas of Storm into Danish.

Magnussen was not, of course, the first translator to contribute to Storm's reception in the Danish-speaking world. We already mentioned earlier Alfred Ipsen. There were also others, presumably more than the ones listed in the catalogue of the Royal Library at Copenhagen. Anonymous translations from foreign tongues appeared at the time in Danish journals in great abundance, for there were then no copyright agreements with other nations.

Yet Magnussen's translations had a different appeal than those of his competitors. For one thing, he had attended school for many years in Husum and possessed a knowledge of the German language as well as the background of Storm's novellas that far exceeded any other Danish translator's. He was also very anxious that his renderings should be advertised as authorized translations. He knew that Storm could read Danish and he wanted, therefore, the benefit of the author's approbation before the translations could appear in print. Storm cooperated fully, not only in giving his approval, but in reading the publisher's proofs and commenting on various Danish renderings of the original German versions.[302]

This was the only time Storm authorized translations of his works into other languages, and it was the only time he discussed in detail with a translator individual renderings. Doubtless this was because he had a better knowledge of Danish than of any other language in which translations of his works were appearing, but it is also likely

---

301 The scholarly interest in Magnussen first surfaced as a result of the re-editing of Storm's correspondence with Heyse. See *Storm–Heyse*, III, 190.

302 See Dieter Lohmeier, "Storm und sein dänischer Übersetzer Johannes Magnussen. Mit unveröffentlichten Briefen," STSG 33 (1984): 53–70.

that these Danish translations helped him sense the remarkable affinity his fictional pieces enjoyed with the Danish mind. How else could one explain that translations of his works were receiving a much greater reception in little Denmark than in any other country, even though the size of the readerships in those nations was much larger? Judging from the tone of the letters exchanged with Magnussen, Storm must have been as eager for the Danes to have an excellent comprehension of his novellas as the translator was eager to gain more readers for Storm in Denmark with meticulously accurate translations.

Storm's critical correspondence with Magnussen continued intermittently for a period of five years, from 1880 to 1885, a time in which he was much impressed, as he said, with the refreshing tone of Danish literature.[303] In 1885, the second of Magnussen's volumes of Storm translations appeared in attractive binding.[304] The correspondence with this "gewissenhaften" (conscientious), "liebenswürdigen" (congenial), and "findigen" (resourceful) Danish literary interpreter,[305] no less than the flattering reception of Storm's works with the kindred Danish reading public, could only confirm to the author from Husum that, once again, it was in his application of the lesson of the Danish novella that he had found his calling as a writer of prose fiction, and that he should continue to answer this calling in his writing, with strengthened determination. *Der Schimmelreiter* would become the paradigmatic example of his renewed calling.

---

303 On November 4, 1881, Storm had encouraged his versatile friend Paul Heyse to continue reading Danish literature, for "es circulirt ein recht frisches Blut in diesem germanischen Jüngling," i.e., in Denmark's literature (*Storm–Heyse*, II, 91).
304 Theodor Storm, *Fem Noveller* (Copenhagen: Schou, 1885). The first volume, entitled *Fire Noveller*, appeared with the same publisher in 1883. Both volumes are in the Royal Library at Copenhagen.
305 See Storm's characterizations of Magnussen in *Storm–Keller*, 105, and in *Storm–Heyse*, III, 44.

g. The specter of impending death

Another factor that contributed to igniting and sustaining the creative flame that produced *Der Schimmelreiter* was the specter of impending death, which almost constantly hovered over Storm in the 1880s. Reading his letters, we learn that as early as 1878 thoughts about the twilight of his life began to consume him. In the summer of that year it was clear to everyone in the family that his eighty-one-year-old mother was fast moving towards death. (His father had already preceded her.) His mother's approaching death, he wrote to Erich Schmidt in January 1879, reminded him of his own mortality.[306] He was only twenty years younger than his mother. Now he would soon be the senior in the family, and the next to go.

Storm had to make the necessary preparations. He would follow in the footsteps of his wife's parents in their old age and withdraw from public life and move to the seclusion of the remote village of Hademarschen in Holstein.

His mother died on July 28, 1879. The sale of the ancestral home followed. With his share of the estate at his disposal, he then retired from his judicial position in Husum on May 1, 1880, and resettled in Hademarschen. He was not quite sixty-three, but his strength was failing, as he wrote to Erich Schmidt in June 1880, and eventide, he felt, was falling.[307]

Despondency over the hopeless lives of his sons Hans and Karl only made him more aware of the descending darkness. Hans, the eldest son, had become an incurable alcoholic. His physical condition steadily worsened. Death finally came to him on December 5, 1886. Karl, the youngest son, was suffering from a venereal disease which by the 1880s had advanced so noticeably that, as the father knew, there could no longer be any hope for a recovery.

Exeunt omnes, words which Storm had frequently used,[308] now became particularly meaningful to him.

---

306 *Storm–Schmidt*, II, 11.
307 Ibid., II, 15.
308 *Storm–Heyse*, I, 67; II, 70; III, 79.

Of course, these words became most meaningful when his own health markedly degenerated. From October 1886 to February 1887 he had been confined much of the time to his bed. As spring came, he seemed to feel well enough to be again at his desk. In the midst of writing, however, he found himself suffering from stomach pains that would not subside. Suspecting the worst, he demanded that his physician be frank with him about the ailment's exact nature. The doctor obliged and said it was stomach cancer. Upon hearing this, Storm collapsed, gave himself over to gloom, and lost all will to continue writing *Der Schimmelreiter*, with which he had been preoccupied intermittently for quite some time.

Fortunately, Storm had a brother who was a physician. This brother, Aemil, organized a hocus-pocus *concilium* of three doctors who quickly pronounced the earlier diagnosis of cancer as wrong; the ailment, they said, was not malignant after all. The trick worked. Storm bounced back and, refreshed in spirit by the positive verdict, returned to his desk once more to work on his great novella.

Still, he knew that time was running out for him. In September of 1887 he reached the biblical age of seventy. He realized, too, that despite the diagnosis of the three physicians, his health was not improving. Indeed, he was always feeling worse. Would he be able to win the race with impending death and finish *Der Schimmelreiter* before it was too late?

This thought certainly must have weighed heavily on his mind while he wrote the novella, and it must also be considered an important factor in making the elements of passing time and evanescence stand out, as we shall see, so conspicuously in the narrative design.

h. Applying once more the lesson of the Danish novella

The combination of many factors made it possible for Storm, with *Der Schimmelreiter*, to bring to a triumphant conclusion the lesson he had learned from the Danish novella. Nothing in this tale alerts us more to its Danish heritage than the strong sense of drama we perceive here. For it was the dramatic component, as we said earlier, which had let the Danish novella assume a different form than the novella of the German tradition.

Criticism has not usually stressed the dramatic quality of this novella, but Thomas Mann — that great judge of Storm — saw it clearly when he said that, in this tale, Storm had elevated the novella "as the epic sister of the drama" to a height never before reached.[309]

Amongst the professional critics it was primarily the Canadian Germanist Hermann Boeschenstein who reminded us of this novella's rich "dramatic structure."[310] This critic addressed himself to what he considered to be the most conspicuous works of German literature in the nineteenth century, and he did not use the epithet "dramatic" to describe any of the other many works of prose fiction he discussed. Boeschenstein, I should also like to point out, was an authority on the novellas of Gottfried Keller; but as impressed as he was with Keller's prose fiction, it did not possess for him the deep dramatic quality that he found so characteristic of *Der Schimmelreiter*. This quality, he knew, made *Der Schimmelreiter* different from the novellas of Keller and from those of other practitioners writing in German. What Boeschenstein perhaps did not realize was that this different quality of Storm's novella derived from the author's Danish literary heritage.

The drama in *Der Schimmelreiter* is, of course, none other than that between the forces of time and memory which we had found to be so constitutive for the other novellas we discussed at some length, only this time it has acquired a far sharper profile than ever before. For now the dramatic conflict assumes a heightened intensity because it is shown through the prism of two opposing *dramatis personae*.[311]

---

309 Mann *Essays*, 286.
310 Hermann Boeschenstein, *German Literature of the Nineteenth Century* (London: Edward Arnold, 1969), 132.
311 The following analysis is a revised and expanded version of the remarks on *Der Schimmelreiter* included in my book *Poetic Realism in Scandinavia and Central Europe 1820–1895* (Columbia, SC: Camden House, 1995). It represents my increased understanding of this novella and its context.

The one is the young, tempestuous dikemaster Hauke Haien, whom most interpreters — focusing on the narrative (German) rather than on the dramatic (Danish) perspective of this novella — have believed to be the one and only main character. He stands out, as we shall see, as the victim of passing time.

The other main character is the old, contemplative schoolmaster who personifies victory over passing time, for he succeeds in rescuing Hauke Haien from the oblivion into which the latter seemingly had been swept.

Throughout the core of this dramatic novella both characters rival one another in counterpoint fashion. In certain stretches of the central story the stage lights shine on one main character, and he becomes the object of our attention. Then a break occurs, followed by a shift in attention to the other main character. The alternating pattern goes on back and forth in the story and does much to highlight its fundamental dramatic structure.

i. Hauke, the victim of time

As soon as we are introduced to Hauke, we are told about the Greek mathematician Euclid. The narrator must have some special reason for making us aware of the science of mathematics at the beginning of Hauke's story. It does not take long to find out why: we soon feel invited to take part in a mathematical exercise: to count the astonishing number of references to chronological time.

In no other Storm novella do references to chronological time play as enormous a role as in *Der Schimmelreiter*. In no other novella do we sense the influence of Steen Steensen Blicher's novella of time as extensively as here. Indeed, we do not even need to prove that Storm had ever read *En Landsbydegns Dagbog* — always a hazardous undertaking in comparative literature — to recognize the parallelism between the two novellas and to assume a genetic influence which, in turn, gives us more reason to count the references to the passing of time in much the same way as does the reader of Blicher's novella.

Hauke's story begins "in der Mitte des vorigen Jahrhunderts" (in the middle of the last century), i.e., in the 1700s. On the next page we read that "die Stachelbeeren ... wieder blühten" (the gooseberries were blossoming again). The long winter season is over, and it is early spring. But early spring does not tarry long, for soon "die Bohnen blühten" (the beanfields were in bloom), and we know then that late spring has arrived. From "Ostern bis Martini" (Easter to St. Martin's Day), i.e., November 11, Hauke works on the dike. We learn what happens "Ende Oktober" (at the end of October). A few lines further it is "Allerheiligentag" (All Saints' Day), i.e., November 1. Two lines later "das Christfest" (Christmas) is mentioned. Next we hear that "es [ist] wieder Winter geworden" (winter has returned again). A whole year has passed. Before long it is "Februar" (February).

And so it goes throughout Hauke's story. Counting these references we become evermore aware of transience, page by page. Particularly at the beginning of paragraphs we are reminded that more time has passed, e.g., "Nach einem andern Jahr" (After yet another year), "mehrere Jahre später"(several years later), "So war der Sommer und der Herbst vergangen" (Thus summer and autumn had passed), "drei Jahre ... [waren] hingegangen" (three years had gone by), etc.

Correspondingly, Hauke's life and his life's happiness ebb away. His is a life that illustrates how the steady (funeral) cortège of passing hours, days, weeks, months, seasons, and years brings disaster in its wake. His life mirrors how the sea's "Gezeiten" (the tides = time, as in even-tide, yule-tide, etc.) — always in either the foreground or background of this narrative drama — ceaselessly pound, weaken, damage, and even destroy the man-made dikes which had been built to preserve all life within their bounds from the *aquis submersus* that Storm detailed in the tale of that title. Significantly, Hauke, the dikemaster, whose profession it is to hold back the tides of time, himself perishes in their restless waves.

Hauke, when he first comes on stage in this novella, spends all of his time, it seems, watching the rising and falling of the tides, and observing how the dikes succeed and fail in preventing the floods from engulfing the land. When he is not near the dikes, he immerses

The Novellas

"Und schon kam unten aus der Marsch der Leichenzug heran, eine Menge Wagen aus allen Kirchspielsdörfern; auf dem vordersten stand der schwere Sarg, die beiden blanken Rappen des deichgräflichen Stalles zogen ihn schon den sandigen Anberg zur Geest hinauf" (And the funeral procession was already emerging from the marshland below, a collection of wagons from all the villages in the parish; the heavy coffin rested on the leading wagon which was already being hauled up the sandy slope towards the uplands by two shiny black horses from the dykemaster's own stable) — *Der Schimmelreiter*.

himself in his Euclid. But this life free from care does not last long. When he becomes a teenager, he has to join the other men in his district and perform hard work on the dikes. That keeps him busy from early spring until late autumn.

But having only to work half the year is a phase that also does not last long for Hauke. The day arrives when he has to take a full-time job. He becomes an apprentice to the dikemaster, which proves to be more of a burden than he could have anticipated. At every turn he feels the ill will of the jealous foreman, Ole Peters. With the passage of more time the rift between the two employees widens. It might have become unbearable for each if Ole had not quit his job in order to marry and assume the duties of managing the farm of his bride.

Hauke is then promoted to the job of his former rival. The joy, however, is short-lived, for one year later he, too, feels compelled to tender his resignation. His father has grown old and feeble, no longer able to take care of himself. Hauke must help him. A few months later Hauke has a death and a funeral on his hands.

Uplifting events follow for a change, but only in order to point in the direction of further, more intense sorrow. Hauke becomes secretly engaged to the daughter of the dikemaster, something which might have brought a sense of joyous relief to the story of gloom and the chronicle of time's inexorable advance. This, however, is not the case, for the mention of the engagement is followed by a most extensive death and burial scene, this time of the bride's father. We sense the gloom in the novella now more heavily than at the time of Hauke's father's passing.

One year later Hauke and his bride are married. It must have been a very lavish wedding, for Hauke had married the richest young woman in the area, and by virtue of his marriage to the daughter of the deceased dikemaster, he himself now becomes the dikemaster, the most prominent as well as the most influential man in the community. Yet, almost unbelievably, there is no mention whatsoever of a grandiose wedding which touched the lives of the bridal couple and of the entire populace of the region. The heavy gloom of the funeral atmosphere we felt when the two older men reached their appointed ends was not to be arrested with the portrayal of a subsequent scene of wedding joy triumphing over the former gloom. On the contrary, in the further course of time, life only becomes more difficult for Hauke. Marital bliss eludes him. The young couple knows nothing but work. Each has less and less time for the other.

Even the landscape in which Hauke and his bride live has a doleful appearance. The sea is always a source of menace, never one of bliss or rejuvenation. In the spring all references to colorful blossoms are noticeably absent. In the summer there is no mention of the stately poplar trees or picturesque windmills which usually give such charm to the North Sea coastal setting just south of the Dano-German frontier, in which the story's action takes place. Neither is there any mention of the wild vegetation or of the melodious flutter of the white seagulls crisscrossing on the northern blue horizon. In autumn the bright purple and rose colors of heather in bloom are nowhere to be seen. We are reminded of the gloom that prevails in Blicher's fictional scene-painting on the other side of the border between Denmark and Germany.

Most revealing for the gloom surrounding Hauke's marriage is the absence of any laughter of children. Many years of married life went by, and it seemed as though no child would ever come. Finally, in the ninth year of the marriage, a child is born. The joyous occasion, however, is short-lived, for as the child grows up her parents discover she is feeble-minded. Sorrow is now added to the loneliness of the marriage.

Hauke's life in the community contributes further to the gloom that deepens in time. A campaign of gossip against Hauke finds more and more adherents. The rumor spreads that Hauke had only gotten the post of the dikemaster because of his wife's money, and not because of any merits of his own. This provokes him to begin the construction of a new dike around reclaimed land in order to prove himself as a dikemaster. The onerous undertaking and the burdensome costs involved breed more discontent amongst the citizenry. When Hauke's last friend, Jewe Manners, dies of old age, everyone in the community, it seems, is against him.

Hauke's battle with both the hostile tides and his no less hostile fellow men eventually becomes more than he can bear. His strength is sapped, and in a moment of weakness, and against his better judgment, he gives in to the opposition and lets the old dike be repaired on a cheaper, but less effective plan. What then occurs is all too predictable. In a storm the inadequately repaired dike breaks at the point where it joins the new dike. The only way to prevent the raging waters of high tide from rushing in and submerging the unprotected village would be to breach Hauke's new outer dike and let the floods disperse in the area lying between the two dikes. Hauke refuses, however, to sacrifice his new dike. Yet this fatal choice gives the narrator the opportunity to demonstrate his point: that human life perishes in the maw of all-consuming time. With the continued rise of the "Ge*zeit*en" and the consequent collapse of the dike, Hauke and his family drown and vanish in the tides of oblivion: *aquis submersus*.

j. The schoolmaster, the victor over time

Yet in the drama of life, according to Storm, there are two opposing forces. We see in this novellistic drama not only the victim of time but just as clearly the victor over time. In *Der Schimmelreiter*, as I said earlier, this victor is the schoolmaster.

The victor over time plays such a conspicuous role here that we, as spectators of the dramatic action, ask ourselves who is the primary character, Hauke or the schoolmaster. The question is a moot one. The schoolmaster is the first to come on stage and he is the last to leave. That gives him an undeniable claim to precedence. On the other hand, Hauke is at the center of the stage longer, and that makes him loom forward in the artistic design.

By recalling the story of Hauke Haien some eighty years after the latter had vanished in the tides of oblivion, the schoolmaster impersonates the power of memory to counteract the action of time that had destroyed Hauke. On seven different occasions in this dramatic tale the schoolmaster puts in his appearance and lets us know that Hauke, his life, hopes, and dreams have not been as totally submerged as we were given to believe.

The song of evanescence, which the tale of Hauke could echo, no longer seems, when the schoolmaster frequently interrupts his story, as dismal as it first sounded. So successfully, indeed, can the schoolmaster-actor bring Hauke to life on stage that we, as well as the entire company of minor characters listening to him, feel that Hauke is never far away from the setting over which the schoolmaster presides.

Prior to the schoolmaster's powerful recollection there were, as we hear, also other attempts made to keep Hauke alive beyond his appointed time in history. The most important of these is doubtless the Frisian saga in which Hauke Haien had lived on, from mouth to mouth and from generation to generation. We are also told that an old housekeeper had preserved in her memory the story of Hauke. Yet neither a teller of the saga nor the housekeeper puts in an appearance on stage to narrate their stories.

Storm chose only the schoolmaster to demonstrate in person the victory of recollection. As a result, the schoolmaster appears to be the most reliable provider of the facts. Storm endows him with a power to bring alive a character from yesteryear that he did not give to the others. The victory of memory that the schoolmaster represents, then, resounds all the more loudly. He plays the part of the chief adversary of Hauke in the drama to outwit time.

k. Compounding the drama

In the battle between time and memory in *Der Schimmelreiter* there are also two important subsidiary *dramatis personae* who have their relevance for the drama: (1) a journalist and (2) Theodor Storm himself in fictional disguise.

The first of these, sitting on the stage together with the schoolmaster, puts into a printed form the story of Hauke that the schoolmaster had kept alive in his memory. With this printed recollection the role of the schoolmaster in the drama changes. Instead of being the victor over time, as we observed him when he alternated with Hauke in the leading role on the stage, he now becomes the victim of passing time by virtue of his impending death from old age. The journalist, preserving the story of Hauke beyond the schoolmaster's lifespan and in the more permanent form of a printed memoir, becomes the new victor.

The same procedure repeats itself with the other subsidiary actor, the fictional figure of Storm. As the journalist could act as the victor over time after the passing of the schoolmaster, then that journalist, too, changes roles and becomes the victim rather than the victor. Now it is the Storm-figure who is the recaller and preserver of Hauke's story, for when he narrates it to us, it is well over half a century after the journalist had committed it to print, and the journal in which it was printed can no longer be found. Both the journalist, presumably no longer alive, and his memorializing essay had fallen, therefore, victim to the further passage of time. The Storm-figure is the new victor.

Yet, the fictional Storm also, in turn, becomes a dubious conserver of former life. He is telling us the story in the year 1888, or shortly beforehand, while writing this novella and knowing full well that his health was failing. Soon he and his ability to remember would also become things of the past. What then?, we ask.

We pause to reflect, and quickly notice that we are not allowed to close the book on a negative note. For in the final sentence we read that a brilliant golden sun had risen over the seascape. This startles us. Throughout Storm's novellistic production, and especially throughout *Der Schimmelreiter*, we had grown accustomed to hearing about the setting of the sun. Why did Storm, only a few months before he died, wish to end this novella, which he surely knew was his last, on an optimistic note?

Death was not to have the final say. The memorializing medium of fiction, the victory of art in the shadow of death, would prevail instead. When Storm mulled over the conclusion to *Der Schimmelreiter*, he must have felt that he had composed an *immortal* work of art: the story of Hauke Haien would not fade into oblivion but would be remembered in the hearts and minds of readers for ages to come. He was not wrong. According to Gerd Weinreich, who has researched this point, *Der Schimmelreiter* is now, in the whole world, the best known and most widely read novella of the German language.[312] The secondary literature on it is vast and keeps growing so that one can hardly survey any longer all of the interpretations that continue to find their way into print.

---

312 Gerd Weinreich, *Theodor Storm: Der Schimmelreiter* (Frankfurt am Main: Diesterweg, 1988), 94.

The Last Months

On February 9, 1888, Storm sent the manuscript of *Der Schimmelreiter* to the publisher Elwin Paetel. The latter was much impressed with what he read. (His flattering comment, in an unpublished letter to Storm dated March 5, 1888, is preserved in the Schleswig-Holsteinische Landesbibliothek in Kiel.) In great haste he handed the pages over to the printer with the (apparently) urgent request to start the printing process immediately. The printer quickly complied, for barely two weeks after Storm had mailed the handwritten text off to Paetel, he was already busy correcting the galley proofs. In the April and May 1888 issues of the *Deutsche Rundschau* he could finally experience the joy of seeing the novella in print.

This joy, however, was not so unbounded as it should have been, for his physical condition had by now gone from bad to worse. He was suffering greatly and hardly knew any more what it meant to have a good night's sleep.

Significantly, when his end was near, he asked his daughter Gertrud to read to him from Hans Christian Andersen's *O.T.*, a novel about life in Denmark in the early decades of the century. The action moves back and forth across the Danish landscape between the royal capital at Copenhagen and Lemvig on the North Sea coast, the town in which Storm's Danish translator Johannes Magnussen lived. With these nostalgic glimpses of Danish life from the time of his youth Storm now, during his dying days, wished to be comforted. It was like a trip to the world of his own yesteryear, and he must have nodded in hearty assent as Gertrud read to him, for — despite the pain he was experiencing — he asked her to keep reading.

On July 4, 1888, Storm breathed his last. It was his wish to be buried in the family crypt in Husum in the graveyard lying next to the almshouse he had immortalized in his novella *In St. Jürgen*. The Governor General of Schleswig-Holstein, Georg von Steinmann, was at the station in Husum on July 7 when the funeral train from Hademarschen arrived. He and a huge crowd then accompanied the coffin to its final resting place.

Selected Bibliography

Collected Works

The best and most convenient current edition of Storm's works is *Theodor Storm, Sämtliche Werke*, eds. K. E. Laage & D. Lohmeier, 4 vols. Frankfurt am Main: Deutscher Klassiker Verlag, 1987–1988.

English Translations

Aquis submersus. Translated by Jeffrey L. Sammons. In J. L. Sammons, ed., *German Novellas of Realism II*. The German Library, Vol. 38. New York: Continuum, 1989.

The Dykemaster (Der Schimmelreiter). Translated by Denis Jackson. London: Angel Books; Chester Springs, PA: Dufour, 1996.

Hans and Heinz Kirch, with *Immensee* and *Journey to a Hallig (Eine Halligfahrt)*. Translated by Denis Jackson and Anja Nauck. London: Angel Books, 1999; Chester Springs, PA: Dufour, 2000.

Immensee. Translated by C. W. Bell. In V. Lange, ed., *Great German Short Stories. An Anthology*. New York: The Modern Library, 1952.

Immensee. Translated by Ronald Taylor. In R. Taylor, ed., *3 German Classics*. London: John Calder; New York: Riverrun Press, 1985.

The Rider on the White Horse and Selected Stories (Der Schimmelreiter, Im Saal, Immensee, Ein grünes Blatt, Im Sonnenschein, Veronika, In St. Jürgen, Aquis submersus). Translated by James Wright. New York: New American Library, 1964.

The Rider on the White Horse. Translated by Muriel Almon. In E. Mornin, ed., *Three Eerie Tales from 19th Century German*. New York: Ungar, 1975.

St. George's Almshouse (In St. Jürgen). Translated by G.W. McKay. In F. J. Lamport, ed., *The Penguin Book of German Stories*. Harmondsworth: Penguin Books, 1974.

The White Horseman and Beneath the Flood (Der Schimmelreiter, Aquis submersus). Translated by Geoffrey Skelton. London: The New English Library, 1962.

The White Horse Rider (Der Schimmelreiter). Translated by Stella Humphries. London & Glasgow: Blackie, 1966. Reprinted in J. L. Sammons, ed., *German Novellas of Realism II*. The German Library, Vol. 38. New York: Continuum, 1989.

Bibliographies

Teitge, Hans-Erich. *Theodor Storm Bibliographie*. Berlin: Deutsche Staatsbibliothek, 1967.
Sobel, Alfred. *Theodor Storm-Bibliographie 1967–1991*. Berliner Bibliographische Bücher, ed. B. Benedikt, Vol. 2. Wiesbaden & Berlin: Sobel, 1993.
The annual *Schriften der Theodor-Storm-Gesellschaft* provide periodic updates.

Editions of Letters

A useful selection can be found in *Theodor Storm. Briefe*, ed. P. Goldammer, 2 vols. Berlin & Weimar: Aufbau, 1972, ²1984.
Theodor Storm. Briefe an seine Braut, ed. G. Storm, Braunschweig: Westermann, 1916.
Theodor Storm-Hartmuth und Laura Brinkmann Briefwechsel, ed. A. Stahl, Berlin: Erich Schmidt, 1986.
Storm als Erzieher. Seine Briefe an Ada Christen, ed. O. Katann, Vienna: Hollinek, 1948.
Theodor Storms Briefe an Friedrich Eggers, ed. H.W. Seidel, Berlin: Curtius, 1911.
Theodor Storm–Constanze Esmarch Briefwechsel, ed. R. Fasold, 2 vols. Berlin: Erich Schmidt, 2002.
Theodor Storm–Ernst Esmarch Briefwechsel, ed. A.T. Alt, Berlin: Erich Schmidt, 1979.
Theodor Storm–Theodor Fontane Briefwechsel, ed. J. Steiner, Berlin: Erich Schmidt, 1981.
Theodor Storm. Briefe an seine Frau, ed. G. Storm, Braunschweig: Westermann, 1915.

Theodor Storm–Klaus Groth Briefwechsel, ed. B. Hinrichs, Berlin: Erich Schmidt, 1990.
Theodor Storm's Briefe in die Heimat aus den Jahren 1853–1864, ed. G. Storm, Berlin: Curtius, 1907.
Theodor Storm–Paul Heyse Briefwechsel, ed. C. A. Bernd, 3 vols. Berlin: Erich Schmidt, 1969–1974.
Theodor Storm. Briefe an Dorothea Jensen und an Georg Westermann, ed. E. Lüpke, Braunschweig: Westermann, 1942.
Theodor Storm und Dorothea geb. Jensen. Ein unveröffentlichter Briefwechsel, ed. G. Ranft, STSG 28 (1979): 34–97.
Theodor Storm–Gottfried Keller Briefwechsel, ed. K. E. Laage, Berlin: Erich Schmidt, 1992.
Theodor Storm–Eduard Mörike / Theodor Storm–Margarethe Mörike Briefwechsel, eds. H. & W. Kohlschmidt, Berlin: Erich Schmidt, 1978.
Theodor Storms Briefwechsel mit Theodor Mommsen, ed. H.-E. Teitge, Weimar: Böhlau, 1966.
Theodor Storm–Wilhelm Petersen Briefwechsel, ed. B. Coghlan, Berlin: Erich Schmidt, 1984.
Blätter der Freundschaft. Aus dem Briefwechsel zwischen Theodor Storm und Ludwig Pietsch, ed. V. Pauls, Heide: Boyens, 1939, ²1943.
Theodor Storm–Heinrich Schleiden Briefwechsel, ed. P. Goldammer, Berlin: Erich Schmidt, 1995.
Theodor Storm–Erich Schmidt Briefwechsel, ed. K. E. Laage, 2 vols. Berlin: Erich Schmidt, 1972–1976.
Theodor Storm–Otto und Hans Speckter Briefwechsel, ed. W. Hettche, Berlin: Erich Schmidt, 1991.
Theodor Storm und Iwan Turgenjew. Persönliche und literarische Beziehungen, Einflüsse, Briefe, Bilder, ed. K.E. Laage, Heide: Boyens, 1967.

Secondary Literature

Ackermann, Friedrich. "Zum Rhythmusproblem: verdeutlicht an Storms Gedicht 'Hyazinthen.'" *Die Pädagogische Provinz* 19 (1965): 26–39.
Albertsen, Leif Ludwig. *On the Threshold of a Golden Age*. Copenhagen: The Royal Danish Ministry of Foreign Affairs, 1979.
———. "Theodor Storm mellem Danmark og Tyskland." *Slesvigland* 5 (1984): 134–135.

Alt, A. Tilo. *Theodor Storm.* New York: Twayne, 1973.
Bender, Hans. "Liebesmüdigkeit" in *Frankfurter Anthologie 5*, ed. M. Reich-Ranicki. Frankfurt am Main: Insel, 1980: 114–116.
Bennett, E(dwin) K. *A History of the German Novelle.* Revised and continued by H. M. Waidson. Cambridge, England: University Press, 1934, ²1974.
Bernd, Clifford Albrecht. *Theodor Storm's Craft of Fiction.* Chapel Hill, NC: University of North Carolina Press, 1963, ²1966.
——. "Wilhelm Petersen." *Schleswig-Holsteinisches Biographisches Lexikon* 3 (1974): 208–210.
——. *German Poetic Realism.* Boston: Twayne, 1981.
——. *Poetic Realism in Scandinavia and Central Europe 1820–1895.* Columbia, SC: Camden House, 1995.
——. "The German Lyric in the Age of Poetic Realism" in *Life's Golden Tree. Essays in German Literature from the Renaissance to Rilke*, eds. T. Kerth & G. C. Schoolfield. Columbia, SC: Camden House, 1996: 171–181.
——. "Vom dänischen Kulturerbe. Um ein neues Verständnis für Storms Lyrik bittend" in *Stormlektüren. Festschrift für Karl Ernst Laage zum 80. Geburtstag*, eds. G. Eversberg, D. Jackson, E. Pastor. Würzburg: Königshausen & Neumann, 2000: 33–45.
——. "Storm's Debt to the Danish Muse and its Disavowal in Criticism" in *Kuriosum als Erkenntnis*, eds. A. Hübener & E. Unglaub. Flensburg: Futura Edition, 2002: 7–12.
Bernhardt, Wilhelm. *Hauptfakta aus der Geschichte der deutschen Litteratur / A Short History of the Poetical Literature of Germany.* New York, Cincinnati, Chicago: American Book Co., 1892.
Bloom, Harold. *The Western Canon.* New York: Harcourt Brace, 1994.
Boeschenstein, Hermann. *German Literature of the Nineteenth Century.* London: Edward Arnold, 1969.
Böttger, Fritz. *Theodor Storm in seiner Zeit.* Berlin: Verlag der Nation, n.d. (1959).
Bollenbeck, Georg. *Theodor Storm. Eine Biographie.* Frankfurt am Main: Insel, 1988.
Borup, M., ed. *Breve fra og til Meïr Goldschmidt.* Copenhagen: Rosenkilde & Bagger, 1963.
Boswell, Patricia M., ed. *Theodor Storm. Aquis submersus.* Oxford: Blackwell, 1974.

———. *Theodor Storm* (Leicester German Poets). Leicester: University Press, 1989.
Brandt, Otto. *Geschichte Schleswig-Holsteins*. Kiel: Mühlau, 1925, [7]1976.
Bruns, Alken. *Übersetzung als Rezeption: Deutsche Übersetzer skandinavischer Literatur von 1860 bis 1900*. Neumünster: Wachholtz, 1977.
Carr, William. *Schleswig-Holstein 1815–48. A Study in National Conflict*. Manchester: University Press, 1963.
Cecil, Lamar. *Wilhelm II. Prince and Emperor, 1859–1900*. Chapel Hill, NC: University of North Carolina Press, 1989.
Christensen, Carlo. *Peter von Scholten. A Chapter of the History of the Virgin Islands*. Lemvig: Nielsen, 1955.
Corrinth, Curt. "Ein unbekannter Bekenntnisbrief Storms." *Deutsche Allgemeine Zeitung*, 29. Juni 1942.
Coupe, W. A. "Zur Frage der Schuld in 'Aquis submersus.'" STSG 24 (1975): 57–72.
Cowen, Roy C. *Der Poetische Realismus. Kommentar zu einer Epoche*. Munich: Winkler, 1985.
Cunningham, Wm. L. "Zur Wassersymbolik in 'Aquis submersus.'" STSG 27 (1978): 40–49.
de Mylius, Johan. "Hans Christian Andersen and the Music World" in *Hans Christian Andersen. Danish Writer and Citizen of the World*, ed. S. H. Rossel. Amsterdam: Rodopi, 1994: 176–208.
Detering, Heinrich. "Produktive Grenzgänge: Literatur zwischen den Kulturen" in *Grenzgänge: Skandinavisch-deutsche Nachbarschaften*, ed. H. Detering. Göttingen: Wallstein, 1996: 11–27.
———. "'In mir segelt und schwimmt noch alles': Hans Christian Andersen in Kiel" in *Kuriosum als Erkenntnis*, eds. A. Hübener & E. Unglaub. Flensburg: Futura Edition, 2002: 45–53.
Döhring, Erich. *Geschichte der Christian-Albrechts-Universität zu Kiel 1665–1965, Vol. III: Geschichte der juristischen Fakultät*. Neumünster: Wachholtz, 1965.
Duroche, Leonard L. "Like and Look Alike: Symmetry and Irony in Theodor Storm's *Aquis submersus*." *Seminar* 7 (1971): 1–13.
Dysart, David L. *The Role of the Painting in the Works of Theodor Storm*. North American Studies in Nineteenth-Century German Literature, Vol. 11. New York: Peter Lang, 1992.
Eaton, John Wallace. *The German Influence in Danish Literature in the Eighteenth Century*. Cambridge, England: University Press, 1929.

Eucken, Rudolf. *Lebenserinnerungen.* Leipzig: Koehler, 1921.
Eversberg, Gerd. "Storms erste Gedichtveröffentlichungen." STSG 41 (1992): 45–49.
Fabricius, Knud. *Sønderjyllands Historie.* Vol. IV. Copenhagen: Reitzel, 1936–1937.
———, and J. Lomholt-Thomsen, eds. *Flensborgeren, Professor Christian Paulsens Dagbøger.* Copenhagen: Gyldendal, 1946.
Fasold, Regina. *Theodor Storm.* Stuttgart: Metzler, 1997.
Feise, Ernst. "Theodor Storms 'Aquis submersus.' Eine Formanalyse." *Monatshefte für Deutschen Unterricht* (Wisconsin) 30 (1938): 246–256.
———. "Berichtigung zu meinem Aufsatz über Storms 'Aquis submersus.'" *Monatshefte* 30 (1938): 334–335.
———. *Xenion. Essays in the History of German Literature.* Baltimore: Johns Hopkins Press, 1950.
Fenger, Henning. *Kierkegaard. The Myths and their Origins.* Studies in the Kierkegaardian Papers and Letters, trans. G. C. Schoolfield. New Haven & London: Yale University Press, 1980.
Field, G. Wallis. *A Literary History of Germany. The Nineteenth Century.* London: Benn; New York: Barnes & Noble, 1975.
Fink, Troels. *Ustabil balance: dansk udenrigs- og forsvarspolitik 1894–1905.* Aarhus: Universitetsforlaget, 1961.
Fisenne, Otto v. "Theodor Storm als Jurist." STSG 8 (1959): 9–47.
Forster, Franz. "Theodor Storms 'Meeresstrand' und 'Die Stadt.'" *Jahrbuch der Grillparzer-Gesellschaft.* 3. Folge. XII (1976): 27–37.
Friis, Oluf. "Den poetiske realismes generation" in *Dansk Litteratur Historie,* ed. P. H. Traustedt, Vol. III. Copenhagen: Politiken, 1976: 11–278.
Freund, Winfried. *Theodor Storm.* Stuttgart: Kohlhammer, 1987.
Geismar, Oscar. *Nogle Digterprofiler.* Copenhagen: Gad, 1906.
Goldammer, Peter. *Theodor Storm. Eine Einführung in Leben und Werk.* Leipzig: Reclam, n.d. (1968), ⁴1990.
Gosch, Charles A. *Denmark and Germany since 1815.* London: Murray, 1862.
Haupt, Richard. *Die Bau- und Kunstdenkmäler der Provinz Schleswig-Holstein.* Vol. I. Kiel: Homann, 1887.
Hausmann, Manfred. "Unendliches Gedicht. Bemerkungen anläßlich der Lyrik Theodor Storms." *Abhandlungen der Akademie der Wissenschaften und der Literatur in Mainz,* 1962.
Hedemann-Heespen, Paul von. *Die Herzogtümer Schleswig-Holstein und die Neuzeit.* Kiel: Mühlau, 1926.

Hedinger, B., ed. *C. F. Hansen in Hamburg, Altona und den Elbvororten.* Munich & Berlin: Deutscher Kunstverlag, 2000.

Hertling, Gunter H. *Theodor Storms 'Meisterschuß' "Aquis submersus." Der Künstler zwischen Determiniertheit und Selbstvollendung.* Würzburg: Königshausen & Neumann, 1995.

Hielmcrone, U. v., P. Zubek, J. Henningsen, eds. *Marienkirche Husum.* Husum: Schrift 7 des Kreisarchivs Nordfriesland, 1983.

Hjelholt, Holger. *Sønderjylland under Treårskrigen.* 2 vols. Copenhagen: Gad, 1959–1961.

———. *British Mediation in the Danish-German Conflict 1848–1850.* Historisk-filosofiske Meddelelser udgivet af Det Kongelige Danske Videnskabernes Selskab 41:1. Copenhagen: Munksgaard, 1965.

Hoffmann, Friedrich. *Das alte Husum zur Zeit des jungen Storm.* Kiel: Institut für Weltwirtschaft, 1957.

Holub, Robert C. "Realism and Recollection. The Commemoration of Art and the Aesthetics of Abnegation in *Aquis submersus.*" *Colloquia Germanica* 18 (1985): 120–139. Reprint in *Reflections of Realism: Paradox, Norm, and Ideology in Nineteenth-Century German Prose.* Detroit: Wayne State University Press, 1991.

Hude, Elisabeth. *Thomasine Gyllembourg og Hverdagshistorierne.* Copenhagen: Rosenkilde & Bagger, 1951.

Jackson, David A. "Die Überwindung der Schuld in der Novelle 'Aquis submersus.'" STSG 21 (1972): 45–56.

———. "The Sound of Silence. Theodor Storm's Son Karl and the Novelle *Schweigen.*" *German Life and Letters* 45 (1992): 33–49.

———. *Theodor Storm. The Life and Works of a Democratic Humanitarian.* New York & Oxford: Berg, 1992.

———. *Theodor Storm. Dichter und demokratischer Humanist. Eine Biographie.* Berlin: Erich Schmidt, 2001. Translation of the English book listed above.

Jäger, Peter. *Postgeschichte Schleswig-Holsteins.* Kiel: Bezirksgruppe Kiel der Gesellschaft für deutsche Postgeschichte, 1970.

Jakstein, Werner. *Landesbaumeister Christian Friedrich Hansen. Der nordische Klassizist.* Neumünster: Wachholtz, 1937.

Jensen, Johannes. *Nordfriesland in den geistigen und politischen Strömungen des 19. Jahrhunderts (1797–1864).* Neumünster: Wachholtz, 1961.

Kamphövener, Martin. "Theodor Storm og Danmark." *Jyske Tidende,* 18 maj 1950: 4.

Köster, Albert. "Einleitung" in *Theodor Storms Sämtliche Werke*, ed. A. Köster. Vol. I. Leipzig: Insel, 1919.

Kuhn, Hans. *Defining a Nation in Song. Danish Patriotic Songs in Songbooks of the Period 1832–1870*. Copenhagen: Reitzel, 1990.

Laage, Karl Ernst. *Theodor Storms Welt in Bildern*. Heide: Boyens, 1988.

——. *Theodor Storm. Leben und Werk*. Husum: Husum Druck- und Verlagsgesellschaft, 1979, [7]1999.

——. *Theodor Storm. Eine Biographie*. Heide: Boyens, 1999.

Laing, Samuel. *Observations on the Social and Political State of Denmark and the Duchies of Sleswick and Holstein in 1851*. London: Longman, Brown, Green, Longmans, 1852.

Löding, Frithjof. *Theodor Storm und Klaus Groth in ihrem Verhältnis zur schleswig-holsteinischen Frage*. Neumünster: Wachholtz, 1985.

Lohmeier, Dieter. "Storm und sein dänischer Übersetzer Johannes Magnussen. Mit unveröffentlichten Briefen." STSG 33 (1984): 53–70.

——. "Die Berichte der Husumer Behörden über Storms politische Haltung während der schleswig-holsteinischen Erhebung." STSG 34 (1985): 39–48.

——. "Theodor Storm und die Politik" in *Theodor Storm und das 19. Jahrhundert. Vorträge und Berichte des Internationalen Storm-Symposions aus Anlaß des 100. Todestages Theodor Storms*, eds. B. Coghlan & K. E. Laage. Berlin: Erich Schmidt, 1989: 26–40.

——. "Kopenhagen als kulturelles Zentrum der Goethezeit" in *Grenzgänge: Skandinavisch-deutsche Nachbarschaften*, ed. H. Detering. Göttingen: Wallstein, 1996: 78–95.

Lorenzen, Vilh. *Vor Frue Kirke. Københavns Domkirke*. Copenhagen: Tryde, 1927.

Lukács, Georg. *Soul and Form*, trans. A. Bostock. London: Merlin, 1974.

Lund, Hakon, and Anne Lise Thygesen. *C. F. Hansen*. Vol. II. Copenhagen: Arkitekten, 1995.

Lund, Hans, Valdemar Ammundsen, Mads Iversen. *Sønderjyllands Historie*. Vol. V. Copenhagen: Reitzel, 1942.

Mainland, William F. "Theodor Storm" in *German Men of Letters*, ed. A. Natan. Philadelphia: Dufour, 1962: 147–168.

Mann, Thomas. *Theodor Storm Essay*, ed. K. E. Laage. Heide: Boyens, 1996.

McCormick, E. Allen. *Theodor Storm's Novellen*. Chapel Hill, NC: University of North Carolina Press, 1964.

Merker, Paul. "Theodor Storm: Meeresstrand" in *Gedicht und Gedanke*, ed. H. O. Burger. Halle: Niemeyer, 1942: 274–287.

Mitchell, P. M. *A History of Danish Literature.* New York: Kraus-Thomson, 1958, ²1971.
Möller-Christensen, Ivy York. *Den gyldne trekant. H. C. Andersens gennembrud i Tyskland 1831–1850.* Odense: Universitetsforlag, 1992.
———. "Hans Christian Andersens Durchbruch in Deutschland: ein wahres Märchen" in *Grenzgänge: Skandinavisch-deutsche Nachbarschaften*, ed. H. Detering. Göttingen: Wallstein, 1996: 132–146.
Momsen, Ingwer E. "Nikolaus Falck. Vor 200 Jahren wurde der große schleswig-holsteinische Jurist geboren" in *Zwischen Eider und Wiedau. Heimatkalender für Nordfriesland*, 1984.
Müller, Harro. *Theodor Storms Lyrik.* Bonn: Bouvier, 1975.
Mullan, W. N. B. "Tragic Guilt and the Motivation of the Catastrophe in Storm's 'Aquis submersus.'" *Forum for Modern Language Studies* 18 (1982): 225–246.
Nielsen, A. Morell. *The Danish Post and Telegraph Museum.* Copenhagen, 1987.
Pastor, Eckart. *Die Sprache der Erinnerung. Zu den Novellen von Theodor Storm.* Frankfurt am Main: Athenäum, 1988.
Paulin, Roger. *The Brief Compass. The Nineteenth-Century German Novelle.* Oxford: Clarendon, 1985.
———. *Theodor Storm.* Munich: Beck, 1992.
Paulsen, Christian. *Det danske Sprog i Hertugdømmet Slesvig.* Copenhagen: Qvist, 1834.
———. *Om Slesvigs indre Forbindelse med Danmark.* Copenhagen: Reitzel, 1848.
Peitsch, Helmut. "Ein Storm aus Blut und Boden? Zur literarhistorischen Biographik aus der Zeit des Faschismus am Beispiel Franz Stuckerts" in *Theodor Storm – Narrative Strategies and Patriarchy*, eds. D. A. Jackson & M. G. Ward. Lewiston, NY: Mellen, 1999: 239–264.
Pitrou, Robert. *La Vie et l'Oeuvre de Theodor Storm.* Paris: Alcan, 1920. 812 pages!
———. "Thomas Mann, juge de Theodor Storm." *Revue germanique* 22 (1931): 257–261.
Pizer, John. "Guilt, Memory, and the Motif of the Double in Storm's *Aquis submersus* and *Ein Doppelgänger.*" *The German Quarterly* 65 (1992): 177–191.
Prater, Donald. *Thomas Mann. A Life.* Oxford: University Press, 1995.
Prawer, S. S. *German Lyric Poetry. A Critical Analysis of Selected Poems from Klopstock to Rilke.* London: Routledge & Kegan Paul, 1952.

Prinzivalli, Lydia. *Theodor Storm*. Palermo: Palumbo, 1958.
Ratjen, H. *Zur Erinnerung an Nicolaus Falck*. Kiel: Akademische Buchhandlung, 1851.
——. *Geschichte der Universität zu Kiel*. Kiel: Schwers, 1870.
Ritte, Hans. *Das Trinklied in Deutschland und Schweden*. Munich: Fink, 1973.
Roos, Carl. "Slesvig, Holsten og den tyske Litteratur." *Ugens Tilskuer* 9 (1919): 140–142, 152–154.
Runge, Johan. *Sønderjyden Christian Paulsen. Et slesvigsk levnedsløb*. Flensburg: Studieafdelingen ved Dansk Centralbibliotek for Sydslesvig, 1981.
Runge, Johann. *Christian Paulsens politische Entwicklung*. Neumünster: Wachholtz, 1969.
Sanders, Wilm. *St. Nikolaus Kiel*. Kiel: Schmidt & Klaunig, 1968.
Scavenius, Bente, ed. *The Golden Age in Denmark* & *The Golden Age Revisited. Art and Culture in Denmark 1800–1850*. Copenhagen: Gyldendal, 1994 & 1996.
Schleiden, Rudolph. *Jugenderinnerungen eines Schleswig-Holsteiners*. Wiesbaden: Bergmann, 1886.
Schmeisser, Felix. *Eine westschleswigsche Stadt in den Jahren 1848–51*. Husum: Delff, 1914.
Schmidt, Erich. *Charakteristiken*. Vol. I. Berlin: Weidmann, 1886, ²1902.
Schmidt, Harry. *Jürgen Ovens. Sein Leben und seine Werke*. Heide: Westholsteinische Verlagsdruckerei, n.d. (1922).
Schneider, Wilhelm. *Liebe zum deutschen Gedicht*. Freiburg i. B.: Herder, 1952, ⁵1963.
Schulz-Behrend, George. "Forever Immensee." *The German Quarterly* 22 (1949): 159–163.
Schuster, Ingrid. *"Ich habe niemals eine Zeile geschrieben, wenn sie mir fern war." Das Leben der Constanze Storm und vergleichende Studien zum Werk Theodor Storms*. Bern: Peter Lang, 1998.
Selbmann, Rolf. "Vergoldeter Herbst. Storms 'Oktoberlied.' Emanuel Geibel und der Realismus in der Lyrik." STSG 45 (1996): 117–126.
Sengle, Friedrich. "Storms lyrische Eigenleistung. Abgrenzung von anderen großen Lyrikern des 19. Jahrunderts." STSG 28 (1979): 9–33.
Sievers, Hans Jürgen. "Zur Geschichte von Theodor Storms 'Singverein.'" STSG 18 (1969): 89–105.
Sievers, Kai Detlev. *Die Köllerpolitik und ihr Echo in der deutschen Presse 1897–1901*. Neumünster: Wachholtz, 1964.

Silman, Tamara. "Theodor Storms Gedicht 'Meeresstrand.'" STSG 25 (1976): 48–52.
Silz, Walter. "Theodor Storm: Three Poems." *Germanic Review* 42 (1967): 293–300.
Simonsen, Anna. *Theodor Storm og Hjemlandet.* Unpublished thesis. University of Copenhagen, 1948.
——. "Theodor Storm og Danmark (med specielt Henblik paa hans Forhold under Krigen 1848–50)." *Sønderjydske Årbøger* 1 (1950): 140–152.
Smidt, C. M. *Arkitekten C. F. Hansen og hans Bygninger.* Copenhagen: Gad, 1911.
Storm, Gertrud. *Theodor Storm. Ein Bild seines Lebens.* 2 vols. Berlin: Curtius, 1912–1913. Reprint, Hildesheim: Olms, 1991.
Strehl, Wiebke. *Theodor Storm's "Immensee." A Critical Overview.* Columbia, SC: Camden House, 2000.
Strodtmann, Adolf. *Das geistige Leben in Dänemark.* Berlin: Paetel, 1873.
Stuckert, Franz. "Der handschriftliche Nachlaß Theodor Storms und seine Bedeutung für die Forschung." STSG 1 (1952): 41–60.
——. *Theodor Storm. Sein Leben und seine Welt.* Bremen: Schünemann, 1955.
Stutz, Elfriede. "Verskundliche Notizen zu Storms Gedicht 'Meeresstrand'" in *In Search of the Poetic Real. Essays in Honor of Clifford Albrecht Bernd on the Occasion of his Sixtieth Birthday*, eds. J. F. Fetzer, R. Hoermann, W. McConnell. Stuttgart: Heinz, 1989: 243–253.
Tanaka, Hiroyuki, and Mari Tanaka, "Theodor Storm in Japan – beliebt und hochgeschätzt" in *Storm – Essays aus japanischer Perspektive. Jubiläumsband aus Anlaß des fünfzehnjährigen Bestehens der Theodor-Storm-Gesellschaft Japan*, eds. H. Tanaka, S. Fukami, M. Ishihama. Husum: Husum Druck- und Verlagsgesellschaft, 1999: 9–23.
Thomas, Calvin. *A History of German Literature.* New York: Appleton, 1909.
Vogel, Frank. "Introduction" in *Geschichten aus der Tonne von Theodor Storm.* Boston: Heath, 1905.
Volbehr, Friedrich. *Professoren und Dozenten der Christian-Albrechts-Universität zu Kiel 1665 bis 1887.* Kiel: Universitätsbuchhandlung, 1887.
Wang, Zhiyou. "Theodor Storm in China" in *Theodor Storm und das 19. Jahrhundert. Vorträge und Berichte des Internationalen Storm-Symposions aus Anlaß des 100. Todestages Theodor Storms*, eds. B. Coghlan & K. E. Laage. Berlin: Erich Schmidt, 1989: 173–175.

Ward, Mark G. "Narrative and Ideological Tension in the Works of Theodor Storm. A Comparative Study of *Aquis submersus* and *Pole Poppenspäler*." *Deutsche Vierteljahrsschrift für Literaturwissenschaft und Geistesgeschichte* 59 (1985): 445–473.

Wellek, René. *Concepts of Criticism.* New Haven & London: Yale University Press, 1969.

Werneke, Franz. "Theodor Storms Oktoberlied – Eine Interpretation." *Unsere Schule* 9 (1954): 223–228.

Wickert, Lothar. *Theodor Mommsen. Eine Biographie.* Vol. I. Frankfurt am Main: Klostermann, 1959.

Wimpfen, C. v. *Ueber die staatsrechtlichen Verhältnisse der Herzogthümer Schleswig und Holstein.* Kiel: Universitäts-Buchhandlung, 1831.

Woldsen, Johan Frederik. *Stamtavle over Slægten Woldsen.* Copenhagen: Mayland, 1932.

Wooley, E(lmer) O(tto). "Gertrud Storm." *Monatshefte für Deutschen Unterricht* (Wisconsin) 28 (1936): 247–249.

———. *Studies in Theodor Storm.* Bloomington, IN: Indiana University Press, 1943.

———. "Four Letters from Thomas Mann to E. O. Wooley." *Monatshefte* 56 (1964): 15–17.

Zachariae, R. "Theodor Storm." *Literatur og Kritik* 1 (1889): 236–240.

Index of Names

Ackermann, Friedrich 128
Albertsen, Leif Ludwig 35 n41
Ammundsen, Valdemar 18 n10
Andersen, Hans Christian 31, 34, 81–85, 99, 140, 168, 215
Augusta Viktoria, Queen Consort of Prussia & German Empress 21

Balzac, Honoré de 77
Bartholdy, Nils G. 73 n111
Baudelaire, Charles-Pierre 77
Bender, Hans 128
Bennett, Edwin K. 171
Bernhard, Carl 33 n36, 149
Bernhardt, Wilhelm 81
Bismarck, Otto v. 45, 162, 164
Blicher, Steen Steensen 31, 149, 157, 158, 162, 205, 209
Bloom, Harold 16
Boeschenstein, Hermann 204
Bollenbeck, Georg 137
Borzikowsky, Holger 44 n49
Boswell, Patricia 116, 190
Brandt, Otto 30 n27
Brentano, Clemens 50
Brinkmann, Hartmuth & Laura 98, 136 n218, 139
Browning, Robert 76
Bruns, Alken 82 n129
Buchan, Bertha v. 57, 128, 129
Burchardi, Georg Christian 61

Carl, Danish prince 57, 58
Caroline, Danish princess 41

Carr, William 28 n25, 72 n108
Cecil, Lamar 21 n11
Chamisso, Adelbert v. 54–56
Christen, Ada 100
Christensen, Carlo 104 n170
Christian VIII, King of Denmark 56, 60, 61, 75, 92–99, 120, 129
Christian August, Duke of Augustenborg 103, 112, 113, 115, 121
Corrinth, Curt 85 n133
Coupe, William A. 190
Cowen, Roy C. 191
Cunningham, William 190
Curtius, Karl 65

de Mylius, Johan 82
Dickens, Charles 76
Disraeli, Benjamin 103
Döhring, Erich 64 n94
Dostoyevsky, Fyodor 77
Duroche, Leonard L. 189, 190
Dysart, David L. 192

Eaton, John Wallace 33 n34
Eckersberg, Christoffer 31
Eichendorff, Joseph Freiherr v. 50, 78
Ernst Günther, Duke of Augustenburg 22, 23
Esmarch, Constanze *see* Storm, Constanze
Esmarch, Elsabe (Woldsen) 75, 76
Eucken, Rudolf 173, 174 n265

Euclid, Greek mathematician 205, 208
Eversberg, Gerd 86, 87 n137, 89 n139

Fabricius, Knud 22 n17, 34 n40, 119, 122 n196, 137 n224
Falck, Nicolaus 28 n26, 59, 60, 62–64, 69–74, 151
Feise, Ernst 188, 189
Fenger, Henning 33 n37
Festersen, Georg 161, 162, 168
Field, G. Wallis 137 n221
Fink, Troels 65 n96
Fischer, Frederik 112
Fisenne, Otto v. 22 n18, 23 n22, 57 n78, 65 n95, 73 n110, 75 n113, 90 n142, 141 n231
Flaubert, Gustave 77
Fontane, Theodor 16, 24, 61, 78–80, 116, 117, 138, 140, 151, 194, 198, 199
Forster, Franz 135 n217
Frederick the Great (Friedrich II), King of Prussia 30
Frederik VI, King of Denmark 36–46, 48, 49, 51, 54, 56–60, 63, 68, 72, 84
Frederik VII, King of Denmark 62, 102–105, 111, 121
Freiligrath, Ferdinand 113–117
Friedrich, Duke of Augustenburg 21
Friedrichsen, Peter 47–51

Gadamer, Hans-Georg 192
Gantzer, Prussian army captain 131–133, 159
Geibel, Emanuel 100
Geismar, Oscar 133 n211
Gerstenberg, Heinrich Wilhelm v. 32
Gillhoff, Gerd 142
Goethe, Johann Wolfgang v. 53, 78, 116, 118, 149, 151, 197
Goldammer, Peter 15
Goldschmidt, Meïr 31, 34
Gosch, Charles A. 34 n40
Grundtvig, N. F. S. 31
Gyllembourg, Thomasine 31, 33, 149, 150, 153, 154, 156

Hacken, Richard D. 39, 83, 87, 95
Hansen, Christian Frederik 32, 42–47
Hardy, Thomas 76
Haupt, Richard 45, 46 n56
Hausmann, Manfred 134
Hedemann-Heespen, Paul v. 34 n40
Heiberg, Johan Ludvig 31, 84
Heine, Heinrich 16, 50, 53, 78, 82
Henel, Heinrich 16
Herrick, Robert 108
Herrmann, Emil 62 n90
Hertling, Gunter H. 192
Heyse, Johann Christian 50
Heyse, Paul 149, 171, 194–196, 200 n301, 201 n303
Hirsch, Emanuel 157 n249
Hjelholt, Holger 34 n40, 35 n42, 102 n167, 121
Hoegh-Guldberg, Frederik 52
Hoffmann, Friedrich 40 n44
Holberg, Ludvig 79
Holub, Robert C. 191
Hude, Elisabeth 150 n235

Ipsen, Alfred 133, 134, 200
Iversen, Mads 18 n10

Index of Names

Jackson, David A. 105, 129 n204, 175 n271, 190
Jäger, Peter 30 n28, n30
Jakstein, Werner 46
Jensen, Doris see Storm, Doris
Johnson, Samuel 139

Kamphövener, Morton 137 n224
Karstensen, Kristen 112
Keller, Gottfried 16, 77, 78, 100, 149, 162, 194, 195, 204
Kierkegaard, Søren 33
Kleist, Heinrich v. 149, 151
Klopstock, Friedrich Gottlieb 32
Koch, Peter Christian 112, 113
Købke, Christen 31
Köller, Ernst Matthias v. 18, 20–23, 65
Köster, Albert 173, 189
Kruse, Laurids 157 n246, n247, n248
Kühl, Emma 57, 87, 89
Kuhn, Hans 111, 112

Laage, Karl Ernst 74 n112, 80, 166
Laing, Samuel 55
Legge, J. G. 114 n182
Lessing, Gotthold Ephraim 161, 197
Lincoln, Abraham 105
Lohmeier, Dieter 33 n35, 128, 129, 166, 200 n302
Lomholt-Thomsen, J. 22 n17
Lorenzen, Vilh. 44 n50
Lowe-Porter, Helen T. 79
Lübker, Detlev Lorenz 41, 51, 52
Lukács, György 151 n236
Lund, Hakon 42 n45
Lund, Hans 18 n10
Lund, Troels 77
Luther, Martin 32

MacIntyre, Carlyle F. 107
Magnussen, Johannes 194, 200, 201, 215
Mainland, William F. 137 n222, n225
Mallarmé, Stéphane 24, 77
Manicus, Emil 36, 49 n61
Mann, Thomas 6, 78–80, 118, 119, 126, 127, 134, 135, 152, 159, 160, 193, 204
Mannhardt, Helen Mary 199
Marie Sophie Friederike, Queen Consort of Denmark 41, 51
Marstrand, Wilhelm 140 n229
McCormick, E. Allen 189, 190
Merker, Paul 135 n217
Meyer, Conrad Ferdinand 16, 77, 78, 149, 162
Meyler, Heinrich August 86
Mitchell, P.M. 32 n33, 140 n229
Møller, Poul Martin 68, 149
Möller-Christensen, Ivy York 85 n135
Mörike, Eduard 16, 50, 78
Mommsen, Theodor 90–92, 102, 117
Mommsen, Tycho 91, 102
Momsen, Ingwer E. 72 n106
Morgan, Bayard Quincy 152
Müller, Harro 111 n177, 116, 117, 135 n217
Mullan, William 188, 190, 191
Mylius, Johan de see de Mylius, Johan

Nielsen, A. Morell 30 n29

Oehlenschläger, Adam 31, 33
Österling, Anders 134

Opitz, Eckardt 72 n106
Ovens, Jürgen 182

Paetel, Elwin 172, 215
Paulin, Roger 157 n249
Paulsen, Christian 22, 62–70, 72, 73
Peitsch, Helmut 53 n71
Petersen, Wilhelm 194
Petrarch, Francesco 24
Pitrou, Robert 65 n95, 118, 168, 193 n291
Pizer, John 192
Prater, Donald 119 n190
Prawer, S. S. 128

Ratjen, H. 64 n94, 72 n109
Rehder, Franz 93
Ringsted, Palle 49 n60
Ritchie, J.M. 153 n245
Ritte, Hans 111 n179
Rodenberg, Julius 174
Romberg, Andreas 119 n192
Roos, Carl 138, 175 n270
Runge, Johan(n) 55 n77, 68 n101, 70 n105

Salinger, Herman 124
Sanders, Wilm 30 n31
Schiller, Friedrich 25, 197
Schindler, Heinrich 141
Schlegel, Johann Elias 32
Schleiden, Rudolph 58
Schmeisser, Felix 104 n169, 121, 130
Schmidt, Erich 137, 161, 194, 197, 202
Schmidt, Harry 182 n273
Schmitz, Victor A. 157 n249
Schneider, Wilhelm 135 n217

Schulz-Behrend, George 152
Schuster, Ingrid 129 n205
Selbmann, Rolf 111 n177
Sengle, Friedrich 116
Shakespeare, William 195
Sievers, Hans Jürgen 120 n193
Sievers, Kai Detlev 21 n12, 65 n96
Silman, Tamara 135 n217
Silz, Walter 111 n177, 116, 117
Simonsen, Anna 122 n196, 136, 175 n270
Smidt, C. M. 42 n46
Steinmann, Georg v. 215
Stendhal, pseud. of Marie-Henri Beyle 77
Stiebeling, Werner 47 n58
Stoltenberg, Gerhard 42 n45
Storm, Aemil (Emil) 203
Storm, Constanze (Esmarch) 75, 98, 128–130, 135, 138, 160, 164
Storm, Doris (Jensen) 98, 99, 120, 129–132, 135–139, 141, 144, 146, 159, 160, 163, 175
Storm, Gertrud 18, 19, 21–23, 64–66, 89 n140, 93, 99 n159, 129, 215
Storm, Hans 202
Storm, Johann Casimir 53, 60, 61, 69, 75, 137, 139, 202
Storm, Karl 202
Storm, Lucie (Woldsen) 45, 75, 76, 202
Storm, Otto 100
Strehl, Wiebke 153
Strodtmann, Adolf, 82
Stuckert, Franz 23, 43 n47, 52, 63, 65 n95, 66 n99, 130 n208, 157 n249
Stutz, Elfriede 135 n217

Swinburne, Algernon Charles 76

Tanaka, Hiroyuki & Mari 15 n2
Tennyson, Alfred, Lord 76
Thackeray, William Makepeace 76
Thomas, Calvin 173
Thomsen, Jacob 112 n180
Thorvaldsen, Bertel 31
Thygesen, Anne Lise 42 n45
Tieck, Ludwig 50, 149, 151
Tobiesen, Ludolph Herrmann 51, 52
Tolstoy, Count Lev 77
Turgenev, Ivan 77

van der Helst, Bartholomeus 182
Verlaine, Paul 77
Vogel, Frank 161 n251
Volbehr, Friedrich 64 n94

Wang, Zhiyou 15 n3
Ward, Mark G. 191

Weinreich, Gerd 213
Wellek, René 81
Werneke, Franz 111 n177
Wickert, Lothar 90 n142, 91 n143–147, 92 n148, 102 n166
Wilhelm I, King of Prussia & German Emperor 162
Wilhelm II, King of Prussia & German Emperor 21
Wilhelmine, Danish princess 57, 58
Wilmowski, Kurt v. 21
Wimpfen, Carl v. 28 n24
Woldsen, August Friedrich 105
Woldsen, Christian Albrecht 105
Woldsen, Ingwer 105
Woldsen, Johan Frederik 105 n172
Woldsen, Magdalena (Feddersen) 45
Wooley, Elmer Otto 18, 19, 23 n19, 65 n97, 129, 152
Wussow, Alexander v. 151 n237

Zachariae, R. 173

North American Studies in 19th-Century German Literature

This series of monographs is about post-Romantic literature during the 19th century in German-speaking lands. The series endeavors to embrace studies in criticism, literary history, the symbiosis with other national literatures, as well as the social and political dimensions of literature. Our aim is to offer contributions by American scholars, to renovate the reformation of the canon, the rediscovery of once significant authors, the reevaluation of texts and their contexts, and a renewed understanding and appreciation of a body of literature that was acknowledged as internationally important in the 19th century.

Vol. 35   Rinske van Stipriaan Pritchett: The Art of Comedy and Social Critique in Nineteenth-Century Germany. Charlotte Birch-Pfeiffer (1800–1868). Forthcoming.

Vol. 34   Ferstenberg Helen: Meditations on Jewish Creative Identity. Representations of the Jewish Artist in the Works of German-Jewish Writers from Heine to Feuchtwanger. 229 pp., 2004.

Vol. 33   Bernd Clifford Albrecht: Theodor Storm. The Dano-German Poet and Writer. 233 pp., 2003, 2005.

Vol. 32   Mornin Edward: Through Alien Eyes. The Visit of the Russian Ship *Rurik* to San Francisco in 1816 and the Men behind the Visit. 125 pp., 2002.

Vol. 31   Kluger Karin: Der letzte Augenblick der hübschen Idylle. Die Problematisierung der Idylle bei Wilhelm Raabe. 199 pp., 2001.

Vol. 30   Browne Christine Geffers: Theodor Storm.
         Das Spannungsverhältnis zwischen Glauben und Aber-
         glauben in seinen Novellen. 155 pp., 2002.

Vol. 29   Van Ornam Vanessa: Fanny Lewald and Nineteenth-
         Century Constructions of Femininity. 192 pp., 2002.

Vol. 28   Marshall Jennifer Cizik: Betrothal, Violence, and the
         "Beloved Sacrifice" in Nineteenth-Century German
         Literature. 265 pp., 2001.

Vol. 27   Hock Lisabeth M.: Replicas of a Female Prometheus. The
         Textual Personae of Bettina von Arnim. 260 pp., 2001.

Vol. 26   Vanchena Lorie A.: Political Poetry in Periodicals and the
         Shaping of German National Consciousness in the Nine-
         teenth Century. 290 pp., 2000.

Vol. 25   Schuchalter Jerry: Narratives of America and the Frontier
         in Nineteenth-Century German Literature. 302 pp., 2000.

Vol. 24   Boehringer Michael: The Telling Tactics of Narrative
         Strategies in Tieck, Kleist, Stifter, and Storm. 204 pp., 1999.

Vol. 23   Anton Christine: Selbstreflexivität der Kunsttheorie in den
         Künstlernovellen des Realismus. 227 pp., 1998.

Vol. 22   McGlathery James M.: Wagner's Operas and Desire.
         312 pp., 1998.

Vol. 20   Arnds Peter O.: Wilhelm Raabe's "Der Hungerpastor" and
         Charles Dickens's "David Copperfield". 202 pp., 1997.

Vol. 19   Justis Diana Lynn: The Feminine in Heine's Life and
         Oeuvre. Self and Other. 247 pp., 1997.

Vol. 18   Taylor Rodney R.: Perspectives on Spinoza in Works by
         Schiller, Büchner, and C.F. Meyer. Five Essays. 170 pp., 1995.

Vol. 17   Wagner Nancy Birch: Goethe as Cultural Icon.
         Intertextual Encounters with Stifter and Fontane.
         220 pp., 1994.

Vol. 15   Morris-Keitel Helen G.: Identity in Transition.
         The Images of Working-Class Women in Social Prose of the
         "Vormärz" (1840–1848). 216 pp., 1995.

Vol. 14 Remak Henry H. H.: Structural Elements of the German Novella from Goethe to Thomas Mann. 341 pp., 1996, 2001.

Vol. 13 Felden Tamara: Frauen Reisen. Zur literarischen Repräsentation weiblicher Geschlechterrollenerfahrung im 19. Jahrhundert. 179 pp., 1993.

Vol. 12 Good Charles F.: Domination, Dependence, Denial and Despair. Father-Daughter Relationships in Grillparzer, Hebbel and Hauptmann. 175 pp., 1993.

Vol. 11 Dysart David L.: The Role of the Painting in the Works of Theodor Storm. 1992

Vol. 10 Pettey John Carson: Nietzsche's Philosophical and Narrative Styles. 1992.

Vol. 9 Mugge-Meiburg Beth L.: Words Chiseled into Marble. Artworks in the Prose Narratives of Conrad Ferdinand Meyer. 1991.

Vol. 8 Lehrer Mark: Intellektuelle Aporie und literarische Originalität. Wissenschaftsgeschichtliche Studien zum deutschen Realismus: Keller, Raabe und Fontane. 1991.

Vol. 7 Danford Karen Pawluk: The Family in Adalbert Stifter's Moral and Aesthetic Universe. A Rarefied Vision. 1991.

Vol. 6 Lund Deborah S.: Ambiguity as Narrative Strategy in the Prose Work of C.F. Meyer. 1990.

Vol. 5 Steiner Carl: Karl Emil Franzos, 1848–1904. Emancipator and Assimilationist. 1990.

Vol. 4 Peters George F.: "Der Große Heide Nr. 2". Heinrich Heine and the Levels of His Goethe Reception. 1989.

Vol. 3 Sammons Jeffrey L.: Imagination and History. Selected Papers on Nineteenth-Century German Literature. 1988.

Vol. 2 Frost Alphonso A. Jr.: Ernst Dronke: His Life and His Works. 1989.

Vol. 1 Franklin Ursula: Exiles and Ironists. Essays on the Kinship of Heine and Laforgue. 1988.